# The Silver Queen

Used by permission, Utah State Historical Society, all rights reserved.

# The Silver Queen

## Her Royal Highness
## Suzanne Bransford Emery Holmes
## Delitch Engalitcheff
## 1859–1942

Judy Dykman and Colleen Whitley

Utah State University Press
Logan, Utah

Copyright © 1998 Utah State University Press
All rights reserved

Utah State University Press
Logan, Utah 84322-7800

Typography by WolfPack
Cover design by Barbara Yale-Read
Cover photograph courtesy of Vadney and Jean Murray

Library of Congress Cataloging-in-Publication Data

Dykman, Judy, 1946-
The Silver Queen : her royal highness Suzanne Bransford Emery
Holmes Delitch Engalitcheff, 1859-1942 /
Judy Dykman and Colleen Whitley.
p. cm.
Includes bibliographical references (p. ) and index.
1. Engalitcheff, Suzanne Bransford Emery Holmes Delitch,
1859-1942. 2. Socialites—Utah—Biography. 3. Utah—Biography.
I. Whitley, Colleen, 1940- . II. Title.
CT275.E542D95 1998
979.2′031′092—dc21
[B]              97-45311
         CIP

*To the Bransford family, the people Susie loved*

# Acknowledgments

The authors thank the many people who allowed us to use their photographs, records, and memories to make this book possible. In particular we thank Susanna Hartman, Susie's niece and namesake; Vadney and Jean Murray, relatives of the Blood family; Stella Inge and Sue Lease, Stella Bransford's daughters; and Anne Newhall, Mary Leader, and Carolyn MacDonald, Wallace Bransford's granddaughters. Extra thanks go to Dr. Harold Lamb for his patience in recalling experiences and explaining relationships in the family and to John Alley of USU Press for his expert guidance.

# Contents

| | |
|---|---|
| Illustrations | ix |
| Prologue | 1 |
| 1 Where It All Began | 3 |
| 2 The Belle of Plumas County | 11 |
| 3 True Love and Tragedy | 20 |
| 4 The R. C. Chambers Affair | 37 |
| 5 A Decade of Adjustment | 48 |
| 6 Entertaining in Style | 61 |
| 7 The Progressive Movement | 81 |
| 8 The Next Generation | 92 |
| 9 A House Divided Against Itself | 111 |
| 10 Three, Two, One . . . | 120 |
| 11 Hard Times | 135 |
| 12 Here Comes the Prince, Again | 143 |
| 13 "To you, my dear Sherrie, I say good bye" | 151 |
| Epilogue | 159 |
| Bransford Family Tree | 164 |
| Notes | 165 |
| Bibliography | 177 |
| Indix | 183 |

# Illustrations

| | | | |
|---|---|---|---|
| Susie, the Silver Queen | ii | David Keith | 41 |
| Susie in an elegant dress | xii | John Bransford family | 43 |
| The Bransford crest | 2 | Tom Kearns | 45 |
| Walter Lee Bransford family | 4 | Jennie Judge Kearns | 45 |
| Milford and Sarah Bransford | 5 | Helen Pearson Corbin | 46 |
| Map of Plumas County, California | 7 | Susie dresssed for the Gilded Age | 47 |
| Milford and Sarah Bransford children | 9 | Sarah Bransford home | 49 |
| Margaret Flourney's autograph | 10 | Knutsford Hotel | 49 |
| Taylorsville School class photo | 11 | Colonel Edwin F. Holmes | 51 |
| Woodcut of stage robbery | 13 | Phoebe Apperson Hearst | 52 |
| Bransford and McIntyre Mercantile | 14 | Women of Bransford family | 53 |
| Greenville, California | 16 | Bransford family portrait | 54 |
| John and Rachel Bransford home in California | 17 | Molly Brown | 56 |
| | | Molly Brown house | 56 |
| Crescent Mills | 19 | Susie on cover of *Elite Magazine* | 58 |
| Albion B. Emery | 22 | Thomas Walsh | 59 |
| Susie and Albion Emery | 23 | Thomas Walsh mansion | 60 |
| Viola Bransford Lamb | 25 | Nellie's wedding dress | 62 |
| Salt Lake City Masonic Hall | 25 | Biltmore House | 63 |
| Louise Grace Emery | 27 | Ida Stingley Newhouse | 64 |
| Willis and Harold Lamb | 28 | Kearns mansion | 65 |
| Willis Lamb and R. C. Chambers | 29 | Thomas Kearns's bowling alley | 66 |
| George W. Emery | 30 | David Keith mansion | 66 |
| Susie's silver calling-card case | 30 | Susie, a queen in Amelia's Palace | 67 |
| Susie when Albion died | 32 | Colonel Holmes at the Gardo House | 67 |
| Silver King Mine | 34 | The Gardo House | 68 |
| Albion's and Susie's parlor | 34 | Amelia Folsom and Brigham Young | 68 |
| Park City | 35 | The "auto house" | 69 |
| Stores destroyed in Park City fire | 35 | Invitation to tea at Amelia's Palace | 69 |
| Park Avenue depot, 1918 | 36 | Gardo House floor plans | 70 |
| Silver King stock certificate | 36 | Gardo House double doors | 72 |
| Robert Craig Chambers | 38 | Gardo front entry and staircase | 72 |
| George Hearst | 39 | Gardo main floor salon | 73 |

| | |
|---|---|
| Gardo main parlor | 73 |
| Gardo dining room | 74 |
| Round table in Gardo House | 74 |
| Susie's suite | 75 |
| Susie's bed | 75 |
| Susie's bedroom set | 75 |
| Gardo art gallery and ballroom | 76 |
| Art gallery stage | 76 |
| Susie's Steinway piano | 77 |
| Gardo hallway | 77 |
| Colonel Holmes's study | 78 |
| Colonel Holmes's bedroom | 78 |
| Bedroom in the Gardo House | 79 |
| Gardo kitchen | 79 |
| Gardo billiard and card rooms | 80 |
| Gardo House exterior | 80 |
| John Bransford | 82 |
| Saltair resort | 82 |
| Salt Lake City from Capitol Hill | 83 |
| John Bransford and automobile | 84 |
| Stockade for legalized prostitution | 86 |
| Belle London | 86 |
| Salt Lake City Police | 87 |
| Salt Lake City fire protection | 87 |
| Lory Snow | 89 |
| Downtown Salt Lake City, 1904 | 90 |
| Harold V. Lamb | 92 |
| Grizzelle Lamb and children | 93 |
| Harold Lamb home | 93 |
| Adele Blood | 95 |
| William Randolph Hearst | 96 |
| Hearst Castle™ | 96 |
| Louise Grace Emery | 99 |
| Wallace Bransford | 100 |
| Car decorated with flowers | 101 |
| Bransford Apartments | 103 |
| Louise Grace Emery Apartments | 103 |
| Susie's Oakwood Estate | 105 |
| Oakwood | 106 |
| Oakwood's avenue of trees | 106 |
| Oakwood used Millcreek's current | 107 |
| Susie's proper serving of meals | 107 |
| Family visiting at Oakwood | 108 |
| Susanna Harris | 109 |
| Oakwood in the summer | 110 |
| Grace Emery recuperating | 111 |
| Grace Emery outdoors | 112 |
| Bransford family in Los Angeles | 113 |
| Party at the Gardo House | 114 |
| Salt Lake County Court House | 116 |
| Adele Blood and Susie at Oakwood | 117 |
| Edna Leonard Bransford | 118 |
| Susie's parties and socializing | 119 |
| Cornelia Snow | 121 |
| Susie, still youthful at sixty | 122 |
| "Birds and Flowers at El Roble" | 123 |
| Wrigley mansion | 124 |
| Susie on cover of *California Life* | 125 |
| Susie again on *California Life* | 125 |
| Susie in one of her stylish outfits | 127 |
| El Roble, 1905 | 128 |
| Postcards of El Roble | 129 |
| El Roble remodeling | 130 |
| Fence and iron gate at El Roble | 130 |
| El Roble patio and fountain | 131 |
| Four-car garage at El Roble | 131 |
| El Roble main entry | 132 |
| El Roble stairway | 132 |
| El Roble gatehouse | 133 |
| Castle-like gatehouse at El Roble | 133 |
| Plaza Hotel | 134 |
| Susie with a "walker" | 136 |
| Dr. Radovan Delitch | 138 |
| Susie and Radovan Delitch | 139 |
| Susie's facade of wealth | 141 |
| Susie and Nicholas Engalitcheff | 144 |
| Prince Nicholas V. Engalitcheff | 145 |
| Susie in *San Francisco Chronicle* | 146 |
| Adele's daughter, Dawn Hope | 147 |
| Adele Blood, Broadway actress | 148 |

| | | | |
|---|---|---|---|
| Susanna Harris in late teens | 149 | Emery-Bransford graves, Mt. Olivet | 157 |
| Susie with paste imitations | 150 | Susie and her four husbands | 158 |
| Culver Sherrill | 152 | Susanna's wedding | 160 |
| Susie's constant travel | 153 | Culver Sherrill's Sicily villa | 161 |
| Three generations of Bransford men | 155 | Milford and Sarah Bransford descendants | 163 |
| Wallace in his later years | 155 | | |
| Susie in 1942 | 156 | | |

Susie in one of her most elegant dresses. Used by permission, Utah State Historical Society, all rights reserved.

# Prologue

Beginning at 3 P.M. on Saturday, August 9, 1942, a steady stream of family, friends, distant relatives, business associates, reporters, and curiosity seekers entered the largest room in the Evans and Early funeral home in Salt Lake City to pass by the casket of Her Royal Highness Suzanne Egera Bransford Emery Holmes Delitch Engalitcheff.[1] But the actual number of mourners was less than anticipated. By age eighty-three Susie, as she was affectionately known, had outlived four husbands, both parents, two siblings, her adopted daughter, and both of her major business partners and their spouses. Many of her close friends had also passed on by 1942. In short, she seemed to have lived too long.

A few of the mourners gasped because they hardly recognized the famed beauty. Her face was puffy; her makeup was different from her usual fashion; and her hair was not styled the way she liked to be photographed. Some also felt her dress was out of character; it was too light, plain, and maybe even outdated. Out of pity or possibly derision or even respect, a few people tossed silver dollars inside the casket as they walked by. After all, they reasoned, a "Silver Queen" should have something silver as a final memento. Years later this action would give rise to the story that the Silver Queen was buried in a silver dress in a casket filled with silver dollars, only one of the many myths that would surround and confuse her memory.[2]

At 4 P.M., Right Reverend Arthur W. Moulton, Episcopal bishop of Utah, conducted the brief formal services. They were very appropriate but seemed an anticlimactic ending for the fabulous life of a woman who rose from obscurity in the gold fields to become a multimillionaire and then mysteriously lost it all. As a five-year-old she crossed the plains in a covered wagon. As a teen she survived a stagecoach holdup. As an adult she traveled around the world, socialized with Europe's royalty, discussed politics with America's presidents, had an audience with Pope Leo, and chatted with Hitler and Mussolini. She was a central figure, once as defendant and once as plaintiff, in Utah courts in two landmark cases concerning women's property rights. Married four times, she outlived all her husbands—two of them millionaires, one a mining magnate, the other a civic activist; and two gigolos, one a Serbian physician and the other a Russian prince—even though one was thirty years younger than she. Her travels, elegant parties, and personal tragedies frequently made headlines—and created myths. Like many other socialites of the Gilded Age, Susie was her own best publicist and cleverly planted news stories to ensure her status. She loved to recount incredible adventures and later was pleased to hear her stories repeated unchallenged.

Even as the lady who loved to make grand entrances to restaurants and parties was quietly lowered into a grave in Mt. Olivet Cemetery next to her first husband, rumors were circulating about her death and her financial problems. What had happened to her many millions, the beautiful jewels, and her fabled elegant clothes? Why was she staying in a small walk-up hotel room in Norwalk, Connecticut, instead of New York City's fashionable Plaza Hotel? Why did the hotel management discover the body? Where was her secretary and constant traveling companion when she died? Why did he and other servants inherit all her money while her family got nothing? All of these and many other unanswered questions, all of the stories she told about herself, and all of her documented exploits have evolved into a body of folklore that still survives today.[3]

The Bransford crest, "No fraud is a safe hiding place," showing Susie's distant connection with English royalty, would become part of her campaign for acceptance by the socially elite.

# 1

## Where It All Began

Susie's saga begins in medieval England, where the Bransfords served the country's royalty as soldiers and government officials, occasionally marrying the landed gentry. A branch of the family emigrated to America and continued to distinguish itself in society as family members acquired large tracts of land in the South, numerous slaves, and recognition in Southern politics.

Thomas Bransford, Susie's great-grandfather, was a strong advocate of the Confederacy in Kentucky's legislature and labored to convince Southern politicians that the South needed an extensive railroad system to ensure its future security. Few people in power shared his progressive views, and the railroads were never built. Later, when the Civil War approached, he criticized those who had doomed the South by their failure to cooperate. When his son Walter Lee married Susan Quessenbury, the next generation gained even more prestige because the Quessenburys descended from British royalty.[1] During the next four generations, at least seven other girls would be christened Susan or Susanna after Mistress Quessenbury. Using a generous endowment from Thomas, Walter Lee and his siblings gained wealth and prominence on their own merits, and each patriarch labored to pass on the legacy and help younger family members succeed.[2]

Walter Lee and Susan continued the family tradition and lived as country gentry outside Richmond, Missouri, until the Civil War. By the mid-1850s two of their sons were working for J. P. Quessenbury Hardware and Grocery. Milford was initially apprenticed to a wealthy Tennessee merchant but soon returned home to marry Sarah Ellen Cooper, a pretty fifteen-year-old orphan who lived with the Quessenburys. Her parents had died years earlier, forcing her to live with friends and family until she married, though she did not come to them simply as a poor relation. Sarah's mother had left her some silver plate, seventy acres of land, and several slaves as a nest egg. This property later supplemented Milford's income and provided a few luxuries, allowing the young couple to live comfortably. On November 8, 1854, Sarah and Milford had their first baby, Joseph Jackson, who died nine months later; however, their next two children, John, born November 8, 1854, and Susie (short for Susan), born May 6, 1859, were healthy and lived to maturity.[3]

As the war approached, Missouri's population became increasingly divided over the issue of slavery, as many newer immigrants were abolitionists and sided with the Union. A minority of the population had most of the wealth and needed slaves to work their large cotton and tobacco plantations. Without question, this small group favored the Confederacy, and many other residents supported them. General Sterling Price, a Mexican War hero, roused the pro-Southerners to attack the nearby Union troops.[4] Southern sympathizers gathered at Price's makeshift headquarters from all parts of Missouri. Few had military

Walter Lee Bransford and his wife, Susan Quessenbury, were prosperous Southerners. Tax records in the 1850s indicate they were one of Richmond, Missouri's wealthiest families. This portrait illustrates their affluence; they are well dressed and could afford a family photograph, a rarity prior to 1850. In the back, left to right, are Albina, Parthenia, Berrell, Milford, Susan, Felix, Walter Lee, and Maria; the youngsters, Armenith and Thomas, are in front. The following year Maria died and Walter Lee Jr. was born. Photograph courtesy of Susanna Hartman.

training, and those with none compensated for their inexperience with their enthusiasm. As weapons were scarce, each man brought his own; consequently, there was an odd variety of hunting rifles, shotguns, and ancient muskets to challenge the better trained and supplied Northern troops.[5]

Sarah had two young children, John and Susie, and was pregnant with another when Milford joined Price's forces in 1861. She feared the worst as she watched him leave but realized he felt obligated to go. Upon reaching Price's camp, Milford and his brothers, older and better educated than most of the recruits, were commissioned as officers. As the months passed, the Bransfords distinguished themselves at Carthage and Springfield. Eventually, however, most of Price's unschooled army was shot or captured; Milford was among those imprisoned on Johnson's Island.

The prison was filthy, the food poor, medical care nonexistent, and many died or contracted tuberculosis before they were released or could escape. When the Bransfords finally returned to Ray County, they discovered their property had been seized by the pro-Union government for taxes, and John Charles Frémont controlled the area. To demoralize the South and strengthen his hold on the region, he threatened to execute all Confederate guerrillas found behind Union lines, seize their land, and free their slaves. When Union troops began gaining ground in the West, many Confederates believed the South had lost, and they deserted in order to harvest their crops; others, however, stayed with the army. Milford's oldest brother, Felix, rejoined Price and followed him to Texas. Most of the Bransfords, however, stayed in Missouri to care for their families and aged parents. When Milford returned home, Sarah introduced him to their fourth child, Jackson Cooper, born March 3, 1862; the boy was several months old when Milford first saw him.

Missouri's 1864 election placed Radical Republicans firmly in control of the state government. Eager for vengeance against Southern sympathizers, they passed the hated Test Oath Law to force supporters of the Confederacy to express loyalty to the Union. Anyone not swearing allegiance to the Union was denied the right to vote and hold office. The Republicans also planned to draft all able-bodied men into the Union army. Fearing the worst, hundreds of Missourians with Confederate ties liquidated their holdings, packed up their belongings, and left. The Bransfords and many of their friends assembled in Independence, Missouri, to form a large wagon train, and Milford, as a respected war veteran, was chosen to lead the group. Like the others, he dreamed of recouping his family's losses by heading west. With rich veins of silver and gold being discovered at every turn, the emigrants reasoned that Colorado, Nevada, and California were lands of opportunity.[6]

Susie was five years old when her family left Richmond to cross the plains. It was the first great adventure of what would become a highly adventurous life. She vividly remembered the day her family started west, describing it years later to a reporter for the *Louisville Courier*. That spring morning Independence had seemed a mass of confusion as people scurried in every direction to assemble provisions and finish last minute repairs. Each family had equipped its wagons with the necessary food, clothing, and other supplies for the six-month trip to California, and everyone, young or old, was anxious to leave. The streets were crowded with wagons, teams of oxen or

Thanks to a legacy, Susie's parents, Milford and Sarah Bransford, lived comfortably in Richmond, Missouri, prior to the Civil War. After they arrived in California's gold country, their good fortune changed. Photograph courtesy of Susanna Hartman.

mules, and other livestock waiting for the captain's signal to move out; the noise and confusion were nearly deafening.

An unpublished family history reports that three of Walter Lee's slaves chose to go with his family rather than stay in Missouri. The oldest, Aunt Emily, acted as a cook and maid for the elder Bransfords, while her sons, Rafe and Carter, drove the wagons. When Aunt Emily was asked why she preferred serving the Bransfords to living as a free woman in Missouri, she scoffed at the idea. She used the Bransford name since she never knew her husband's family name, and she did not like the idea of being separated from the elderly Mrs. Bransford as the woman now needed her help. Concerned her sons might leave, she told them that they owed the Bransfords their loyalty. Walter Lee, concerned for the comfort and safety of his aged wife, built Susan a ramshackle ox-driven cart so she would not have to walk. As the group headed west, the small cart frequently led the wagon train.

The long trip was uneventful until Susie's three-year-old cousin, Minnie Richardson, suddenly became ill and died.[7] The group paused at a stage station's small cemetery long enough to prepare the body and hold a brief funeral. Milford's brother Zerrel fashioned a coffin out of a large wardrobe, and the Bransford women lined it in black silk and dressed the child in a beautiful white dress. After the burial the group continued on to Salt Lake City. Along the way they encountered bands of Indians but had no major problems. When they arrived in the Salt Lake Valley, they joined other wagon trains camped on Washington Square. The three-day stop allowed the animals and emigrants a much-needed rest and a chance to buy additional supplies. Several weeks later, in early November, their wagon train disbanded near Quincy, California, to wait for the spring thaw.[8]

After crossing the harsh Great Basin in covered wagons, the Bransfords saw the valleys of the Sierra Nevada Mountains as a paradise. Each valley lay approximately three to four thousand feet above sea level, and most were surrounded by high, tree-covered mountains. The wetlands and streams teemed with wildlife and fish, providing the immigrants a pleasant respite from their previous diet of dried foods. The native Maidu were not aggressive people and seemed in awe of the Whites who rushed into their valleys to mine, cut trees, build homes, and farm. Powerless to stop the newcomers, they had watched the first Whites pass through on their way to the west coast, only to return in greater numbers when gold was discovered in the late 1840s. When tensions between the races developed into open conflict, the natives thought to be responsible were quickly punished to discourage further problems. Whites, however, transgressed on Indian lands with few consequences.

By the mid-1860s Plumas County could provide the new settlers several comforts of home. Thus, during the summer months, it appeared a safe haven from the ravages of the Civil War. The winter months, however, could be brutal. More than one lone traveler froze or starved to death in the Sierra's deep snows and subzero temperatures. In 1846 Donner Lake, less than sixty miles south of Quincy, had been the scene of a terrible tragedy. Many of the eighty-seven members of the Donner Party either starved to death in the deep snows or resorted to cannibalism to stay alive. Snowdrifts more than ten feet high often blocked the Sierra passes until the spring thaw. Those immigrants who reached Reno, Nevada, after mid-October were forced to winter in one of the mountain valleys or stay in Reno. Fortunately for the Bransford party, the guide wisely chose the lower Beckwourth Pass to take them into the wide American Valley and the town of Quincy.

In Plumas County young Susie probably watched snowshoed expressmen or dog teams carry mail and ore shipments to the lower western valleys during the winter. The same expressmen also brought supplies and mail back to the high valleys until warmer weather permitted wagons to be used. One inventive stage driver trained his horses to use specially designed snowshoes so his stage could traverse the snowy canyons. The stage, mounted on skis and loaded with passengers and freight, glided over the deep drifts.

After the spring thaw the Sierra Nevada Mountains were deluged with rain for several weeks, turning the roads into a muddy quagmire. The large express wagons soon became mired to their axles in sticky muck, making the journey to Reno or points west a nightmare. Despite the mud, several hearty teamsters reached the mountain valleys with supplies, though the trip tested their endurance and skill. Plumas County residents were isolated nearly four to five months each year, so it was no wonder they eagerly awaited the arrival of the railroad; they saw it as the answer to their transportation problems. By the mid-1860s railroad lines crisscrossed the eastern states, giving Californians hope that they would soon be connected with the rest of the country.[9]

During their first winter in California, the Bransfords holed up in a small cabin in Indian Valley while Milford and his brothers helped a friend build a house and barn. By 1865 Indian Valley had scarcely 350 people in its three settlements, and most of these were lumbermen or miners. There were some families, but few had children for the Bransfords to play with. There was, however, a Maidu *ku'm* (hut) near their cabin, and Susie and her siblings spent many hours with the two boys who lived there. The cold weather and snows that wearied the adults provided a wonderland for the children, who sledded, built snowmen, and played on the frozen ponds.

The isolation depressed Milford's wife, Sarah, who had enjoyed a busy social life in Missouri and missed her friends and their activities in Richmond. Before the war Richmond's large, well-stocked mercantile stores carried the latest eastern fashions, a variety of foodstuffs, and other conveniences. The town had two churches, a good school, graded roads, dependable mail and freighting services, as well as a number of year-round social activities to entertain the residents. By contrast, California's infant Sierra towns were hard pressed to provide the necessities of life during the winter months. There was also the matter of good medical care. Richmond had a number of capable physicians and a hospital, while Plumas County had few doctors and no hospital until 1880. As a mother with small children, Sarah constantly worried about these deficiencies.

Milford, meanwhile, enjoyed life in Indian Valley and viewed California as a place of opportunity. He assured himself that their early hardships were temporary. Local miners had reported successful strikes in the surrounding canyons, and many thought the outcroppings of quartz in Indian Valley's mountains yet concealed deposits of gold. Prospects for the area's growth seemed good.

In no time Milford made friends and was offered a bookkeeping position in a mercantile. Short of funds and eager to work, he took the job. He reasoned that if he worked hard, he could build a home and provide a good income for his family. Masonry and politics were family traditions, so he was glad opportunities for both existed. Milford undoubtedly shared his excitement with Sarah, but she still viewed California as a harsh land and a major disappointment. What chance would the children have for a good life in such a rough area? She wanted the family to move to the coast, where schools and medical care existed.

When the thaw came, the Bransford families moved to Sonoma County and sought work. Milford's brother Zerrell purchased a piece of land with a house and tried farming in Petaluma. Walter Lee apprenticed Milford's brother Tom to a merchant in Ukiah, a small town in Mendocino County. By 1865 Walter Lee and Susan were both feeling the strains of age, and they gratefully settled in Ukiah, where the milder climate was kinder to Susan, now crippled with arthritis. Their youngest son, Walter Lee Jr., was enrolled in a local school. As Susan's oldest son, Milford felt obligated to watch over his aged parents and rented a small house in Petaluma. Despite this sense of obligation, he quietly wrote friends from Missouri living in other California or Nevada cities asking about jobs in those areas when he was unable to find work nearby. Unfortunately, none of his contacts provided any leads, and he constantly worried about being dependent on his father and brother for support. Growing up with such economic instability undoubtedly affected Susie; years later she told her niece, Susanna Hartman, that she had known poverty and vowed never to be poor again.[10]

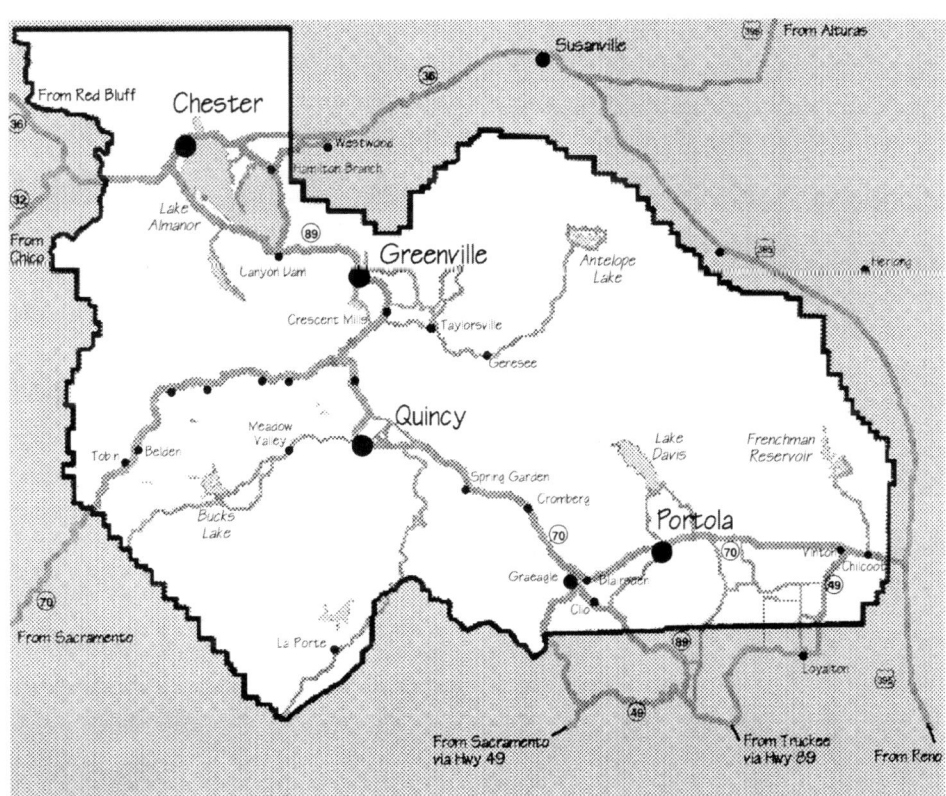

This map of Plumas County, California, shows the proximity of Greenville, Crescent Mills, and Taylorsville, all cities familiar to the Bransford family. Map courtesy of Feather River Publishing Company, Quincy, California.

Milford was not alone in his concerns. Records show that many emigrants from the East were disillusioned with California; it was not the Mecca they had expected. Jobs were hard to find and gold mining had yielded little by the 1860s. Unscrupulous Western propagandists had painted California as a veritable garden of Eden, but the reality of its limitations embittered settlers. Though some left for Utah and other western states, many settlers stayed in California, and, surprisingly, a number of Missourians returned home to take their chances with the Radical Republican government. Under these conditions, Union Colonel Patrick Connor easily raised an army in 1862. Offering unemployed Californians a job with a regular paycheck, three meals a day, a place to sleep, and warm clothing, he found more than enough recruits. Colonel Connor took his new soldiers to occupy Utah, where they were assigned to protect the telegraph lines and stagecoach routes and to make sure the Mormons remained loyal during the Civil War.[11]

To please Sarah, Milford looked for work in Sonoma County until the fall of 1865. When none was available, he accepted a bookkeeping position in Taylorsville, a small town in Plumas County. Sarah was not pleased with his decision, but the firm of Cunningham & Holthouse offered steady work. Nine months later she followed him back to Taylorsville with their young family—possibly it was the death of their youngest child that convinced her Petaluma couldn't guarantee a safe future. She had fought hard to save four-year-old Jackson but helplessly watched him die. Despondent and weary after the funeral, she packed up their furniture and personal possessions for the third time in two years. A little over thirty-one, she had buried two babies in ten years and had two surviving children, John, twelve, and Susie, ten. Stoically she accepted the fact that frontier life caused a woman to age before her time, and she prayed for God's help and mercy.

No record survives to report how Sarah felt when their wagon reached Taylorsville in the summer of 1866, but things had improved in Indian Valley during her year in Petaluma. Taylorsville was still small, with less than 250 souls, but now there were more women and children for companionship. A school held regular classes part of the year and a church provided Sunday services. A sawmill, blacksmith shop, flour mill, hotel, and general store existed to provide some of the basics needed for a comfortable life. Several mines and some logging operations also provided temporary employment for men who wandered through the area on their way to the West Coast or Reno—and steady jobs for those who stayed. A stage connected the city with the rest of the valley and points east and west, and mail was delivered weekly if not daily. That fall Milford wrote in a letter to a friend that Sarah now accepted life there.

The Bransfords first rented a home in Taylorsville until Milford saved enough money to buy a piece of land one block from the city's main intersection, where he hoped to build a home when their financial situation improved. Enthusiastic and optimistic about the future, they happily drew plans for their future home. A devoted husband, Milford wanted a home Sarah could be proud of and in which she could entertain. Meanwhile, John and Susie proved resilient and quickly made friends with the Bloods, Flournoys, and Cooks. Within a few months Sarah also felt at home and appeared content. She found Taylorsville to be a small, close-knit community whose citizens depended upon and supported one another. The towns of Crescent Mills and Greenville, which were less than ten miles away, provided many other close friends.

The family's financial situation gradually improved; within a year Milford became a respected member of the community and the local Masonic lodge. One day he single-handedly foiled a shoot-out in the store where he was working. Impressed, Mr. Smith, a wealthy rancher and miner, offered Milford a business partnership in a new mercantile. The owner of two quartz mines and the local quartz mill, Smith easily financed the new store. To cover his share of the partnership, Milford sold the land he had been saving for Sarah's new house. After some discussion the men named the store Bransford and Smith Mercantile, as Milford would spent the most time with their customers. The store opened in no time, offering groceries, furnishings, mining implements, and other sundry items.

Months later when a larger home, the McGinnis house, was available in nearby Crescent Mills, the Bransfords moved again.

Milford and Sarah Bransford had four children who lived to be adults: John, Suzanne (Susie), Viola (Ola), and Nellie. Photographs courtesy of Susanna Hartman.

Sarah was pregnant a fifth time so more bedrooms were needed. On January 19, 1868, Sarah delivered a fair-haired baby daughter. The infant was healthy and proved a delight to her family, who christened her Viola Crescent in honor of their new home in Crescent Mills. During this time Milford daily commuted the four miles to his store in Taylorsville on horseback.[12]

Through judicious management, the Bransford finances steadily improved, and by 1872 Milford managed to buy a piano. A piano was a status symbol on the frontier; it not only cost a great deal, but the freight bill to bring it by wagon to Indian Valley was expensive. Elated, Sarah entertained her family and friends with melodies from the period, and their home soon became a popular place for dances. Susie also loved music but proved a poor student when Sarah tried to teach her to play. She amused her mother by dancing about the piano and soon proved she could dance to any melody. She looked forward to dances because they provided opportunities to socialize.

By 1872 Milford had decided that sixteen-year-old John needed a career. So John left Plumas to study business in San Francisco, as did many of the children from the county because the local school did not offer older children advanced courses. Sarah was filled with mixed emotions as she watched her tall, handsome son leave home for the first time. He would stay with friends in San Francisco or live in the dorm until he finished the business course at Heald's Business College. Sarah had confidence in his ability to live away from home but found it hard to see him go. Fortunately, he could now travel to and from San Francisco easily on the biweekly stage. Sarah also had her two daughters for companionship. Viola was four and required constant supervision, and fourteen-year-old Susie was always on the go. A tall, shapely brunette with a mind of her own, Susie already received a lot of attention from miners and loggers and loved to flirt.[13]

Many young women in the late nineteenth century kept autograph books where friends wrote messages. Susie's friend, Margaret Flourney, wrote this coded message offering a challenge: "I defy you to read this, Mr. Murray, and it is well for your piece [sic] of mind that you are unable to translate it. Each word is sepperated [sic] by a comma. Maggi." With questionable or missing words or letters in brackets, the simple letter-substitution code reads, "My sweetey, you are the dearest litt[l]e angel in the wor[l]d. [?]eel and I adore you though we dare not say so. Our heart palpitates when we hea[r] your fo[o]tst[e]p on the stairs, and your footstep on the stairs. From your [beloved] Gretie." Autograph courtesy of Vadney and Jean Murray; decoded by Colleen Whitley.

## 2

## The Belle of Plumas County

Fortune alternately smiled and frowned upon Milford Bransford during the 1870s and 1880s as his investments and income fluctuated. Through it all Sarah did her best to make their homes in Taylorsville and Crescent Mills comfortable and to keep their lives on an even keel. Under Sarah's watchful eye, Susie and Viola trained to be good homemakers and learned how to make themselves attractive. Like their brother John, the girls attended the small Taylorsville and Crescent Mills schools where they learned penmanship, reading, writing, and simple mathematics. Both participated in plays, parades, and pageants and gave recitations with the other pupils. When inclement weather or other problems closed the school for weeks or months at a stretch, Sarah tutored her children at home. She was determined her children would have an education and enjoyed helping with their lessons or reading with them. Many years later Susie told a friend that her mother taught her to read by reading with her in the evenings before bedtime.

As a teenager Susie grew tall and developed a shapely silhouette. With her thick, light brown hair and expressive eyes, she became one of the local beauties. Undoubtedly her parents had a difficult time managing her adolescent activities. Growing up in a predominantly male world, Susie felt at ease with men and never lacked friends of either sex. The Blood, Flournoy, and Brown families had several young daughters for her to socialize with, and she developed several friendships that apparently lasted many decades. Like all young girls of the period, Susie collected autographs, beginning as a teenager and continuing into her adult years. The autographs were not simply signatures, however; friends and relatives wrote messages as well as their names, and the entries in Susie's book give insights into her life during this period. She loved being out of doors and enjoyed being a tomboy as much as she loved dressing in pretty clothes. On one occasion she bragged that her father let her swing the first pick when he opened a new shaft of the Green Mountain Mine. This was a dubious honor for a proper young lady, but like other Western women, Susie learned to be independent and tackled chores Eastern women would probably never have considered.[1]

The class photograph of Taylorsville School, 1889–1891. The Taylorsville School District was formed in August 1863 and by 1865 included Genesee and Crescent Mills. Photograph courtesy of Plumas County Museum.

When Susie turned sixteen, her parents decided it was time to send her to San Francisco for more education. Gifted with enthusiasm and a lively personality, Susie needed a chance to polish her social skills. While no record confirms the name of the school her family chose, Susie later talked of attending a woman's seminary in Oakland. The school was probably Field's Seminary for Young Women in Oakland, which offered a very impressive course of study. Field's was a finishing school and an academic institution with outstanding credentials. Its students learned poise and social skills and were well prepared for college and life, according to an 1880 advertisement in a San Francisco Blue Book.

It is hard to know how many Indian Valley families sent their daughters to this or similar schools in the 1870s and 1880s, but Susie was most likely not the only one attending that year. Like John, she probably boarded with family friends or stayed in the school's dormitory. During quarter breaks she used the stage to travel home to Indian Valley. Sarah was concerned about her attractive daughter living in sophisticated San Francisco, but she worried more about denying Susie the chance to meet "the right people." She ultimately bridled her fears and allowed Susie to venture forth. Records do not show whether Susie graduated from the school, but if Sarah had her way Susie probably attended as long as the family had funds for tuition.

During these exciting months of freedom, Susie had one of the greatest adventures of her life—she survived a stagecoach holdup. Always a flirt, she had persuaded the driver to let her sit in the driver's seat instead of riding in the cab with the other passengers. As the stage rounded one of the Sierra's steep canyon ridges, outlaws stepped out into the road and blocked the stage's path. The men wore masks and hats to conceal their identities, but were obviously local boys. One of them recognized Susie and called her by name when she screamed. Surprised to see a favorite amidst the passengers, he assured her she had nothing to fear and took the other passengers' money instead. Susie was flattered by the experience and frequently told friends about her brush with California's outlaws. She claimed not to have recognized the voice as it was muffled by the man's bandanna. The story sounds a bit contrived, and given Susie's later penchant for embellishing her experiences, it may have been. But it could well be true—the stage was the major means of transportation in northern California for many years until a railroad connected Plumas County to Reno and San Francisco. As long as the stages carried mail, freight, and passengers with pocketbooks, robberies were a fact of life.[2]

Two years later in 1877, as Susie turned eighteen, thirty-nine-year-old Sarah delivered her sixth and last baby. Susie and Viola undoubtedly helped their mother during her confinement since Milford's brothers and sisters lived many miles away and had families of their own to care for. After having lost two sons, Sarah was grateful this baby girl was healthy and survived infancy. Susie developed a special bond with the infant, and eventually the sisters became close friends. Milford named the baby Nellie, and she soon became one of her mother's greatest treasures. Now Sarah's family extended from twenty-year-old John to eighteen-year-old Susie, nine-year-old Viola, and the tiny infant, Nellie.

Nellie's birth came in the midst of the Bransfords' financial struggles. Eager to get a foot in the door of local politics and the developing mining interests, Milford had invested in several enterprises. After establishing himself as a Taylorsville merchant, he affiliated with the Imperial Quartz Mining Company and ran its stamp mill. Few of the local miners found pay dirt, so it was no surprise when the mine didn't make money during the next few years. Meanwhile, when a friend felt he had a claim that looked promising, Milford would grubstake him with food and other supplies from the mercantile's inventory. None of these smaller investments proved successful, and Taylorsville's Bransford & Smith Mercantile was gone by 1874.[3] However, one of the men Milford grubstaked, R. C. Chambers, a former sheriff of Plumas County, eventually became wealthy and repaid the favor many years later in Utah.

Milford was not as fortunate as Chambers, however; he fell behind on his taxes and had to sell his investment in the Quincy-Indian Valley Road in 1879. He and a partner, William G. Young, had contracted with the legislature in 1870 to complete the road William H. Blood had started before his death. Unfortunately, the legis-

This woodcut by Orville Carroll from the *Louisville (Kentucky) Courier Journal*, 8 March 1942, illustrates one of the great adventures of Susie's life. During her youth in California, bandits robbed the stage on which she was riding; one of them, however, recognized Susie and did not take her money. Courtesy of *Louisville (Kentucky) Courier Journal*.

lature underestimated the project's cost and did not provide enough money. When the money was gone, Milford and his partner paid the workmen from their own funds. For years this road was an important thoroughfare in Plumas County, but neither of the men gained much satisfaction from the project.[4] Both lost money and had nothing to show for their efforts.

In 1878 Crescent Mills's Green Mountain Mine, where Milford was superintendent, had a major fire. For several days rescuers attempted to reach four men who were trapped in the mine, but finally abandoned the search for their companions, knowing they must have already died from the poisonous smoke. The mine was closed to smother the fire, then reopened several weeks later and production resumed.

During the next four years the mine had better luck but went through alternating periods of prosperity and stagnation. In 1882 it was sold to a New York City firm because local investors overextended their credit trying to make needed improvements. When the mine management was reorganized later that year, Milford was in New York representing the Taylor Plumas Mine.[5] He returned several months later, assured that the mine's financial problems were over. No record of the Taylor Plumas Mine now exists, probably because it was absorbed by the Green Mountain Mining Company years later. In any event, Milford didn't make money in any of his mining ventures. And his financial problems only worsened during the next few years.[6]

Few of Milford's investments succeeded, though many, like the $100 he gave Western Union Telegraph Company for a local telegraph line, initially seemed sound. Local merchants were guaranteed free telegraph privileges proportionate to the amount they contributed to the project. Although Plumas County had a hard time maintaining its lines in the deep snow, the project eventually succeeded. Meanwhile, Milford lost other properties in several lawsuits. A Mr. McKinney sued him for indebtedness and took his holdings in

Milford eventually gave his interest in the Bransford and McIntyre Mercantile to his son, John. Photograph courtesy of the Plumas County Museum.

the Southern Eureka Mining Company, forcing him to sell his interests in the Bransford and Taylor Quartz Mine and Crescent Tailings Placer Claim. The pressure of these and other debts and obligations forced him to give his interest in Greenville's Bransford and McIntyre Mercantile to his son John. Amazingly, despite one disaster after another Milford maintained high spirits and focused on public service. The governor appointed him to be a notary public, and in 1884 he found work with a Mr. Mills. This impressive list of misadventures does suggest that Milford was often a failure but not that he was lazy; he was overly ambitious and plagued with bad luck. Like many others, he optimistically put too many family assets into risky ventures that didn't succeed. Another problem may have been his health. Some family members believe he contracted consumption, or tuberculosis, as a Confederate prisoner on Johnson's Island. If he spent much time working in any of the mines, the dank mine air probably aggravated his condition. A Utah obituary eventually listed "la grippe" (consumption) as the cause of death.[7]

To ease the family's financial problems, Sarah turned their home into a boarding house. The money she provided supplied a small but steady income. Still, running a boarding house in a rough country was not the life Sarah would have chosen for her children. She was painfully aware of Plumas County's backwardness and her family's financial problems. Her own youth had been dismal due to the early death of both her parents. Orphaned at eight and living with relatives or friends, she may have been passed from one relative to another until she married Milford at fifteen. Mindful that her mother lacked an education and signed her will with an "X," Sarah valued her own education. Fortunately, those who cared for her made sure she received the land, money, slaves, property, and silver plate her mother had bequeathed to her. Someone also provided her with piano lessons, but by marrying at fifteen she missed many opportunities she might have had. She wanted better for her daughters and could see that life in a mining camp offered few opportunities.

If Susie had been raised in the Old South in the 1870s and if her parents' financial situation had been more stable, she would have lived the life of a Southern belle. By age eighteen she would have been formally introduced to society at a "coming out" party, where all of her parents' friends and the eligible young men of Missouri would have attended. The following year she would have made the rounds to parties and balls dressed in elegant, stylish clothes. She might even have joined other Southern daughters on a European Grand Tour to London, Paris, and Rome. In the midst of all this activity, many young Southern women met eligible bachelors and became engaged. Following an appropriate engagement that could last months or even years, they married and started families. Unfortunately, none of these opportunities were available in California's mining communities.

To compensate her daughters for the dances and parties they missed by living in California, Sarah made the effort to be a proper Southern hostess. According to Charles Mulholland, a family friend, the Bransford home was recognized in Indian Valley for its hospitality. When the family wasn't entertaining, they were guests at some neighbor's home. Newspapers in nearby Greenville frequently praised the Bransford dinners or parties and the dances that generally concluded each evening. All this is not to say the county didn't provide its own social outlets for its citizens. There were weekly church services, spelling bees, recitation nights, quilting bees, and lectures on timely issues. Major holidays provided an excuse for a community dance. Plumas County also provided a variety of social and political clubs, such as the Masons, a dance club, a drama group, a temperance society, and the Prevaricators Club.

Like her parents, seventeen-year-old Susie loved to mingle and became an enthusiastic "joiner." In 1876 she helped to organize Taylorsville's Rescue Lodge 215, I.O.G.F. Her enthusiasm for all of Plumas County's activities earned her the affectionate title, the "Belle of Plumas," and one of the *Greenville Bulletin*'s journalists wrote the following blurb in the local newspaper when she came to visit friends:

> Friends in all the aged she finds
> And lovers in the Young.[8]

When the family's finances turned sour during the 1880s, Susie worked as a seamstress to

The main street of Greenville, California, prior to 1900 was unpaved and had wooden sidewalks. Photograph courtesy of Plumas County Museum.

bring in more money. The following excerpt from the Rogers's family history appeared in a Plumas County publication:

> Susie E. Bransford, long the belle of the valley, but forced through pecuniary reverses to do fine dressmaking, built the wedding gown. She also did up the bride's hair.[9]

Although she later denied having worked as a common laborer, Susie used her ability as a seamstress and skill as a hairdresser to aid women in northern California. When work in Indian Valley was unavailable, she traveled to other locales, where she advertised by word of mouth that she could sew clothes, design hats, and style hair.

The summer of 1881 may have been one of the most significant times in Susie's life. She performed in a Taylorsville lyceum and received praise for her performance. But more importantly, she may have been dating her first great love. In July 1881 Joseph Holz, perhaps only a drifter passing through the valley but possibly a boarder in the Bransford home, wrote a romantic autograph to Susie pledging his "undying love and devotion."

> To Miss Susie E. Bransford
> Only to love you, nothing more,
> No larger boon I ask;
> Only to love you o'er and o'er,
> And in your smile to bask;
> Only to catch the light that lies
> With your grace divine,
> Only to see you tho' your eyes
> May wander not to mine.
> Only to hear you, though your words
> Be not to me addressed;
> Their sound can thrill the fondest chords
> That tremble in my breast.
> Only to love you, tho' your love
> Be not bestowed on me,
> Only to breathe the name of *Susie*
> Thro' all eternity
>     From a True Friend,
>         May 11, 1881            Joseph Holz[10]

John and Rachel Blood Bransford lived in this home in Quincy, California, until they moved to Salt Lake City. Photograph courtesy of Plumas County Museum.

We will never know if Susie returned his feelings or if there was a romance, since no diaries or letters have survived from this period. However, several newspaper articles and other autographs suggest Susie had numerous admirers. In November 1881 Susie visited Maggie Flournoy, a friend from Genesee who was living in San Francisco; she stayed for five months and then returned to Crescent Mills. The trip to the Bay area is couched in mystery; no one knows its purpose. Was she vacationing, looking for work, or was there a far more personal reason for the extended visit?

During her stay in San Francisco in 1881–1882, Susie had a significant experience of some kind, as evidenced by many entries in her autograph book. Ever an enthusiastic autograph collector, she had a page signed by Dr. John Sheets, March 28, 1882, which simply stated

> Remember Your—,
> City and County Hospital, San Francisco.

In the corner, she added a strange comment: "There endeth the 1st lesson." This vague message raises several questions, considering the history of the previous several months. Had she been ill or injured in an accident? Plumas County had opened a hospital between Quincy and Indian Valley in 1880; why, then, did she travel to San Francisco? Also, a dominant theme that runs through several of the later autographs suggests she was depressed. Many friends wrote notes to her after 1882 trying to cheer her by reminding her she had a bright future to look forward to.

> O let us as we pass through life
> Be always glad and cheery,
> For though some hours are dark and cold
> They can not all be dreary.
> —Your Mother

> True friendship, is like phosphorus,
> whose light glows brightest when
> all around is dark.
> —W. G. Lamb

> Bright are the days in store for you.
> —John A. Fitzgerald

All of these verses suggest something traumatic happened during the five months she spent in San Francisco early in 1882. The signature from a doctor giving his hospital address suggests an illness or hospitalization of some sort; however, a careful check of the City and County Hospital Archives shows that Susie Bransford was not treated at the facility under her own name. She may have used an assumed name or Dr. Sheets may have made a house call to attend her.[11] He could, of course, simply have been a friend, and she might not have needed his professional services at all. Much later, however, her first husband, Albion Emery, also wrote a verse in her autograph book that is puzzling:

> Life is too short for any vain regretting;
> Let dead delight bury its dead. I say.
> And let us go upon our way forgetting
> The joys, and sorrows, of each yesterday.
> —Albion Emery

Perhaps we will never know what this body of circumstantial evidence indicates. If letters or diaries were available, we could better interpret these autographs and the unusual events of 1881 and 1882. Certainly the possibility of pregnancy cannot be ignored. During the nineteenth century unwed mothers were social outcasts or were closeted away by their families. One family member feels it would have been impossible for Susie to keep an illegitimate child, a miscarriage, or an abortion a secret from the others, especially since Susie was very close to her mother until she died in 1905. Older members of her family may have been privy to the circumstances of the trip, of course, but simply decided not to discuss it with younger members. Such an incident would have been an embarrassment to Susie and her family if it became public knowledge. The fact that Susie never had a child of her own also gives this possibility a tragic and ironic twist.[12] A second explanation might be that Susie was infatuated with Dr. Sheets and was rebuffed because he was a struggling medical student, especially since three corners of the page containing his autograph suggest a meeting after dark in the nearby park. Little information exists about his medical career or private life after he finished his medical training in 1887 and moved to Buckley, Washington. Maybe Susie met Dr. Sheets while she and Maggie visited friends. After witnessing her father's financial problems, the security of being a doctor's wife

This view of Crescent Mills, probably taken before 1900, shows the view of the valley from the city cemetery. Eventually Susie's sister, Viola, was buried here. Photograph courtesy of Plumas County Museum.

might have appealed to her. Her friend Maggie Flournoy doubtless knew what happened because Susie was staying with her. Susie's older brother, John, wrote the following vague warning in Maggie's autograph book in February 1884:

> To Maggie
> Hard times are coming on Maggie,
> and the ground is covered with snow. So be
> careful and don't throw your heart away.

John may have been warning Maggie to be careful about choosing suitors because he had witnessed his sister's heartbreak two years earlier; or he may have had a premonition that bad times were coming when he wrote the autograph.

The Plumas County Museum reports the county's mining industry struggled during the late 1880s when hydraulic mining was outlawed in northern California. John had seen his father and many other good men struggle and then lose everything. In each case the wives carried a heavy burden as the families struggled to survive. Whatever this warning to Maggie or the mysterious entries in Susie's autograph book may have meant, something happened to Susie during that winter in San Francisco, and it may have been part of her motivation to leave California two years later.[13]

# 3

## True Love and Tragedy

Susie grew restless as she neared her twenty-fifth birthday in the spring of 1884, two years after returning from San Francisco. When not sewing a dress, making a hat, or styling hair, she helped Sarah run the boarding house. Several neighbors and friends commented that it was odd the "Belle of Plumas" was still single and good-naturedly teased her, as in this entry in her autograph book:

*Dear* Susie,
It has been a long time since I last saw you, and if it is as long a time as this ere I see you again, you will have become an *old maid*—that is if you do not get married.
    Yours in haste,
    Warren H. Blood

By this time most of her friends had spouses and children. Six years earlier her older brother, John, had married Rachel Blood, and they now lived in Greenville with two children. Her younger sister, Viola, now sixteen, was a budding scholar whose high scores were recognized in the newspaper. A natural beauty with light brown hair, Viola was also beginning to give Susie serious competition for beaux. Suddenly, Plumas County's young men had two eligible Bransford girls to choose from. W. G. Lamb, one of Milford's business associates, spent many hours at the Bransford home courting Viola and regularly volunteered to escort her when a Crescent Mills or Greenville group sponsored parties or dances. Nearly twice her age, he was uncomfortable about publicly declaring his intentions until she was older. Nevertheless, everyone knew there would soon be a wedding announcement. Viola, or "Ola" as she was sometimes known, had turned sixteen in January. Nellie, the baby of the family, was seven and was quite independent.[1]

As summer approached, Susie wrote several relatives and friends for information about relocating; it seemed time to make a change. Most of her friends and loved ones were happily married or content, while her life seemed stalled in a shallow backwater. She longed for a chance to meet new people and find steady work, but none of her return mail sounded promising until letters from the Chambers and Aschheim families arrived. Both were then living in a Utah mining community called Park City and invited her to visit. Park City was a small town, but it was only thirty miles away from Salt Lake City, a well-established larger city. The only drawback was that Salt Lake City and most of Utah were not like San Francisco, Sacramento, or Reno. A large conservative Mormon population controlled the region, and non-Mormons were a minority. Still, the Jewish Aschheim family was content and happy living there, and R. C. Chambers felt the area offered many opportunities.

By midsummer Susie was on her way to Utah. Because it was socially unacceptable for a woman to travel alone, she may have traveled with R. C. Chambers, who was spending half his time in Utah and half in California. He made the trip frequently and was a good friend of the family. Susie's first trip twenty years earlier had taken several weeks by covered wagon; the trip across the hot, dry Nevada desert in 1884 was much easier. By then the railroad connected Reno, Nevada, and Park City, Utah; and it took about two days to travel between the two cities if there were not too many stops along the way. Temperatures in Nevada's and Utah's lower valleys were ninety to one hundred degrees, so Susie must have found Park City's cool mountain air a pleasant reprieve.[2]

Prior to the 1870s, early settlers had called Park City, or Parley's Park City, "the Robin's Nest of the Wasatch." It was scenically located on the east side of the Wasatch Mountains at the base of Treasure Mountain. The meadows surrounding the city were filled with sagebrush, columbine, Indian paintbrush, and many varieties of wildlife. Up the canyon a small reservoir collected water that drained from the mines, but there were very few trees. Logging for timber to fortify the walls of the mines and to fuel the steam-powered water pumps had stripped the mountains around Park City of the few trees that grew there. By the 1880s logging crews were traveling more than fifty miles to cut timber in the Kamas and Strawberry Valleys. The city's residents also depleted the fragile landscape by cutting lumber to build their homes and businesses—the stark contrast with Plumas County was unsettling. Many of the hillsides were covered with sagebrush and log stumps instead of the lush greenery Susie was accustomed to.

Park City was incorporated in 1884 after years of haggling about its location and a debate over Utah's voting laws. The city had one major road that extended up the center of town. Overburden from a number of the city's mines was used to pave this and many smaller side streets. Wood, brick, and stone buildings lined the main road and crawled up the steep slopes above the city. There were several large hotels, a school, lots of saloons, a butcher shop, livery stable, blacksmith shop, assay office, post office, some banks, boarding houses for the miners, a few department stores, a commercial club, a library, a few churches, an opera house, and even a Chinatown. Park City was the third mining town in the country to obtain a telephone line to connect it with the rest of the country and allow its mining companies better access to their scattered mines. Originally, there were few women to civilize the city other than the "ladies of the night," but by 1884 the number of women and children had dramatically increased. Lastly, but very importantly, the town had its own weekly newspaper, the *Park Record*, which humorously and sometimes viciously editorialized about topics in local, national, and international news.

Despite its sparse appearance, Park City had become quite civilized by the time Susie arrived. There was still a lawless element that "shot up" the town on occasion, but the days of vigilante justice were basically gone. Each of the town's many ethnic groups favored a particular spot to congregate, such as Riley and Toweys, Finn Hall, Swede Hall, Pape, and Bowmans. After the hanging of Black Jack Murphy in 1883 for the murder of Matt Brennan, the town built a town hall and a large secure jailhouse, complete with a dungeon and leg irons, to warehouse criminals. And most of the city's "loose women" now discreetly plied their trade in the Deer Valley area. The town's "decent" citizens also had a variety of entertainments to choose from. The Palace Restaurant stayed open day and night and offered five-course meals for twenty-five cents. The town's opera house offered productions including *The Golden Giant* and *Under the Gaslight*. Well-known performers such as Buffalo Bill, the violinist Edouard Remeny, and boxer John L. Sullivan entertained the populace. Professor H. B. Younger periodically staged grand balls that featured the two-step quadrille. In addition, several Masons chartered the Uintah Lodge, which eventually included a woman's auxiliary for socializing.[3]

Little information remains about this period of Susie's life because years later a number of Eastern society leaders shunned her after learning she had once worked as a common laborer. The experience so humiliated her that she vowed to reveal only part of her previous life and conceal the rest. From then on Susie fabricated parts of her personal and family history to meet her needs and cautiously spoke with interviewers. Eventually, she instructed loved ones to burn her letters and destroy any diaries she may have kept. Consequently, most of the books and articles about Susie's Park City experiences are primarily speculation.[4]

The M. S. Aschheim family, which operated a large store on Park City's Main Street, had been

Bransford family friends before selling their ranch in Indian Valley. During the 1870s they moved to Utah and entered the lumber and mercantile business with the help of R. C. Chambers, their friend from Plumas County. Susie probably accepted the Aschheims' hospitality and boarded in their home rather than live by herself, since single women had to be very careful to protect their reputations and good names near the turn of the century. Early advertisements in the *Park Record* mention that Aschheim's mercantile carried reasonably priced men's and women's clothing and offered alterations if needed. With her years of experience as a seamstress, it is likely Susie worked in their alterations department or worked with one of the town's dressmakers in a small shop. Working as a seamstress was tedious work with long hours, but the work was steady and allowed time in the evening to socialize. The Aschheims also may have introduced Susie to the great love of her life, their store's part-time bookkeeper and secretary, Albion Emery.

At thirty-eight, Albion cut a dashing figure. He was tall, charming, handsome, and self-confident with the gift of gab. He had an impressive family tree that extended back to 1635 in Massachusetts. Thirteen years Susie's senior, he was born June 22, 1846, in South Berwick, Maine. Some women might have worried about his employment record, but Susie had learned to live with the uncertainties of employment while growing up in California. Albion seldom stayed with a job more than a year, but he generally found better opportunities each time he moved. After graduating from Comer's Commercial College in Boston in 1865, he worked as a carpenter in Massachusetts and in the Chicago area. A few years later adventure lured him to Idaho's Fort Hall Indian Reservation, where he worked as a carpenter and tried prospecting.

The following year Albion moved to Utah and tried mining in several of the Oquirrh Mountains canyons until 1874. Sometime that year he contracted rheumatic fever and was forced to take desk jobs. He moved to Tooele, where he was appointed the first non-Mormon county clerk and deputy county recorder by the non-Mormons' Liberal Party. Next he worked for Waterman Smelting Company off and on for three years. During this time he served as the foreman of the grand jury that investigated Salt Lake City's finances in 1876. Later that year he returned to Maine to visit family for a few months. Following his return west, he tried prospecting in Arizona and later in Idaho for a second time. By 1880 he had returned to Salt Lake City and Park City and found work as a bookkeeper. He now renewed his ties with Utah's Liberal Party and the Masonic lodges in the area. In 1881 he was given a presidential appointment to be town postmaster for three years. In the midst of all this activity, he took time to serve as Bingham's delegate to the national convention for nominating the president of the United States.

Before serving as Park City's postmaster, Albion had worked briefly at the town's railroad station as a baggageman. Although his frequent moves from one job to another hint he was a dreamer, he was also a hard worker who tried to take advantage of every opportunity that came along. In spare moments he voraciously read history and the classics, and he faithfully studied the newspapers to keep abreast of current issues. His good-natured disposition, gift for oratory, and

Albion B. Emery was Susie's first husband and the great love of her life. Used by permission, Utah State Historical Society, all rights reserved.

An Ogden photographer took this picture of Susie and Albion shortly after they were married in 1884. Photograph courtesy of Stella Inge.

generosity attracted friends, and Albion rapidly advanced in Park City's Uintah Masonic Lodge and the Liberal Party. He loved to debate and generally had an opinion on all major issues of the day. Like many mining men, Albion sometimes drank excessively, but he was discreet and earned the respect of many.

After arriving in Utah, Susie had a chance to meet many men, including some she had known previously in California, but none impressed her as did Albion. With his good looks, intelligence, ambition, and charm, he was everything she had been seeking in a husband. Susie's conversational ability, sense of fun, and attractiveness also impressed Albion, who wooed her until she accepted his proposal of marriage. They were married on November 11, 1884, and, being frugal with their limited funds, honeymooned in Ogden, where Albion presided at the opening of Ogden's Masonic Hall. A day later friends held a small reception for them in one of Park City's hotels. The *Greenville Bulletin* printed a notice of the wedding, and the *Park Record* published the following announcement:

> On the 11th of November, Miss Susie E. Bransford was married to Mr. A. B. Emery of Park City, Utah. We wish the young couple much happiness. It is a real surprise to Albion's friends, and a most happy one. He is of the salt of the earth and will be a blessed benedict if there ever was one on earth. The heartiest congratulations of all the old gang go out to him and his bride. May they live forever and never grow old.[5]

Following their marriage, the Emerys rented a small house from Mr. Gulliver in Park City. Sometime later they purchased their own small home at 721 Woodside Drive. Surprisingly, the house is still standing—despite two fires prior to 1900 and a recent plan to demolish it to make way for a ski bridge through town.[6] The Emerys' marriage was surprisingly happy even though they hadn't known each other long. Albion resigned from the post office and began working for the Daly Mines as a bookkeeper. Bookkeeping for John Daly's mine paid more and offered more opportunities to hear of mining investments. Equally ambitious, Susie probably continued working; their home was comfortably decorated with popular furnishings and boasted a piano. Both realized they needed a nest egg for investing and worked hard to save money. Albion wrote a letter to Susie's parents soon after they married that provides insight into their relationship:

> The smile on Susie's face is daily becoming broader and my intelligent grin has become perpetual, so no good reason why this agreeable state of affairs should not continue . . . we intend that it shall.[7]

Eight months later, in 1885, Susie's sister Viola and Willis Lamb announced their engagement. They married that June at the bride's home in Crescent Mills. The bride was seventeen and very much in love. Willis was her first romance and had good prospects as an employee of the Green Mountain Mining Company. Following the marriage they planned to purchase a home near her parents and start a family. Sarah was delighted with her daughter's engagement and planned a lovely wedding. The Bransford home was decorated in grand fashion, and family and friends gathered from far and near to celebrate the event and wish the couple well. The next day, following the ceremony, the newlyweds left for a week-long honeymoon in San Francisco.

Viola announced she was pregnant less than six months later. Milford and Sarah were thrilled for her but felt sad for Susie. Nine years older than Viola, Susie was beginning to wonder why she was not pregnant after two years of married life. The next several months passed quickly, and Viola's pregnancy seemed normal. On September 26, 1886, Viola delivered a healthy baby boy at her parents' home, and Sarah lovingly supervised the care of her daughter and grandson.

The proud parents named their firstborn Harold Bransford Lamb and happily planned for his future. But then there came signs that something was terribly wrong. Weeks passed and Viola continued to pass blood, growing steadily weaker. The exact cause of the problem is still unknown, but modern physicians have speculated that the placenta was not completely expelled after the baby was born. Viola was bedridden for several weeks, the slow constant loss of blood draining all of her strength. Throughout the ordeal local doctors remained optimistic she would recover, but Viola died November 20, 1886.

Susie's sister, Viola Bransford Lamb, died shortly after childbirth. Her son, Harold, was sent to live with Susie, who greatly enjoyed mothering him, and his grandmother Sarah. Photograph courtesy of Harold Lamb.

Willis, Milford, and Sarah were devastated by Viola's unexpected death. Sarah assumed the responsibility for the baby because Willis was in no condition to care for an infant. Friends and family gathered at Crescent Mills for the funeral and the Greenville Band supplied music for the services. Viola was laid to rest in a small cemetery overlooking Indian Valley. The following appeared in the *Greenville Bulletin* on November 24:

> Life lingered until 3:00 P.M. Saturday when she breathed her last, surrounded by relatives and friends. Mrs. Lamb [18 years old] had a wide circle of friends whose love and respect she always enjoyed. She was the second daughter of Mr. and Mrs. M. B. Bransford, and was born at Crescent Mills in this county. The funeral took place at 2:00 P.M. Monday, and it was largely attended by sympathizing friends from all over the valley.

A few weeks after the funeral, Milford and Sarah sold their home and possessions and moved

Albion served as the grand master of Utah's Masons in Salt Lake City's Masonic Hall. Used by permission, Utah State Historical Society, all rights reserved.

to Utah to be near Albion and Susie. Sarah, now forty-eight, was grateful that Susie offered to raise Viola's baby and wanted to be nearby. Milford didn't mind leaving Plumas County; Utah offered more opportunities. The Bransfords held an auction, liquidating their assets to raise funds for the trip and even selling their luggage. One relative believes they were left with little after paying their creditors, but at least they cleared the balance sheet. Friends from the surrounding cities gathered to bid them farewell as they left for Utah.

Upon arriving in Park City, Milford was hired by his old friend, R. C. Chambers, to work as a bookkeeper for the Ontario Mine. Susie helped her parents find a house at 463 Park Street and saw to it that Nellie was enrolled in school. After her family was settled, Susie devoted herself to little Harold, Viola's baby. Motherhood appealed to her and she spent many hours caring for her nephew. Harold also helped to fill the lonely hours when Albion was frequently out of town on Masonic business. Soon she began pressing Albion to adopt if they could not have their own child.

In 1888, a year after Milford and Sarah brought Harold to Utah, the Emerys traveled to Massachusetts to visit Albion's family. While in Boston Susie and one of his sisters quietly visited several orphanages to find a baby. Susie realized forty-year-old Albion was not interested in starting a family, but she hoped to persuade him to adopt anyway. Albion's sister was very sympathetic and agreed to help Susie convince him. Susie later reported that she found a beautiful two-year-old girl in an orphanage and instantly fell in love with her. The two women took the child home and told Albion the baby's tragic history. Both knew he would be moved with compassion when he heard she had been abandoned on a Boston doorstep shortly after birth. The policeman who found her named her Louise and gave her his own surname. With Albion's family as allies, Susie soon convinced her husband to adopt the baby, and the three returned to Utah. A year later, in 1889, when the adoption was finalized, the couple named her Louise Grace Emery.

Susie was delighted with the child and enjoyed dressing her in pretty dresses and ribbons. Some time after the adoption they dropped the name Louise and called her Grace. Albion may have had his doubts about parenthood initially but soon became very attached to both Grace and Harold. The threesome spent many hours playing together when he was home from his frequent trips. Albion enjoyed reading to them and wrestling with them on the floor, even though his health problems limited many of his activities.[8]

During the late 1880s, when he was not clerking for the Daly Mine, Albion immersed himself in politics and Masonry. A Mason since the age of twenty-five, he had participated in several different lodges in many different cities. He had been one of the founders of Park City's lodge in 1880, and later became its senior deacon and senior warden. The following year he was made the lodge's master. By the time he married he had become Utah's junior grand warden and held many responsibilities. His friends recognized him as an expert on Masonic laws, rituals, and history. Since Masonry was so important to her husband and her father was an active Mason, Susie may have been a member of the Eastern Star because a chapter was organized in Park City while they lived there. Eventually, Albion began spending several days and evenings each month in Salt Lake City working with that lodge as well.

To keep in touch while he traveled, Albion wrote brief letters. In one note written in the late 1880s, he warned Susie to save every penny because they might need their nest egg sometime soon. The note proved prophetic; in July 1889 Albion and two friends, W. V. Rice and John Judge, had a chance to buy out three of the Mayflower Mine's original stockholders. The men had tired of the mine's constant legal entanglements and wanted to sell their share of the lease, but to take advantage of the opportunity, Albion needed eight thousand dollars immediately. The problem was that despite his efforts to save money, Albion had sizable debts and poor health. He first approached his boss, John Daly, for a loan, but Daly was leery of lending him money under these conditions.

Family stories suggest Albion eventually managed to raise the eight thousand dollars by borrowing the money from friends. With time running out, some speculate that Susie approached R. C. Chambers, her father's friend, for help. There is no record of the agreement, but Utah Supreme Court records suggest that Albion eventually met with Chambers privately and negotiated an arrangement for the eight thousand dollars he needed. According to one source, he agreed to be a "front" for Chambers and his friend, George Hearst, as they invested in the Mayflower Mine. One of the other owners, David Keith, also probably had Chambers's help when he bought an interest in the mine nine months earlier. By contrast, Thomas Kearns, recognized for his expertise as a mine operator, bartered his management skills for a share in the Mayflower.

During the next three years, the Mayflower and its new owners were involved in several lawsuits. The root of their problem was that as they tunneled deeper into the mountain, the Mayflower's incredibly rich vein merged with other veins or strayed into nearby claims. Folklorists quote Kearns's solution to the problem: "If the ore goes into another claim, buy it if you can, but if you can't buy it, take it anyway!"

Whether Kearns actually said this is immaterial because he apparently took any ores he stumbled upon, disputed or not. During the three years of the Mayflower's most critical lawsuit, *Northland Mining Company v. Mayflower Mining Company*, Kearns continued to take disputed ores from the Northland Mine. The courts finally ruled in favor of the Mayflower Mine and allowed them to buy out the Northland Mining Company for less than fifty thousand dollars. Some claim that by this time the stolen ore was worth many times

Susie and Albion adopted Louise Grace Emery in 1889. A shy, quiet girl, her personality sharply contrasted with Susie's flamboyance. Photograph courtesy of Stella Inge.

Although Susie and Nellie were Harold's primary caregivers, Willis Lamb was very involved in raising his son and was an integral part of the Emerys' lives. Photograph courtesy of Harold Lamb.

To be near his son, Willis Lamb, shown on the right, moved to Park City and worked for R. C. Chambers, seated on the left, as bookkeeper for the Ontario Mine. Photograph courtesy of Harold Lamb.

this amount, but Northland's owners were not aware of the theft until it was too late to protest. Following the settlement the Mayflower's peace was short lived; within a year the wandering vein now headed in the direction of the Silver King Mine. Keith and Kearns wisely approached the Silver King's owners and asked to lease the property. Unaware of the bonanza they possessed, the Silver King's owners agreed to the lease. Six months later, in 1892, the Mayflower Mine was incorporated as the Silver King Mine for three million dollars. The mine's stockholders soon became millionaires.[9]

As his money problems disappeared, Albion's political career took off. As an active Mason, he was a loyal supporter of the Liberal Party and was in the thick of the debate on statehood issues. A man of definite opinions, Albion entered the race for Summit County's seat in the Utah House of Representatives in 1893 and, with his general popularity, easily won the election. Albion's election and the election of several other non-Mormon candidates startled some, as non-Mormons grew more powerful in the House of Representatives with each election. When the legislature opened in January 1894, Albion was unanimously elected speaker of the Territorial House of Representatives. When the session ended, his peers presented him with a mahogany gavel with all their names engraved upon it. His fellow Masons also recognized him for his years of faithful service. He was elected grand master of Utah's Masonic lodges and became Utah's highest-ranking Mason.

After their first major dividend from the Silver King Mine in 1893, Susie and Albion paid off their creditors and moved the family to Salt Lake City. Now Albion could cut back on traveling between Park City and Salt Lake City, and Susie could spend more time with him. She found a large, two-story adobe home on First South and 350 East and eagerly purchased furnishings to fill the rooms. Her dreams of wealth, true love, and security had come true; she could now buy all the clothes she wanted and could travel all over the world.

Susie was also becoming important in society. When some prominent Utahns, including R. C. Chambers, promoted a Utah exhibit for the Chicago World's Fair in 1893, Susie was given a responsible position with the delegation. She and several other Park City women helped pick

Albion's older brother, George W. Emery, served as territorial governor of Utah and is the only governor of the state to have a county named for him. His influence may have helped Albion when he, too, entered politics. Used by permission, Utah State Historical Society, all rights reserved.

materials for the exhibit and later traveled to Chicago to represent Utah in the festivities. On the way home the Emerys and their friends stopped in several large cities and toured the sights. They enjoyed having money to spend after scrimping and barely getting by for many years, but they found themselves still scrambling to learn all the rules of etiquette of the nouveaux riches, the social class that emerged along with the great fortunes of the late nineteenth century.[10]

At the start of the Civil War, only a few Americans could rightfully be called millionaires, but in 1892 a New York newspaper listed over four thousand. This new class of millionaires created what Mark Twain called the "Gilded Age." It is difficult to put precise dates on the Gilded Age. The term is often applied loosely to the last decades of the nineteenth century, with the arrival of the Progessive Era in the early twentieth century marking its demise by increased regulation of business and wealth, especially the income tax provided by the Sixteenth Amendment in 1913. The transatlantic effects of World War I seriously undermined the power and influence of old elites, although many of the entrenched wealthy families found ways to hold onto their fortunes. In many ways, though, the glittery social milieu and cultural values associated with Gilded Age wealth survived until the Great Depression of the 1930s delivered another critical blow to them. Susie's life spanned the entire period and lasted until the Gilded Age had turned completely to dross; and like many others, she didn't seem to realize the era had passed.

The Gilded Age was marked by ostentatious display of possessions, vulgarity in taste, and corruption in both business and government, stemming in large part from materialism and pursuit of wealth at all costs, including the ruthless exploitation of natural resources. Labor organizers would add that the ruthless exploitation extended to

As the Emerys rose in society, Susie needed calling cards to leave at the homes she visited. She kept them in this silver case, monogrammed with SBE, for Susanna Bransford Emery (and, probably, later for Engalitcheff). Courtesy of Harold Lamb.

workers as well. Many Americans made fortunes by mining, manufacturing steel, refining oil, shipping, building and running railroads, and creating food items like cereal or chocolate candy. Others turned to real estate, banking, or stocks and bonds; and some made a great deal of money very quickly. Men such as John D. Rockefeller and Commodore Cornelius Vanderbilt were criticized for their ruthless business practices as they made millions and built their fortunes. Others, such as Andrew Carnegie, Milton Hershey, and Phoebe Hearst, were lauded for their philanthropy and service to others. Many Americans young and old admired them, and all seemed to be fascinated by them. Born in humble circumstances, these people rose from obscurity to the ranks of the rich and famous by using their intellect and aggression. They epitomized the American dream and demonstrated that America truly was the "land of opportunity." Several authors, including Edith Wharton and Henry James, wrote novels about the nouveaux riches and their relationship with the old guard, or established social elites.[11]

Since the early settlement of the United States, an American aristocracy, like but less formally recognized than its British counterpart, had been based upon ancestry and kinship as much as wealth or accomplishment. Inclusion into that select society took years, often generations, during which family members not only earned money, but served the state or the country in government or the military. The standards for belonging were strict: gentlemen upheld strict moral principles, honor, integrity, *noblesse oblige*, and forbearance, although some might observe that such principles were applied only within their own class and not at all in business practices. Ladies shared all of these standards and, in addition, could not talk loudly, run, gesticulate, argue, contradict anyone (especially not a man), nor do anything extraordinary.

The nouveaux riches had suddenly become wealthy through commerce or manufacturing or, as with the Emerys, mining, but the established elites were not about to accept upstart tradesmen easily. Consequently, in frequently futile attempts to impress the old guard, the newly rich developed a fierce competition among themselves to see who could build the most elaborate house, throw the most fabulous party, wear the most exquisite clothes, or own the most expensive jewels. It was a lifestyle guaranteed to breed narcissism. The problem was that no matter how artificial, expensive, and sometimes downright silly the standards became, nearly everyone with wealth found themselves embroiled in the competition to some extent. At this point Susie was only wading along the shore; in future years she would swim in the deepest waters, accepting the values and lifestyle of the Gilded Age wholeheartedly.[12] If her life is viewed through the prism of her narcissism and her attempts to be accepted by an even more narcissistic group, many of her otherwise bizarre behaviors appear logical.[13]

For now, Susie and Albion were relieved because it seemed the years of struggle and hardship were finally over. Unfortunately, the wave of success the Emerys were riding rested on Albion's health. For years he had complained of chest pains. He found reclining in bed difficult, sometimes choking when he laid down, so he often slept sitting up in a chair. Albion's precarious health made the time he had with Susie during these months very important. Mindful that he was living on borrowed time, he frequently reminded her and their friends, "Why live life if you can't enjoy it?" As early as 1889 many had expected him to succumb to breathing and kidney problems, but he miraculously rebounded. Early in 1894, however, it became obvious he was failing, and he sought medical advice. Some have suggested the problem was a kidney disorder known as Bright's Disease; others wondered because of his lung problems whether he had consumption. The doctor prescribed a trip to Hawaii to relieve his suffering because the disease had progressed too far for treatment. This prescription may sound odd, but it was common for people to travel to lower elevations and warmer climates to relieve their tubercular symptoms.[14]

Susie arranged for a sitter to care for the children and took Nellie to help her with Albion. They spent a few weeks in Hawaii before they were forced to return to California. They reached San Francisco, and Albion collapsed after checking into the Belle Vista Hotel. Two doctors and several nurses cared for him during the next few weeks, but none could alleviate his suffering. He had been living on nervous energy and liquor for the last few years; now his body was too weak to fight the disease any longer. Albion's liquor bill the last three

Susie was about 35 years old when Albion died. Used by permission, Utah State Historical Society, all rights reserved.

weeks of his life was extraordinary: he consumed nearly four dozen bottles of hard liquor and several cases of seltzer water. Some authors have accused him of living a debauched life during his last year, but much of the alcohol he consumed doubtless served as a pain killer. At one point the doctors cautiously suggested he might bounce back and fully recover as he had several years earlier when a doctor thought he had contracted diphtheria. Through it all Susie tried to comfort him, but her own spirits were down, as if she sensed she would soon be a widow. His Masonic eulogy describes the Emerys' touching last moments together: "And when the parting hour came his dear companion watched over his failing breath, smoothed his pillow and closed his eyes."

For Susie this was a second tragedy that compounded her grief: three weeks earlier, on May 25, her father, Milford, had died in Salt Lake City. He had suffered from several bouts of tuberculosis since acquiring the disease during the Civil War. Shortly after the Emerys left for Hawaii, he was hospitalized for the last time. When the cablegram arrived to tell them of Milford's death and funeral, Nellie left to attend the funeral in Salt Lake City and to comfort Sarah. Susie was devastated, feeling guilty that she could not be with her grieving mother, but Albion was too ill for her to leave him even briefly. Susie grieved that she could not pay her last respects personally at the funeral and also wept that she could not confide in both of her parents about Albion's impending death. Willis Lamb and John Bransford handled the arrangements for Milford's funeral and burial. Susie sent word that she would like to have him buried in Mt. Olivet Cemetery, not far from Albion's future grave, in a plot she was establishing for all of the family.

Albion died on June 14 and Susie plummeted to the depths of depression. Now that Milford's funeral was over, Sarah and Nellie were on hand to help her during her ordeal. But the hardest reality remained: the two men she most relied on were gone. The loneliness and sense of responsibility were also overwhelming. Fortunately, David Keith,

Thomas Kearns, and Willis, her brother-in-law, offered to make the arrangements for Albion's funeral. She was overwhelmed by the number of people who loved Albion. There was such an outpouring of support from Park City that the men arranged for a train to carry mourners to and from the funeral. The viewing was held in the Masonic Hall and the funeral was conducted in the Congregational church. The Masonic graveside service was equally impressive. Dozens of Masons took part in the ceremony, and Albion was laid to rest with all the pageantry befitting his rank.

Days later, with the initial shock of Albion's death hardly past, Susie's new business partners, David Keith and Tom Kearns, told her more bad news. Albion had left no will to settle his estate, and his business affairs were in disarray. It is likely he expected to survive this latest attack of Bright's Disease, as he had in 1889 when several doctors had predicted his death. Fortunately, this blow was tempered by a $12,500 life insurance policy which would cover expenses until his estate could be probated. But if Susie thought the worst was over, she was wrong. She would soon be embroiled in a major court battle for her husband's estate that would smear the Emery name in Utah's newspapers and turn her public image from a grieving widow into a greedy, ungrateful friend.[15]

The Silver King Mine was the source of Susie's enormous wealth. Photograph courtesy of Park City Museum and Historical Society.

The parlor of Albion and Susie's home reflected the tastes and expectations of the 1890s. Note the piano on the right; some people believe Susie could not play, and yet her homes consistently included a piano. Photograph courtesy of Park City Museum and Historical Society.

Park City sits on the east side of the Wasatch Mountains and was incorporated as a city in 1884. Eventually its rich silver lodes produced $400 million and made twenty-three of its mine owners millionaires. Photograph courtesy of Park City Museum and Historical Society.

In 1898 a fire destroyed much of downtown Park City, including most of these stores. The Aschheim family had lived in Plumas County and probably knew the Bransfords well. Susie probably worked in their store as a seamstress and milliner when she moved to Park City. Photograph courtesy of Park City Museum and Historical Society.

The railroad was an important asset to Park City miners. They needed it to ship their ore out and bring their supplies in. In this picture of the Park Avenue depot, taken about 1918, the train stands ready to receive ore from Silver King Coalition Mine. Photograph courtesy of Park City Museum and Historical Society.

Stock in the Silver King Mine made Susie rich, but it lost its value during the Depression of the 1930s. Photograph courtesy of Park City Museum and Historical Society.

# 4

# The R. C. Chambers Affair

Like many western mining communities, Park City had several powerful personalities who dominated its mining operations, local businesses, and politics. Names such as John J. Daly, John Judge, Colonel William F. Ferry, W. S. McCornick, and, eventually, David Keith, Thomas Kearns, and Albion Emery became well known throughout Summit County and Utah Territory. Many had earned the admiration and respect of the local citizens, while a few, like Robert Craig Chambers, drew mixed reviews. For years Chambers had been the subject of controversy, and his name was associated with many questionable activities. Surprisingly, he was oblivious to his unpopularity until being defeated for election to Summit County's seat in the Utah Constitutional Convention in the fall of 1894. After making a sizable contribution to the Republican Party, he confided to its secretary that this was his first and last bid for election. He claimed he had entered the election to please "the boys," not because of personal ambition. When the election returns were announced, he was shocked and embarrassed to discover he had been defeated by a wide margin. For most people, however, the only mystery was why he had expected to win at all.

Chambers had worked in Utah for over a decade but had made little effort to make friends. On one occasion he had even offhandedly commented to a friend that he wished Park City would go to hell! Possibly one of the reasons he failed to form a strong bond with the Parkites was that he lived on a citrus ranch in Palermo, California, or in a home in San Francisco about six months out of each year. Those who knew him well realized his negativism and unusual political or business decisions were typical of his personality. He enjoyed being unpredictable and liked to keep people guessing, and it is highly likely that many who voted for his opponent in the election did it to spite him for many questionable business practices.

It was hard for many Park City residents to forgive Chambers for repeatedly favoring his California partners over them. One incident that particularly embittered them dealt with a controversial survey of Park City several years earlier. The city's original residents had neglected to survey the town properly and did not have legal title to their buildings and property. When the problem was discovered, a man named Nims and a few unscrupulous individuals arranged to delay the government survey and title registration process until they had filed an application with the territorial government to control the townsite. This gave the scoundrels title to all of Park City's real estate and left the town's residents at their mercy. Chambers made a deal with the scoundrels to protect his title to the Ontario Mine's land and then used his influence to pressure the townspeople to buy their land back from the men who had stolen it from them. Many lost money, businesses, and homes in the shady transaction and never forgave Chambers for helping the crooks cheat them.[1]

A second shady transaction that hurt Chambers's reputation in Utah involved the

Robert Craig Chambers was a good friend of the Bransfords until he filed suit against Susie for part of Albion's estate. Used by permission, Utah State Historical Society, all rights reserved.

Union Pacific Railroad. For several years the Union Pacific had bilked customers by charging exorbitant fees for carrying coal to Park City's mines and to the Salt Lake Valley via the old Utah Central Railroad. Any time an effort was made to break the Union Pacific's monopoly, the company forced its competition out of business. By 1879 the Church of Jesus Christ of Latter-day Saints (the LDS or Mormon Church), many Park City businesmen, and other Utah investors, fed up with the situation, incorporated to build a narrow-gauge railroad line to connect Coalville, Park City, and Salt Lake City through Parley's or Emigration Canyon, hoping the new line would offer all concerned much better freight and coal prices.

The shareholders in the new railroad managed to raise most of the capital needed but lacked enough money to finish the track into Park City. At that point some Park City businessmen approached R. C. Chambers for a $186,000 loan and were surprised when he readily responded. The road was finished a few months later in December 1880. During the next three years, the new Utah Eastern managed to survive some stiff competition and even thrived despite the fact that the Union Pacific now had a parallel rail line into Park City. The Utah Eastern had a few large contracts which offset the Union Pacific's many small customers.

Building on his initial investment, Chambers quickly moved up in the company and soon became the president. Once in control, he quietly gave one of his California partners, James Ben Ali Haggin, a large share of the company's stock. Just as secretively, Haggin turned around and sold the stock to the Union Pacific at a profit. In 1883 the Union Pacific suddenly notified the Utah Eastern's shareholders that the company had a new board of directors. Angry and resentful, the many small stockholders watched in disbelief as the UP began dismantling their company. The Union Pacific also took over the Utah Eastern's freighting contracts, so that the business soon became insolvent and was forced to close. Four years later the company was again ravished when the Union Pacific held an auction to sell the Utah Eastern's equipment and pull up its tracks.

When the dust settled, no one knew whether Chambers had lost money in the deal, but his

Local Indians referred to George Hearst as the "boy the earth talked to." He owned interests in some of the most important mining claims in the United States, including the Comstock Lode in Nevada, the Ontario silver mine in Utah, the Homesake gold mine in South Dakota, and the Anaconda copper mine in Montana. Photograph courtesy of Hearst Castle™/Hearst San Simeon State Historical Monument.™

power and prominence in western mining circles seemed to increase, not decline, with the demise of the Utah Eastern. Meanwhile, many Parkites and other Utahns were ruined financially. Once again they saw that Chambers put his California friends and interests above his loyalty to themselves. So many people were hurt in this debacle that few would ever forget or forgive him in the future.[2]

Within months of Albion Emery's death, Chambers committed what many saw as another grievous sin: he decided to sue Albion's widow. Soon after Albion's funeral, Willis Lamb, David Keith, and Tom Kearns had begun the probate process to settle his estate. A few weeks later, on July 28, 1894, Susie filed a bond in probate court to qualify as administratrix of the estate. Four of

Albion's friends, W. S. McCornick, Emanuel Kahn, Matthew Cullen, and W. H. Dodge, guaranteed her bond as a gesture of moral support.

Notices were then printed in several Salt Lake City newspapers and the *Park Record* informing people that the probate process had started, allowing creditors to present their claims for payment. Most of the bills submitted were very minor, like the one from Judge, Ivers, and Keith Livery for carriages or those from several Salt Lake City mercantiles for groceries and clothing.

By contrast, on September 21, 1894, Chambers's attorney, Parley L. Williams, filed a civil lawsuit claiming that the Emerys owed R. C. $174,712.57 in cash and stocks. Stunned by the lawsuit, Susie sought the help of Judge W. H. Dickson, one of Salt Lake City's most capable attorneys. Many insiders were amazed to hear that the shrewd Chambers could not take the money outright because he lacked written record of his deal with Albion. All of Park City was surprised to hear of Chambers's plans to sue Albion's widow. The large fund of anger that had cost him the election became evident; the Emerys, on the other hand, had many friends in Park City.

Dickson agreed to tackle the case single-handedly even though he was pitted against the formidable firm of Bennett, Marshall, Bradley, and Williams. Within a matter of days, he notified Chambers's attorneys that Susie refused to recognize R. C.'s claims. Realizing the burden of proof rested with the plaintiff, he now openly challenged Chambers to prove his allegations. Charges and countercharges were quickly exchanged. The attorneys for both sides were at loggerheads; neither would concede to the other. The only thing all agreed upon was that a judge, not a jury, should decide the matter. Albion's estate could not be settled and his bills could not be paid until the lawsuit was settled in court.

Meanwhile, Susie, still reeling from the deaths of her husband and father, felt lonely, angry, and apprehensive about the future. She had a mediocre education and was inexperienced in handling large sums of money. In the past Albion or her father had handled the money, paid the bills, and made investments; now she would have to make these decisions. Depression dogged her as she realized she shouldered so many responsibilities alone. Such an adjustment might be difficult enough for a woman in the 1990s, but in nineteenth century America, where many women could not vote or hold property in their own names, it was a major challenge. Fortunately, Sarah, Willis, and Nellie were on hand to provide encouragement and suggestions. During the next several months Susie tried to appear confident while waiting for the trial to begin, but as it neared, she became content to allow Judge Dickson a free hand in court and quietly took a back seat in the matter.

The trial was covered extensively by Utah's papers, and, despite the fund of goodwill Albion and Susie had built, many of the stories were critical of the Emerys and deeply hurt Susie. People watched this trial not with just the prurient interest of voyeurs seeing the wealthy fight among themselves, but because "apart from the magnitude of the demand, it is one of the most important cases from a legal standpoint that has ever come before any court in the West. . . . If Mr. Chambers should win the suit, no man in this territory can ever die with the assurance that his family will be allowed to enjoy the benefits of the property he may leave behind."[3]

The trial started December 18, 1894, and was heard in Judge S. A. Merritt's courtroom in Coalville. To prepare for the trial, Judge Dickson carefully analyzed all of Albion's financial records and interviewed Susie at length about her memories of Albion's dealings with Chambers. Dickson then formulated a game plan for the defense and patiently waited. From the outset he decided to deny all of Chambers's claims to the Emery money and then to sue Chambers to recover the twenty thousand dollars Albion had paid him in interest and principle for the money he borrowed. Later, as the plaintiff's attorney laid out his case in court, Dickson methodically attacked each point and discredited Chambers by challenging each witness. After hearing Dickson's objections, the judge ordered the testimony of John L. Weber, one of Chambers's chief witnesses, stricken from the record. He also threw out one of Chambers's important pieces of physical evidence: bonds Chambers had posted for the Silver King Mine during the seemingly endless chain of lawsuits in the early 1890s. The judge ruled that simply signing for or posting such bonds did not necessarily prove that Chambers actually owned an interest in the mine.

There was no way Dickson could stop Chambers's attorneys from calling David Keith, Richard Mackintosh, A. T. Moffatt, and James Glendenning to testify. Each man claimed to have had conversations with Albion five years earlier in which he admitted having a partnership with Chambers, but Dickson argued that their testimonies should be discounted because so many years had lapsed since the alleged conversations had taken place. Too much was at stake for vague recollections of their conversations to be seriously considered. Dickson also argued that details such as facial expressions and voice inflections must be considered to determine Albion's intentions. The judge also agreed that these could not be accurately replicated for the court. Dickson made it clear he was not challenging the men's honesty—they were pillars of the community—time and human frailties were the issues. After so many years it would be easy to inaccurately recall the conversations with Albion.

To counter, the plaintiff produced additional witnesses, Solon Spiro and M. S. Aschheim. Both had known Albion well when he worked for Aschheim's Mercantile in Park City, and both testified that Emery was ill and in debt in 1889. Under those conditions it was unlikely he could have arranged a loan with anyone. A third witness, A. T. Moffatt, foreman of the Ontario Mine, testified that Albion first tried to borrow money from John J. Daly, but was refused because of poor health and no security. Borrowing money from Chambers was a desperate, last-minute gesture. Moffatt recalled that Albion told him on several occasions that Chambers owned part of his fifth interest in the Mayflower Mine.

In response, Susie's attorney next pointed out that it seemed unusual that a shrewd, cautious businessman like Chambers would overlook the necessity of a written agreement to spell out the terms of any business arrangement. It was also common knowledge in Park City and Salt Lake City that Albion was ailing and might not recover from his latest illness. Despite Albion's illness, Chambers never approached him for his share of the stocks and money before Albion left Utah for Hawaii in March 1894. It seemed unfair that he would wait until Albion was dead to press his widow for the money.

Chambers was forced to admit that he could not produce a written agreement between the two parties. Dickson next pointed out that the check stubs Susie had saved had the word "loan" written near the bottom. These were strong evidence that there had been a loan and that it had been repaid with interest. A note enclosed with one of the cancelled checks also suggested Albion had lent Chambers money because he was overdrawn by thousands of dollars in several local banks.

During cross-examination Keith raised the issue that Albion had suspected Chambers of double-dealing his partners in the Silver King Mine; he reportedly paid two men, Mr. Wilson and Mr. Thompson, to promote the Northland lawsuit against the Mayflower/Silver King Mine interests. The situation had so angered Albion that he decided he would not give Chambers more money until R. C. asked him for it personally. The suggestion that Albion felt Chambers was crooked helped

David Keith, one of Albion's business partners, helped Susie through the *Emery v. Chambers* trial. Used by permission, Utah State Historical Society, all rights reserved.

to dispel some of the negative inferences Chambers had made about Albion's character, but no one's reputation emerged from the cross-examinations without sustaining some damage. Instead, as the trial progressed, this incident seemed to suggest many of Park City's mining deals were made behind closed doors and some were not only unethical but probably illegal as well.

As the end of the second day neared, the evidence presented by both sides served only to muddle, not clarify, the issues. The situation might have become even more heated had Dickson not used a surprising ace that abruptly ended the trial. In an ironic twist of fate, Dickson had been one of the Mayflower's attorneys in the *Northland v. Mayflower* lawsuit two years earlier. Consequently, he knew Chambers had either perjured himself in that case or was lying now. When the attorneys for the Mayflower Mine had called him to testify as an expert witness in the Apex Mining Law case, the Northland attorneys moved to have him excluded as a witness because of an alleged conflict of interest. One of the Northland attorneys had asked him directly if he owned any interest in the Mayflower Mine or if he had grubstaked Albion Emery. To avoid problems and to protect his friends at the Mayflower Mine, Chambers had denied his claims to Albion's stock and claimed that Albion had repaid the borrowed money with interest. Now, in the *Emery v. Chambers* trial, Dickson surprised Chambers by calling him to the witness stand.

Dickson first asked Chambers if he remembered being cross-examined by the Northland attorneys. He did. Next, Dickson asked whether he had told the truth under oath. Chambers, of course, said he had. Finally, Dickson asked Chambers whether, during the earlier trial, he had denied owning any Mayflower stock in his testimony. Chambers's face turned a deep red as he cleared his throat to answer. He realized he was caught in a legal vise. In the earlier trial his testimony had helped the Mayflower win the lawsuit and had ruined the Northland company. Now he could not reverse his earlier testimony without risking a civil lawsuit from the former owners of the Northland Mine and possibly facing criminal actions as well.

When Chambers answered that he had been honest in his earlier testimony, Dickson pounced. If his earlier testimony were true, was the money he gave Albion a loan or a grubstake? If the money were lent, he could not claim any ownership in the mine; if he had grubstaked Albion, his claim might be legitimate, but he had committed perjury in the former trial. A hum filtered through the courtroom as the audience realized Dickson had tricked Chambers into denying his claim to Susie's money. Both attorneys made lengthy closing arguments the next day. Judge Merritt listened attentively and then announced that he needed time to consider the issues and would have his decision when the court reconvened in January after the holidays.

In the interim, Park City had plenty to talk about. Insiders were amazed that Chambers was emerging as a fool. How could he have failed to record the agreement when so much was at stake? Those who hated him because of his ruthless business practices laughed at his legal and financial difficulties. After his many years of double-dealing Park City's residents and even his business partners, George Hearst and James Ben Ali Haggin of the Ivanhoe Holding Company of California, it seemed fitting that he was getting his just due.[4] When newspapers reported that Chambers's attorney had called David Keith as a witness, some speculated that Chambers had also secretly grubstaked him. People debated whether such an agreement existed, but there was much evidence to support the idea. Keith probably could not have raised the eight thousand dollars in 1889 to invest in the Mayflower Mine without outside help.

When the attorneys and their clients met again on January 21, 1895, Judge Merritt awarded Susie and her eight-year-old adopted daughter all of Albion's money. Although Chambers was beaten, he was not yet willing to concede defeat. He promptly directed his attorneys to appeal the matter to Utah's Territorial Supreme Court. Hoping the justices would see his side of the argument and award him some of the money, he claimed that Dickson had tricked him and that the judge had not allowed some of his witnesses to testify. Nearly two years later, Utah now having become a state, the State Supreme Court upheld the lower court's decision and barred Chambers from making further appeals. The justices ruled that it was wrong to assume an agreement existed if no document could be found to substantiate the claim. They also felt that intervening in the rights of inheritance would set a bad precedent for future

Although Susie's brother, John, lived in California, he was still important to her. In a few years his family would become one of the most important factors in her life. This picture, dated from about 1894, shows his family: his wife, Rachel; son, Wallace; John; and daughter, Stella. Photograph courtesy of Vadney and Jean Murray.

litigation and be a miscarriage of justice to all widows. Furious that he had lost a fortune as well as the election several months earlier, Chambers returned to California and subsequently played a much smaller role in Utah's history.[5]

When news reporters released the judge's decision and the details of the trial, some believed Albion and Susie were innocent victims of Chambers's scam. Others took Chambers's side and viewed Susie as a cheat for refusing to honor her husband's obligations. They also criticized her attorney for putting Chambers in a spot where he had no choice but to deny his claim to her money or face the possibility of more legal trouble. Surely ten percent of the famed Silver King Mine's revenues was adequate to care for her family!

Once the trial and appeal were behind her, Susie doubtless breathed a sigh of relief and rejoiced at her good fortune, but her ecstasy was short-lived. She had another weighty problem to deal with: her adopted daughter, Grace. When Grace and Harold were both very young, Susie had enjoyed her motherly role and carefully watched over them. Later, she had enrolled both in a Park City school, dressed them in stylish clothing, and gifted them with everything her resources allowed. The children thrived under her care, even though Grace was frequently absent from school with one childhood illness after another. Even when they were young, Susie noticed Grace was shy and craved adult attention, while Harold easily moved back and forth among his father, grandparents, and Susie with few problems. He seemed a happy, healthy, well-adjusted boy. Grace, however, was developing deeply seated insecurities. She had been two when the Emerys adopted her and had spent those two years in a orphanage; it is hard to know what kind of care she received there and how much the lack of bonding in those very early years affected her personality. Still, it almost seemed she sensed when she was young that she really was not Susie's flesh and blood and constantly wanted reassurance that she was loved.

When Susie moved the family to Salt Lake City in 1893, she transferred Grace to Rowland Hall, a prestigious private school. Susie selected the school because it offered a quality education and because most of Salt Lake City's wealthy families patronized it. Although Grace was enrolled in the school, she spent most of the next year and a half at home with her mother or a governess as her frequent illnesses continued. Her absences from school made it difficult for her to keep up with schoolwork, and her grades suffered. Her high absenteeism and low grades convinced some teachers that she was slow, but intelligence was probably not the issue. Each time Grace returned to school after a long absence, she was too shy to ask the teacher for help or to say when she didn't understand something. The school setting also aggravated her insecurities instead of relieving them. She did not learn how to relate to other children her age. She avoided talking or playing with them; instead, she followed the adults around or played by herself.[6]

At the same time, Susie was becoming less and less available to her daughter as she traveled and socialized, and Grace reacted badly to her mother's absences. For years Albion had left Susie home with the children while he worked or traveled, but now that they had money and she could afford a governess, Susie often left Grace home. She apparently didn't feel guilty about leaving Grace with a governess because other wealthy women used governesses as well. Susie had discovered that many wealthy women sent their children to boarding schools or hired tutors to care for them and educate them at home. Some even selected a governess with a foreign background so that their children would learn a foreign language and a different culture. From Susie's own perspective, she was a good parent. She was sure that the governess adequately nurtured Grace while she traveled.

Social historians Stephen Burningham and Mary Cable have pointed out that wealthy parents of this time generally hired servants to become their children's surrogate parents. Mothers as well as fathers spent many hours traveling, doing charity work, partying, or socializing. Some spent only moments each day with their children or left them in the care of a governess for several months at a time. One of the most widely recognized victims of this sort of parental neglect was "little Gloria" Vanderbilt. In a recent televised biography of her life, Gloria discussed her estrangement from her natural mother and attachment to her governess. Following the death of her father, Gloria's maternal grandmother was publicly criticized for trying to take her away from her mother. The trial was brutal, with the grandmother's attorney calling Gloria to testify against her mother in an effort to prove that the young woman was a negligent parent. After weeks of testimony, the judge decided to place Gloria in her mother's custody. Gloria's mother won a moral victory, but Gloria was the real loser in the ordeal: she lost her closest friend, her devoted governess, in the court battle.[7]

The Vanderbilts' was an exceptional case, but even in less dramatic instances the system could be difficult for children. Parents tended to give their children gifts in place of time and attention. In Southampton children were given cars and allowed to drive at ten or eleven years old, the only restriction being that they could not go beyond the boundaries of the village. One such child observed, "The only time you got into trouble was if you hit someone or a farmer's cow." Craig Mitchell of New York refers to himself as a survivor. "It was as bad an upbringing as you could possibly get. . . . I was rotten spoiled—a lot of us were. I grew up totally undisciplined." His parents bailed him out of one problem after another, but he finally learned discipline at a boarding school—following several beatings from schoolmates and school personnel.[8]

Obviously, if all families had faced such problems, the systems of boarding schools and governesses would have collapsed long ago; instead, it thrives all over the country, although "nanny" has been substituted for "governess." The fact is that most children fared very well under this system. In Utah families as well, many children grew up healthy and well-adjusted although they were frequently separated from their parents. Jack Gallivan, long-time publisher of the *Salt Lake Tribune*, was raised by Jennie Judge Kearns, Tom Kearns's widow. He remembers that she often left him with governesses or in boarding schools while she traveled, and he recognized it was simply the way of life among the families he knew. He and many others who knew Jennie regarded her as an excellent mother.[9]

Since governesses were so commonplace, hiring one for Grace had seemed the best solution to Susie's child care problems, but tragically it

Tom Kearns, another of Albion's business partners, became an influential figure in Utah politics. Used by permission, Utah State Historical Society, all rights reserved.

After Albion's death Grace could not seem to accept his loss. She clung to his image and would not accept comfort. As her emotional problems escalated, she also developed headaches, nausea, and St. Vitus Dance, which caused involuntary, uncontrollable twitching in the face and limbs. To Susie, who was totally overwhelmed with the situation—Albion's and Milford's deaths, her mother's needs, Chambers's demands—Grace's needs were frightening. The little girl's moodiness and possessiveness distressed Susie to the point that she confided to Sarah on several occasions that she was disappointed with Grace's temperament. Had she made a terrible mistake in adopting her? Grace was pretty and sweet but lacked a happy disposition and the ability to mingle with people. Sarah told Susie it was natural for Grace to have a different temperament because she had different genes. Susie would have to be patient with her and help her as best she could. When Susie observed Grace shying away from aggravated Grace's insecurities instead of relieving them. The problem had begun just before Albion's death but became worse after he died. Each time the Emerys traveled together, Grace had became more possessive of her parents' time when they returned. She cried when her parents left and resented them for traveling without her. It seemed unjust to her that she was relegated to staying with servants when her parents traveled, but Harold went to stay with his father and his father's second wife. Willis had married Helen "Corby" Pearson Corbin, a woman from a prominent Eastern family who was very popular in Park City. They had no children of their own and welcomed Harold's visits, so he saw the Emerys' trips as happy holidays for himself as well. Grace, however well she was cared for by the governess, felt no such joy. When her parents left on their last trip together, a number of people tried to explain Albion's problems to her, but she was too young to grasp that her father hoped to recover by traveling to Hawaii.

Jennie Judge Kearns helped her husband in his political career, but she was also a philanthropist and civic worker in her own right. Used by permission, Utah State Historical Society, all rights reserved.

After Viola's death Willis Lamb married Helen Pearson Corbin in 1894 in Park City. Daughter of a wealthy Boston family, Helen was affectionately called "Corby" and was an extremely popular socialite. Newspaper articles from the time indicate she was invited to at least one party per week and often three or four. Photograph courtesy of Harold Lamb.

people in social functions, she would try to involve her in the activities. But being the center of attention terrified Grace, and the more Susie tried to push her into the limelight, the more Grace retreated into the shadows. Despite Susie's efforts to reassure her, Grace could not feel loved. A chasm began to develop between the two, and it would never be bridged.[10]

At the time she met Colonel Holmes, Susie was already moving into Gilded Age society and dressing the part. Her magnificent dresses would become one of the hallmarks of her social image. Photograph courtesy of Vadney and Jean Murray.

# 5

## A Decade of Adjustment

The years immediately following Albion's death presented Susie and Grace with many challenges. Victorian etiquette dictated strict guidelines for how the bereaved were to grieve for family members. Widows were expected to mourn for a year, though some mourned longer. The mourning period for one's child or parent was also a year, while the time required for a grandparent or sibling was only six months. During the first month the bereaved was only allowed visits to church; after thirty days an individual could leave the house without censure if she avoided celebrations or pleasurable occasions. Friends and relatives frequently visited those in mourning to help them deal with their loss and to relieve the social isolation many experienced. Mourners were also expected to wear black for a year; the next year a woman could wear gray, purple, and white, but her clothing had to be conservative. If jewelry was worn, custom dictated that it be as simple as a strand of pearls, semiprecious stones, or black stones.[1]

To compound the problem, poor sanitation, inadequate medical care, and the vulnerability of children made death a constant fact of life in the nineteenth century. For example, in New York City in 1853, forty-nine percent of deaths were children under the age of five. Utah also had high infant mortality rates; during the 1850s approximately one-third of the recorded deaths were very young children. The average life-span for adults in this time period was also short, particularly for women. Many expired before the age of fifty-five, and a good number died before their children reached maturity.

Though the National Board of Health reported conditions in Salt Lake City in 1882 were better than or on par with other cities (60 of 177 cities surveyed had lower mortality rates, while 117 had higher rates), struggling with death and illness still united many nineteenth century Utah families. Some women spent a good part of each month calling on ailing friends or relatives and attending funerals.[2] Like many other families, the Bransfords and their in-laws closed ranks to support each other following the deaths of Albion and Milford. Susie and her mother became particularly close as they kept each other company during their mourning periods.

After losing the two most important men in her life so suddenly, Susie worried that she would next lose her mother, and the prospect overwhelmed her. Her family, particularly her mother, had been very important to her; without them she felt adrift. The problem was that after years of hard work and nursing others, Sarah, now nearly sixty, was exhausted and failing.[3] During the next decade Susie did everything she could think of to prolong her mother's life. Susie frequently took Sarah to doctors or on vacations and pampered her with expensive gifts. Knowing her father's resources had been limited, Susie also invited her mother and her sister, Nellie, to live with her in her home on First South.

A few years later Susie sold the home she and Albion had shared and built a larger, more elegant, two-story house two blocks east at 521 East First South. It was very spacious but did not provide the privacy the three women needed, so Susie and little Grace soon moved to the fashionable Knutsford Hotel, where they had their own apartment. To ensure her mother's comfort and security, Susie gave her the new home and quietly provided her with an income.4

Living in a hotel may seem odd in the late twentieth century, but residential hotels were extremely fashionable at the turn of the century. The Plaza in New York City still maintains a few residential apartments. Many of Salt Lake City's wealthy citizens had homes but retained suites in downtown hotels as well. David Jackling and Samuel Newhouse regularly reserved suites in the Hotel Utah, and David Keith died there in his usual apartment. At the time Susie and Grace moved into it, the Knutsford was Utah's finest hotel and ranked as one of the finest facilities west of the Missouri River, a distinction it held almost until its demolition in 1912.5

Like Grace, Nellie struggled with the loss of her father, but at seventeen, she accepted her loss much more easily than Grace, who was only eight. When Nellie and Susie had lived together with their mother, signs of strain soon developed between the two sisters despite their efforts to be considerate of one another. Nellie misunderstood her older sister's good intentions and felt Susie was trying to mould her into someone she was not. Nellie also felt her older, very attractive sister was using her to reenter society. This may have been one of Susie's motives, but Susie also worried that Nellie, who was very shy, was missing social opportunities.

Susie also enjoyed spending money on her family. Thus, when Nellie turned down most of their party invitations and frequently refused the pretty dresses she offered, preferring her own more modest attire, Susie was amazed and hurt. It was hard for outgoing Susie to understand Nellie's shyness, and they quarrelled. With their mother, the music lover, as an ally, Susie eventually convinced Nellie to accept her offer to pay for music school. Following much discussion Nellie reluctantly agreed to attend the Boston Conservatory to study voice and piano. She did not like to play for others, though she did sing frequently. Years later Nellie came to appreciate

Susie built this home for her mother, Sarah, and on Sarah's death gave it to Nellie and Jay Harris. It was located at 521 East First South in Salt Lake City, where the Eaton Kenway Building now stands. Photograph courtesy of Harold Lamb.

Susie and Grace moved into the fashionable Knutsford Hotel, one of the finest facilities west of the Missouri River. Used by permission, Utah State Historical Society, all rights reserved.

Susie's efforts in her behalf and both adjusted to their new situations.[6]

But while Nellie matured, Grace lapsed into a profound depression that would linger for years. Doctors a century later might have recommended psychiatric counseling or a medication, but nineteenth century medicine was powerless to relieve her suffering. More and more, she seemed a small, lost soul with few friends. Susie tried to help but repeatedly failed; they were just too different to communicate effectively. Fearing that no one loved her, Grace clung to her dolls, mother, and adults.[7]

It is also highly likely that friction erupted when Susie began accepting male callers a year after Albion's death. Such a reaction could be expected from any child who loses a parent, and Grace had idolized Albion. She deeply resented any man for trying to take his place in her mother's life, but Susie was a socially active adult. Eventually, Susie's business partner, Tom Kearns, introduced her to Colonel Edwin F. Holmes in the summer of 1895.[8] Like Susie, Holmes had been widowed in 1894. He had retired from his lumber, shipping, and mining interests to travel shortly before his wife became ill and died. When he visited Utah to check on his holdings in the Anchor Mine, he met Susie, sixteen years his junior, and the attraction between them was immediate.

Susie was charmed by Edwin's handsome appearance, courtly manner, and the many things they had in common. It also helped that he was the father of four children, even though the youngest, Carleton, was fifteen. In addition to discussing mining and business, they could talk about the problems of parenthood. After a few outings it was obvious that they were attracted to one another. But despite the Colonel's protestations of love, Susie would not commit to a serious relationship for several years; she wanted time to venture out into society before settling down in a second marriage. She also probably needed time to resign herself to marriage with another man. Albion had been the great love of her life.[9]

The next year, 1896, Utah's courts declared Susie to be Grace's legal guardian, so she "officially" assumed the responsibility for raising her daughter and managing the money each had inherited. Although by the judge's ruling it was actually two separate inheritances, Susie simply managed all of it together; her daughter was, after all, still very young, and their personal relationship remained the same. In a time when many women were still dependent upon their husbands or a male family member to control their money, Susie was very proud to own and manage her property. Several newspaper articles in her scrapbook mention her boasting about single-handedly directing the investment of her stocks—a practice that seems unlikely because she had no experience in handling large sums of money. Undoubtedly, Willis Lamb, David Keith, and Tom Kearns continued to advise her as they had during the Chambers trial.

Still, focusing on her business interests, on Colonel Holmes, and on her nephew, Harold, helped to take her mind off her other problems. She encouraged her nephew to visit often now that he lived with his father, Willis Lamb, most of the time. Unlike Grace, Harold was a happy child, a good student, and a relaxed companion. Susie enjoyed doting on him, and, with his father's consent, planned to enroll him at Exeter, a prestigious boys' boarding school, after he finished his studies at St. Mark's, a boys' school later integrated with Rowland Hall.[10]

After Grace spent two more unimpressive years at Rowland Hall, Susie withdrew her from the school. Susie was upset that Grace did poorly in school and showed no interest in trying to improve. It concerned her that Rowland Hall's principal, Miss Clara Colbourne, also believed Grace was slow and might be uneducable. Determined to make her daughter a better student, Susie enrolled her in a boarding school for girls near Berkeley, California. The prestigious private school guaranteed more individualized attention, so she hoped Grace would do better academically. Whether she was advised by the school, by Grace's doctor, or simply acted on her own intuition, Susie also decided to have Grace stay in the dormitory with a nurse rather than stay with her in her San Francisco hotel suite. Susie hoped Grace would make friends with the other girls and become less dependent upon her. Sadly, the plan failed; Grace became hysterical at the idea of being separated from her mother and sobbed as soon as Susie left the building. Grace's nanny and companion immediately contacted Susie at her hotel suite, but Susie did not return to

Colonel Edwin F. Holmes became Susie's second husband and one of Utah's most prominent citizens. Used by permission, Utah State Historical Society, all rights reserved.

the dormitory. Reasoning that a few weeks apart would resolve the problem, Susie decided to leave Grace alone with the other girls and her nurse, a classic application of the sink-or-swim philosophy.

While her daughter was in school, Susie probably visited friends in San Francisco. Years later she told reporters she knew Phoebe Hearst and several of the other wealthy notables of San Francisco well. She also visited with her brother John's son, Wallace, a bright, talented student pursuing a business degree at nearby Berkeley. When Susie told him about Grace's problems, Wallace offered to help and visited Grace at her dormitory to see if he could cheer her up.[11]

Wallace was shocked when he saw his young cousin; the effects of St. Vitus Dance and her tear-stained face touched him with pity. He also perceived that the nanny was frustrated with Grace's anxieties and had little patience with her. Only six years older than Grace, Wallace didn't understand all that passed between mother and daughter, but he asked his aunt if he could take Grace to Indian Valley to stay with his parents. Having already tried so many other alternatives, Susie gladly consented; maybe the trip would calm Grace. Susie was still concerned about her daughter's education but decided to put off dealing with the issue until later. Several days later Wallace and Grace arrived in Quincy, where his parents, John and Rachel, now lived. John was the town sheriff, having given up merchandising and mining. After seeing Grace, Rachel was also touched by her anxieties and devoted herself to eliminating them. Ironically, Grace's arrival probably helped Rachel deal with her own sense of loss; a few years earlier her youngest daughter, Erma Ellen, had died at the age of nine. Now she had another little girl to dote on for a few months. Perhaps Wallace recognized that his grieving mother could also benefit from the visit when he suggested it to Susie.[12]

Grace thrived in Quincy; she developed a tan and put on several pounds from her aunt's home cooking. The sole object of her aunt's and uncle's attention, she soon relaxed and began to enjoy the life of an only child in the house. The small town environment and Rachel's extended family, the Bloods, welcoming her were just what Grace needed to build her self-esteem. Never a large metropolis, Quincy had more than doubled in size since Susie and her family left the area over ten years earlier. Yet it still had several of the old social groups, such as the Prevaricators Club, and many church and school activities in which Grace could participate. Grace also enjoyed the outdoor activities, like hiking and fishing, readily available in Quincy. Emotionally starved, Grace eagerly bonded with her aunt, older cousin Stella, and the Blood cousins. In years to come she would never

Phoebe Apperson Hearst married George Hearst at the age of nineteen. Formerly a schoolteacher from Missouri, she became one of the most important philanthropists at the turn of the century. She was co-founder of the Parent-Teacher Association (PTA) and the first woman regent of the University of California, serving actively on the board from 1897 to 1919. Susie proudly claimed her as a friend. Photograph courtesy of Hearst Castle™/Hearst San Simeon State Historical Monument™.

Rachel Blood Bransford entertains the women of her family in front of the Bransford home in Quincy about 1898 or 1899. Rachel is in the center, at the head of the table, and Grace is second from the right with a very flushed face. Grace's visit to Quincy improved her health and her spirits. Photograph courtesy of Stella Inge.

forget their many kindnesses and would think of them as her own family.

In February 1899 John brought Grace back to Utah, along with the rest of his family. Though the Bransfords had apparently been happy and respected in Plumas County—John served as both county sheriff and county treasurer—the rest of his family was now in Utah. John purchased a home near his mother and Nellie, and he became Susie's business manager. John handled all of Susie's business affairs in Utah and her stocks and interests in other areas as well. A business school graduate, he proved a capable administrator. He also purchased a floral business and began working at Utah's stock exchange to provide additional income and investment opportunities for his family.

Susie was proud of her brother and eagerly introduced him to her friends and business partners when he arrived. John soon sought opportunities to work in Utah's politics. He found politics enjoyable, and his friendliness, natural business acumen, and honesty encouraged friendships. Eventually, he joined many of the former members of the Liberal Party to form the new American Party and was elected the party's president. Tensions still existed between some factions of Mormons and non-Mormons, and some members of the American Party were openly anti-Mormon. However, John was new to Utah, and though he was sensitive to the old issues between the warring groups, he had not been part of their earlier battles. As a result, he easily mingled with both groups and could serve as a mediator to prevent more friction from developing. His universal popularity was evident at his funeral forty years later: an attorney friend read the eulogy, a Mormon apostle dedicated the grave, and LDS

A Bransford family portrait. Left to right: Wallace Bransford, Sarah E. Bransford, J. Tarvin Harris, Louise Grace Emery, unidentified man, Nellie Bransford Harris, and Susie. Although there is no date on this photograph, since Sarah, the mother of the clan, is still alive, it dates prior to 1905. Given how young Wallace and Grace look, it was probably taken even earlier. Susie is noticeably taller than the other women; judging by pictures like this and by the clothes she gave to the Daughters of Utah Pioneers, she was probably at least five feet and eight inches tall. Photograph courtesy of Harold Lamb.

President Heber J. Grant mourned his passing in a lengthy press release.[13]

Shortly after John and Rachel moved to Utah, Susie began traveling again. Whether Grace was enrolled in a boarding school or left with a governess is not clear, but the likelihood is that she remained with her Bransford relatives. She later spoke with much affection of John and Rachel, and she seemed to thrive during this period, so she was doubtless under their supervision.

Meanwhile, Colonel Holmes had been patiently waiting for Susie to marry him. One autumn evening in 1899, while they were eating dinner with some Utah friends at Delmonicos in New York City, he decided to force the issue. One bit of folklore claims he plucked a red rose from the table's centerpiece and tossed it to Susie. Then he told the stunned group that he and Susie would soon be married at the Waldorf Astoria. Susie was speechless. She had never accepted his proposal, but now that he had announced the marriage, she decided it was probably a good time to accept.[14]

Edwin Holmes was an excellent example of the self-made man of the Gilded Age. For one thing, his assets totaled seven million dollars. He was ambitious and hard working and determined to accomplish something in his life. Born in Orleans, New York, in 1843, he had few chances for an education, but at an early age he decided to become a gentleman and worked hard toward that end. With little instruction, Edwin had learned to read and write and began collecting an extensive private library of the classics that became one of his greatest treasures. After working all day in the lumber camps or shipping yards, he hungrily absorbed the contents of his books each evening. Many years later his Utah friends marveled at his tenacity in researching issues that concerned him.

At nineteen he had enlisted in the Union army, rising from private to captain before being honorably discharged at the end of the Civil War. Impressed, his commanding officers recommended him for a brevet commission, which he declined; he wanted a business rather than a military career. The title of colonel, which he used throughout his life, was an honorary one. After returning home from the war, he began working as a lumberman in Michigan. In a few years he and his partner established several large lumbering camps and a mill that operated day and night. From this success he turned to shipping on the Great Lakes. Several years later he was building ships, eventually operating a large fleet of ships on the lakes, with large freight contracts. Holmes's restless spirit next pointed him west, where he invested in a number of timber and mining properties. One of his most valuable properties, the Anchor Mine in Park City, would eventually lead him to Utah and to Susie. Through his life he maintained business contacts and operated companies across the country.

Even though he was driven to become a successful gentleman, Holmes had taken time out to fall in love and marry in 1870. During his twenty-four year marriage, he and his first wife, Jenny, raised three daughters and a son. His family was a major priority in his life and he doted on every member of the family. By the time he proposed to Susie his daughters were all young adults. His son, Carleton, was barely fifteen and spent much time with his father when he was home from school. The Colonel often took him along on business trips, hoping that his son would follow in his footsteps and eventually manage his businesses. Concerned for his children's welfare, Holmes frequently brought them to Utah to visit, provided them with an income for life, and made sure each received a good education.[15]

In light of Grace's anger and anxiety, it would be interesting to know how she felt about Susie's marriage to the Colonel. Those who remember him feel he was a very warm, caring person who was patient almost to a fault. It would not have been in his nature to be anything but kind to Grace. When he took his children on vacation, he made sure the outing was timed so that his single children and Grace were home from school and no one was left out of the activity. As for Susie, he called her "Madam" and treated her like royalty.[16]

Holmes and Susie were married October 12, 1899. She sent engraved notices of the marriage to their many friends and family around the country. They rented one of the small dining rooms in the Waldorf-Astoria and had it decorated with many potted plants and flowers. Since the decision and the arrangements were both made so quickly, fewer than two dozen people attended. Susie's brother, John; her business partner, David Keith, with his wife; Mr. and Mrs. W. S. McCornick; and one of the four Bamberger brothers represented their Utah family and friends. The ceremony was brief and tastefully managed, after which the Colonel hosted a dinner for the guests in the hotel's main dining room. Following a brief stay in the hotel, the Colonel surprised Susie with several beautiful pieces of jewelry and some new dresses, and then he took her to Europe for a honeymoon that lasted six months.[17]

Their European honeymoon was typical of the grand tours of wealthy Americans in the Gilded Age. They crossed the ocean in a luxury liner, visited most of Europe's capital cities, sampled numerous exotic foods, danced, met countless members of European society, and tramped through many museums and art galleries. The pace they set for themselves was exhausting.

Many times both felt very tired, but the overall experience was marvelous. In a Moscow art gallery the guide was prolonging the tour with long-winded comments about each masterpiece they viewed. At one point the Colonel broke into the guide's commentary to ask how much longer the tour would take. Ever quick with a comeback, Susie whispered a sharp reply, "About three years at this pace." Whether the guide was really so very long-winded or whether the Holmeses were simply anxious to get on with their trip is an open question. Like many people today, Gilded Age travelers were often as concerned with bragging to their friends about the great number of places they visited as they were with the actual experiences.[18]

While traveling across Russia on the Trans-Siberian Railroad, they met many interesting members of the nobility and shared some meals

Like Susie, Molly Brown, from Leadville, Colorado, made a fortune from mining and moved into society. She was regarded as an upstart Westerner but became famous when she survived the sinking of the *Titanic*. Photograph courtesy of Colorado Historical Society.

Molly Brown spent her fortune on travel, clothes, jewels, and this fabulous house in Denver, Colorado. Photograph courtesy of Colorado Historical Society.

with the czar's brother, the grand duke. With his help they were able to meet Czar Nicholas II and the czarina, Alexandra. Days later, as the Holmeses were riding near Peterhof in St. Petersburg, they passed the czar and czarina in their elegant carriage. Both couples smiled and waved. Thrilled to be acknowledged, the Holmeses sent the royal couple a large bouquet of flowers. When Susie and the Colonel left Russia sometime later, the czar sent them a set of twelve gold-jeweled goblets to match some golden plates Susie had purchased. Susie was overwhelmed with his generosity and was later told the shy czar seldom extended such courtesies to strangers.[19]

While they were in London, Susie had hoped to be received by Queen Victoria, but she never was. There is an invitation to Edward VII's coronation in Susie's scrapbook, but newspapers reported the coronation was cancelled when Edward developed appendicitis; he was later simply taken to parliament, where he swore an oath and was declared king. However, Susie did meet the Scandinavian kings, who were, she said, less pretentious.[20]

Many months later, when their luxury liner steamed into New York's harbor, Grace and her uncle John met Susie and the Colonel at the pier. Susie had no sooner started down the gangplank than Grace ran up to her with an armful of flowers and embraced her. Susie later said how thrilled she was to have Grace greet her so affectionately. She was also glad that Grace, now fourteen, had put on a little weight, smiled, and seemed calmer. Mother and daughter embraced and kissed for several minutes before they walked down the gangplank together.[21]

Their time together was short-lived, however. Susie had made plans to put Grace in a private school that Colonel Holmes had recommended, the National Park Seminary. His niece, Henrietta, was attending the school, and he was very impressed with its curriculum and the opportunities it afforded its students. After hearing his glowing reports of the school, Susie was convinced it was the best place to help a shy, insecure girl get an education. National Park Seminary was a large complex of eighteen buildings resembling a modern college campus in the suburbs of Washington, D.C. Its program promised individualized attention and offered a well-rounded education tailored to the needs of each girl. Students gathered there from around the United States and a few foreign countries, all bearing outstanding references. In addition to offering the "three Rs" and a good background in Christian principles, the girls were given a chance to travel, develop social graces, study other cultures, and learn about American government. Colonel Holmes raved about his niece's success at the seminary and was sure the new and revitalized Grace would feel comfortable there also.[22]

But she did not. However much healthier and livelier Grace appeared, it is questionable whether Susie's relationship with her daughter had improved more than superficially. By now Grace had become a teenager and probably was experiencing all of the emotional ups and downs that come with that level of development. For her part, Susie later complained of feeling distant from Grace at this time. Now that Grace was older, Susie would have loved to take her traveling and show her the world with its many beautiful landscapes and fascinating people, but Grace showed no interest. She was still basically shy and disliked having her picture taken. She simply preferred to stay at home where she felt comfortable.[23]

After enrolling Grace at the National Park Seminary, Susie found a suite of rooms for herself nearby in a Washington, D.C., hotel. An Eastern newspaper in Susie's scrapbook mentions that she and Grace were well received when they arrived and both were applauded on their attractiveness. The same clipping mentioned that Grace was a credit to her mother socially, even though she was very young and shy.

After a few weeks both settled in and appeared to have made friends. A clipping from the *Buffalo Courier* reports than an almost unceasing series of entertainments were given in Susie's honor. By now Susie had traveled to the east and west coasts and was aware of the names of the old guard, the prominent monied families, who were constantly in the newspapers. Now that Susie was also wealthy, she dreamed of being accepted by them and enjoyed attending their elegant and impressive functions, though that was not easy to do. Few Westerners were ever accepted, and Southerners, still carrying the stigma of the Civil War, never were. The rules for social inclusion in the East were much more rigid than they were in

Susie's appearance on the cover of Chicago's *Elite Magazine* indicates her prominence in Midwest society. Used by permission, Utah State Historical Society, all rights reserved.

Thomas Walsh, an innkeeper from Ouray, Colorado, made a fortune and became famous for his elaborate parties in Washington, D.C. Photograph courtesy of Colorado Historical Society.

the Midwest, the West, or the South. Southern society accepted people based on family and tradition much more than on money or status. Jews, ostracized in most circles, formed their own social elite, giving precedence to people of Sephardic origin. To her disappointment, Susie soon discovered she was considered just one of the nouveaux riches who would have to prove herself to the Astors, Vanderbilts, and others.[24]

Through traveling and attending numerous social functions, Susie quickly discovered that acceptance was not the only issue: the nouveaux riches were not only busily competing with each other to catch the eye of the old guard, but those who penetrated the barriers jealously protected their position from intruders *they* deemed unacceptable. If one of the group gave a party that received lots of attention in the press, the others felt duty-bound to top it and have a more spectacular party. The same competition could apply to the homes they built, the trips they took, the jewelry they wore, and even the people their children married. Some realized the game of one-up-manship was becoming excessive and almost ridiculous, but no one made an effort to curb it. Susie recognized they were scrutinizing her and would continue to do so for several years to see if she could measure up. One indication that she was being evaluated is found in a half-page news clipping from the *New York Herald* which included pictures of her Salt Lake home and made the following observations:

> Now comes Mrs. Emery-Holmes, the "Silver Queen of Utah," From Salt Lake, with a determination to outshine the prince of entertainers [Tom Walsh of Colorado]. She is yet unknown in the capital, but she expects to fight for social supremacy to the very last nugget yielded up in her Silver King mine before she relinquishes the attempt to eclipse the Walshes in her dazzling entertainments. . . . It is just possible that a few staid Easterners, a few of the blue blooded in Washington, may object to Mrs. Holmes installing herself as queen of society. The potion may not assimilate, for this Western woman has everything money can buy except family lineage to back her, and even her escutcheon is soiled by the sinister Bar of labor. She was a milliner.[25]

The source of this damning bit of information may well have been Tom Walsh himself. An innkeeper from Ouray, Colorado, he too had made a fortune in mining and struggled to be accepted by the old guard. Since one of the tactics used to hold one's position in society was to prevent others from moving up, he could easily have dished this piece of dirt to embarrass and, worse, discredit her, because the article goes on to say there was "war to the bottom of the purse" between the King of Entertainers (Walsh) and the Silver Queen. Walsh invited the king of Belgium to a party, and Susie countered by inviting the brother of the emperor of Germany. The reporter's comments angered Susie and she became determined to prove she belonged.

By the turn of the century, the old guard had two basic requirements for belonging: lineage and wealth. As far as money was concerned, Susie knew she qualified, or soon would, thanks to the Silver King Mine. Now she just had to show her tie to European aristocrats through the Bransford genealogy. She knew her family descended from several generations of wealthy, prominent Englishmen; her grandparents and parents had told her stories about them when she was a child. America's wealthy, however, required proof of ancestry, so Susie hired a genealogist, Harry Beverley Deas, to authenticate her family tree. Several days later he brought her a document proving that both the Bransfords and Quessenburys were descended from Edward III of England.[26] Thrilled with his results, she encouraged Deas to publish his findings, along with her family's crest, in the newspaper. Now she would show those who had demeaned her that as far as lineage was concerned, she had every right to belong to America's aristocratic class.[27]

Tom Walsh's huge mansion in Washington D.C., is now the Indonesian Embassy. Photograph by Judy Dykman.

# 6

## Entertaining in Style

Days after arriving in Salt Lake City, the Colonel started house hunting. In Salt Lake, as in the rest of the country, one of the measures of social acceptance was a splendid house. In the interim, the Holmeses lived in the Knutsford Hotel. During this period, Susie's youngest sister, Nellie, surprised the Bransfords with news of her engagement. She had met Jay Tarvin Harris, a young civil engineer from Illinois, and was eager to marry. After Jay's father died, his mother had remarried and the family moved to Idaho Falls. Unable to find work as an engineer in Idaho, Jay had moved to Salt Lake City and worked for the Tribune Printing Company. Susie and the family were impressed with Jay and thrilled for Nellie. He would make a good husband, father, and companion. He was good looking, ambitious, not overly pious, kind, possessed a university degree, and had some wealthy relatives in the East.

The family immediately began planning a large wedding for Nellie. Susie purchased a wedding dress made of antique satin and lace and helped arrange for the reception and flowers. On October 10, 1900, the wedding ceremony was held in the Congregational church, and, because the Gardo House was not yet ready for occupation, a reception followed in one of the large rooms at the Knutsford Hotel. News clippings from the period describe the church the day of the wedding as decked in beautiful green flowering plants with yards of ribbons and many elegant bows. The whole affair was one of Salt Lake City's major social events that season. The Knutsford Hotel reception was also impressive and was the talk of Salt Lake City for weeks. Following the reception, Susie also gave Nellie fifty thousand dollars in mining stocks for a nest egg. When questioned about the wedding's expenses years later, Susie admitted the whole affair cost more than a hundred thousand dollars by the time the trousseau and wedding dress were paid for. Following the reception, the Harrises left on a honeymoon that lasted several weeks. When they returned to Salt Lake City they took a suite of rooms in the Knutsford Hotel until they could find a suitable apartment.[1]

A short time later, in 1901, Holmes purchased the Gardo House, probably Salt Lake City's finest mansion and one of its most historic buildings, from the Mormon Church. Like many buildings from that era, the Gardo was a Second Empire design, built of plastered adobe brick and a stone foundation. Brigham Young had started the building on the southwest corner lot on State and South Temple across from the Beehive and Lion Houses in 1873, intending to use it as his official residence and a social center for the Mormon Church. Up to that time, the church had used the home of merchant William Jennings for such affairs, but now Young felt it needed its own facility close to the Beehive House and large enough to accommodate public functions and provide housing for visiting dignitaries. Since he planned to have his youngest wife, Amelia Folsom, live there and act as official hostess, some later called the house "Amelia's Palace."[2]

When her sister Nellie married Jay Harris, Susie treated her to a fabulous dress, ceremony, and reception. Photograph courtesy of Harold Lamb.

Joseph Ridges, the builder of the famous Salt Lake Tabernacle organ, and William H. Folsom were commissioned to design the new edifice.[3] The house was far from complete when Brigham Young died in 1877. After Brigham's estate was probated, his heirs sold the structure to the Mormon Church. John Taylor, who followed Young as the third president of the church, finished it for thirty thousand dollars. Taylor lived there briefly during the 1880s, and, to avoid being arrested by polygamy marshals, on several occasions he was forced to use one of the hiding places the architects had built into the home: in the walls, under the staircases, and in the beds.

Wilford Woodruff, who became president after Taylor's death, preferred to live in his own house, so the church rented the home out to help pay some of the sizable debts it had incurred during the 1880s. The federal government had taken control of the house in 1887, when the Edmunds-Tucker Act allowed it to confiscate all of the Mormon Church's property, including Temple Square, and charged the Mormons rent to use their facilities. At one point the Mormons paid the federal government $450 per month to use the Gardo House. Although the Supreme Court upheld the government's seizure of church property, most of it was eventually returned after Utah Territory became a state. In the interim, however, the government had neglected or abused many of these properties so badly that their value had decreased considerably. This scheme to cripple the Mormon Church and force it to conform to American social, political, and economic practices nearly bankrupted the church and caused widespread suffering throughout Mormondom in Utah, Idaho, and other areas in the West.

During its twenty-three year history, the Gardo House had passed through a number of hands. California financier Issac Trumbo and his family first leased the home, but they left the area when he failed to be elected one of Utah's first senators. The Alfred McCune family next rented the home while their mansion on Capitol Hill was being built. Though only a temporary resident, Mrs. McCune had added many stylish touches to the house, but took all of her furnishing when they moved.

In 1901 the Mormon authorities were forced to sell the Gardo House at a loss to Colonel Holmes. The *Salt Lake Herald* claimed that church leaders felt it was worth a hundred thousand dollars, but they accepted his offer of forty-eight thousand with one stipulation: they wanted an option to buy the home back if the Holmeses eventually sold it. The money helped the church take care of its daily business expenses during a very difficult period. The Colonel gave Susie the deed to the house as a birthday present on May 6.[4]

Susie was thrilled with the Gardo House; it had an aura of dignity, prestige, formal beauty, and history that fascinated her, and it had no equal between Denver and San Francisco. Sitting on a large lot, 200 by 250 feet, surrounded by lawn and an elaborate black, wrought iron fence, it had four stories, including a big basement and an imposing tower. Susie promptly hired William Sinclair from Chicago's Marshall Fields to supervise redecorating the forty-three rooms. While traveling through Europe she had purchased several pictures and some mementos for the home, but many more furnishings were needed. Sinclair spent seventy-five thousand dollars to send decorators to Utah to supervise the remodeling work and dispatched others to scout American and European cities for furniture, fabrics, and light fixtures. Because it would be used to entertain the Holmeses' many future guests, it had to be magnificent but not overdone. They were keenly aware that a spectacular home was one of the chief requisites for impressing the people who really mattered in society. One was expected to entertain and to do it in style.[5]

Ostentatious houses have often been a mark of the wealthy and the aristocracy, but house building in the Gilded Age reached proportions unknown since Louis XIV decided to build a quiet little chateau at Versailles. Across the nation, the newly rich frantically competed to see who could build the biggest, most ornate, and, by modern standards, most gaudy houses. As in much else, the Vanderbilt clan led in the frenzy. William Kissam Vanderbilt's wife, Alva, was a daughter of the old South, so their "cottage" at Newport features the stately columns typical of plantation mansions, except that theirs were patterned after the Temple of the Sun at Baalbek, only bigger. Alva had William Hunt design their New York home; its entrance hall reminded visitors of Milan Cathedral. The prize for most ostentatious home, however, goes to another Vanderbilt, George Washington. His Biltmore estate has been called America's largest private residence. It originally covered a hundred thousand acres, and its architect noted that the surrounding North Carolina mountains are "in scale with the house."[6]

In the same spirit of excess, aristocrats in Washington, D.C., and New York City earned a reputation for their elegant and sometimes outrageous parties. One hostess, Mrs. C. K. G. Billings, could have taken the prize for the most ostentatious entertainment with her formal hunting party. To create a country setting, trees, shrubs, fences, and mounds of soil were arranged in the ballroom of a hotel to appear to be a grove of trees. Before she had dozens of horses brought in, special tarps were installed to protect the floor from the inevitable horse manure. She then instructed her guests to dress in their riding habits and had them seated on the horses, where a several course evening meal was served using specially built tables to hold their plates, silverware,

George Washington Vanderbilt's estate, Biltmore, near Asheville, North Carolina, has been called the largest private residence in the United States. Its one hundred thousand acres are now a part of Pisgah National Forest, and the magnificent home is open to the public. Photograph courtesy of Biltmore Estate, Asheville, North Carolina.

and glasses. Each guest's food was cleverly packed in a saddlebag strapped to the horse's back.

Not to be outdone, another hostess had her guests seated at a table with a pile of sand running down the middle. Each guest was given a tiny silver pail and shovel to dig for the diamonds, emeralds, rubies, and sapphires buried in the sand. Other socialites responded with parties featuring lavish decorations and costumes. Women and men unabashedly spent thousands of dollars on elaborate wigs, dresses, suits, furs, shoes, and jewelry for formal social affairs. Several suits of party attire could have easily competed with the special effects used by twentieth century film makers. In an obvious effort to upstage her friends, Frances Appleton of Boston had a taxidermist kill and stuff a white cat for her to wear as a hat to a New York costume ball. Undoubtedly, her hat gained lots of attention that evening from animal lovers.[7]

Even Western cities like Salt Lake City or Denver, far removed from the large population centers in the East, were not immune to social intrigue. Most Western socialites imitated their

Eastern counterparts, but on a smaller scale. The following article from Salt Lake City's *Goodwin's Weekly* appears in Susie's scrapbook and provides humorous insight into the social affairs of Utah's capital city:

> Is there a leader of society in this city? To you who remember when everything south of Third [South] was an apple orchard or a field of sagebrush, the question may seem a little previous, but they're discussing it at the teas and fighting over it at the dinners, and there you are. Opinions are so widely different and so many sides of the question are being brought up, that it is a wonder that there aren't more cliques and clashes, but the ladies are still resting under a white flag, though an undercurrent of unrest pervades the social atmosphere.
>
> Society leaders are not made, they're born, but their cohorts must be well officered, and their scouts ever attentive, from the little hen party to the public reception for someone with a cunning hammer all tied up in baby ribbon is rambling around ready to "knock" at the slightest opportunity.
>
> A society leader must know how to advertise, where to place the matter, and how to write it. This art is the first qualification. The next thing of importance is tact, and without it, she might as well go back to the cozy corner. It is a most essential ingredient in the make up of a leader. . . . If you are not secure in your position on the throne, look out for the lady behind the fan. . . . Miss saying the right thing in the right room, at the right time, and you stick a trident in your own ambition.
>
> But for the leader locally. There's Mrs. Victor Clement. . . . In perfect innocence, she occasionally invites warring factions the same night, and then again she does not entertain enough to be a real leader. A stunning woman, and one of the smartest in the smart set is Mrs. Jacob E. Bamberger, but she does not take an active part in enough of the winter gaiety to be the recognized captainess. . . .
>
> Mrs. E. F. Holmes [Susie] is a charming hostess, who gives the nicest kind of affairs in her Palace home. Her dinners are dreams and her invitations are a great privilege to the fortunate ones, but she does not entertain enough to lead. . . . The first lady of the State, Mrs. Heber M. Wells, is a good hostess, and a lovable woman but she too—if she has an ambition to be leader—lacks activity in the giving of affairs.
>
> Mrs. O. J. Salisbury is most skillful in the art of making friends, and there is always a pleasant anticipation in going to her pretty home, but she does not concern herself with enough factions to receive a unanimous vote.
>
> Mrs. David Murray is an expert on informal affairs which have a charm about them all their own, but when she doesn't like people she . . . says so, and that is not a leader. . . .
>
> And the leader, I hate to tell you, but there isn't one.[8]

Ida Stingley Newhouse was a leader in Salt Lake City society and, if the rumors were true, one of the many mistresses of Edward VII of England. She is shown here in a painting by Pierre Troubetzkoy. Used by permission, Utah State Historical Society, all rights reserved.

Many of Utah's affluent citizens were as competitive as their Eastern peers and the European royals. They were just smaller fish in the great ocean. They were also a diverse lot. Some had a Mormon background, such as William Jennings, the Walker families, or the Alfred McCunes. But the majority were non-Mormons who made their money in mining, merchandising, and the railroads. Couples such as the E. F. Holmeses, the James Ivers, the David Keiths, the Thomas

Kearnses, the John Judges, the Thomas Weirs, the Samuel Newhouses, the Enos Walls, the O. J. Salisburys, or the Simon Bambergers fit in this category. Their large, impressive homes lined Brigham Street/South Temple and First South and extended from Second West to about Tenth East. Others, like the McCune mansion, were built in the avenues near the state capitol building.[9]

Salt Lake City's leading newspapers, the *Deseret News*, *Salt Lake Tribune*, *Salt Lake Herald*, and the *Salt Lake Telegram*, followed the parties, travels, and philanthropic activities of the elite in their society columns. The following news clipping appeared in one of these newspapers and was pasted in Susie's scrapbook sometime in 1902 or 1903:

> Much flitting is going on in the city, the beginning of Lent being a time of great unrest in physical as well as religious circles. The largest and handsomest houses of the city are all empty, the Amelia Palace being completely deserted for a period of perhaps a year. The beautiful Weir home on Brigham Street will not be open again till the return of Mr. and Mrs. Weir from a cruise of the Mediterranean. The Keith home is also empty while its owners are sojourning in New York. Mrs. Judge and Miss Katherine will probably not return for some months and the Kearns Mansion will doubtless stay closed until late in the spring season. . . . All in all, the town has never been in so unsettled a condition in a social way as it is at the present time, and there are few prospects for a revival of gaiety till after the return of at least a few of the Salt Lakers who are enjoying sights abroad.[10]

In Susie's climb to social prominence, the Gardo was a critical rung on the ladder. Of course, she could not even live in the house, much less entertain, while it was being remodeled. For nearly a year, Susie, Grace, and the Colonel remained in a suite of rooms in the Knutsford Hotel.[11]

Holmes, Susie, and Grace finally moved into the Gardo House late in 1901, after months of waiting for the last workman to finish remodeling. Descriptions from the time indicate it was well worth the wait. *Elite*, an exclusive society magazine from Chicago, gave a detailed description of the house, its new decor, and the lovely furniture. Each of the rooms was tastefully decorated; even the tower had a lounge and bookshelves. A number of ornate, gold-colored chairs and Susie's richly carved dark wood bedroom set were purchased from Brigham Young's estate, the pieces having been ordered years earlier when Brigham first commissioned the construction of the Gardo House.[12]

Like their Eastern counterparts, many of Utah's wealthy families equipped their homes with entertainment centers.[13] Senator Kearns's impressive mansion about six blocks east of the Gardo House was typical of Salt Lake's large mansions. It had a ballroom that took up nearly all of the top floor of the home and a bowling alley in the basement. Next door, David Keith had a smaller ballroom on the third floor of his home and a large, Tiffany glass-domed foyer for receptions. Across the street the Walker mansion had a large organ installed in the entrance foyer to delight guests at parties or receptions. It also had a large room that doubled as a ballroom and a recital hall for entertaining. The Enos Wall mansion, which eventually became the L.D.S. Business College, also had many impressive features, such as a large ballroom, an elevator, and a built-in vacuum system.[14]

Senator Thomas and Jennie Judge Kearns built this impressive gray stone mansion near the turn of the century at an estimated cost of $150,000. In this picture it is decorated for the arrival of Theodore Roosevelt. The building, located at 600 East South Temple, was given to the state and used for a time as the home of the Utah State Historical Society; today it is the Governor's Mansion. Used by permission, Utah State Historical Society, all rights reserved.

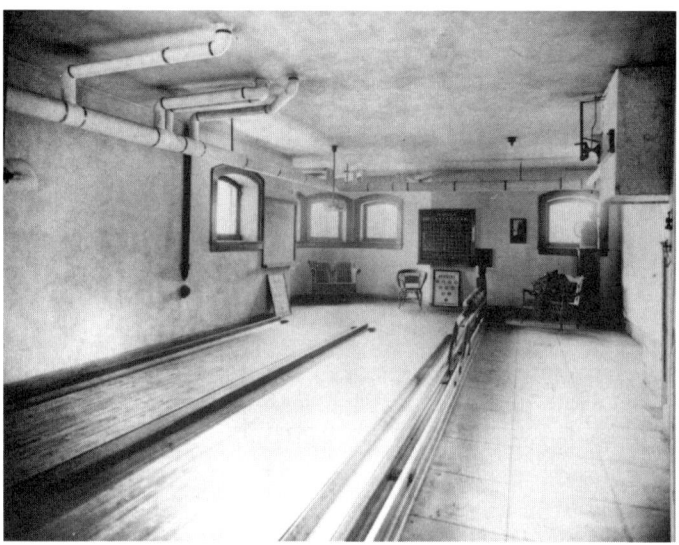

Like all of the newly rich, the Kearnses gave their home some distinctive features, like this bowling alley in the basement. While the building housed the State Historical Society, this room was filled with shelves for books and records. Used by permission, Utah State Historical Society, all rights reserved.

The David Keith mansion was also located on South Temple, a block west of the Kearns mansion and five blocks east of the Gardo House. It was built of gray stone and has beautiful lead glass and stained glass windows. One historian believes this home was built for $100,000. Used by permission, Utah State Historical Society, all rights reserved.

To properly christen the house, the Holmeses planned a large open house for the Christmas season on December 26, 1901. Some claim it was one of the most brilliant affairs ever hosted in Salt Lake City. Special invitations were sent to all of the city's most prominent citizens. The food was a culinary delight, and the music was provided by stringed instruments. Susie played hostess in one of her most dazzling dresses made especially for the occasion. Colonel Holmes proudly directed the guests to chairs or the punch bowl. By the end of the evening, Susie had established herself as one of Salt Lake City's premier hostesses.

During the next twenty years the Gardo House became known for its wonderful entertainments. Flowers were always present. Susie ordered dozens of flowers weekly for the house, usually from her favorite florist, Huddart Floral. During festive occasions she favored red roses by the dozens and often had a red carpet rolled down the front steps. The centerpiece for one of her parties was a pyramid of June's wreath, with fruits beautifully stacked. The top of the piece had roses with yards of satin bows. One fourth of July she used flags from five nations in the centerpiece. Each table had cherries in crystal bowls, napkins folded like tents, toy soldiers, and cannons with chocolate balls for ammunition. Outside the house she had fifteen flags displayed on the veranda.

Susie also hired several small chamber orchestras to provide music for her parties, dinners, or dances. Two of her favorite groups were the Deseret Mandolin Orchestra and the Niles Mandolin Orchestra. She also hired vocalists such as Karl Scheid, Martha Royle Kind, and Fred Graham to entertain. Nellie was a frequent musical guest and seemed to enjoy entertaining the guests with her beautiful voice. When the Salt Lake Theatre sponsored plays or musicians, Susie and several of her peers enjoyed inviting the entertainers to their homes for "sneak previews." Susie's large dance and art museum had a stage at one end for just such occasions. World renowned pianist Alberto Jonas played for Susie and her guests and for the Walkers and their friends.[15]

Invitations to one of Susie's teas or receptions were prized possessions as the Gardo became a primary gathering place for Utah's wealthy or prominent people. Her parties and activities were mentioned in the society sections of the leading newspapers almost weekly when Susie was in town. The newspaper blurbs, which might be as brief as a few lines or fill a column, included descriptions of the food served, entertainment offered, Susie's dress for the occasion, attention of the press. Oscar Wilde in his play, *A Woman of No Importance*, summed up the dilemma all socially conscious people faced at the turn of the century in the following dialogue:

> Gerald: I suppose society is wonderfully delightful?
> Lord Illingworth: To be in it is merely a bore. But to be out of it is simply a tragedy.[16]

Susie truly reigned as a queen in Amelia's Palace. Used by permission, Utah State Historical Society, all rights reserved.

Colonel Holmes enjoyed the wide veranda of the Gardo House. Used by permission, Utah State Historical Society, all rights reserved.

the decorations used, and a list of those assisting the hostess. Some reporters even listed the people who attended each affair so that those who faithfully read the daily society columns would know what was happening. Socially conscious women also realized they must entertain and be invited to other people's parties to maintain their status. To be left out or overlooked would be devastating; thus, they competed with each other for the

*Entertaining in Style*

The Gardo House, built in Second Empire style, was one of the most famous and magnificent homes between Denver and the west coast. Used by permission, Utah State Historical Society, all rights reserved.

The building is sometimes called "Amelia's Palace" because Brigham Young originally intended it to be the home of his youngest wife, Amelia Folsom, as well as a place for the Mormon Church to entertain guests. Used by permission, Utah State Historical Society, all rights reserved.

Susie added the small, square building on the right to the Gardo House. The bottom floor was a garage or "auto house," while the second floor housed the art gallery and reception room. Photograph courtesy of Anne Bransford Newhall.

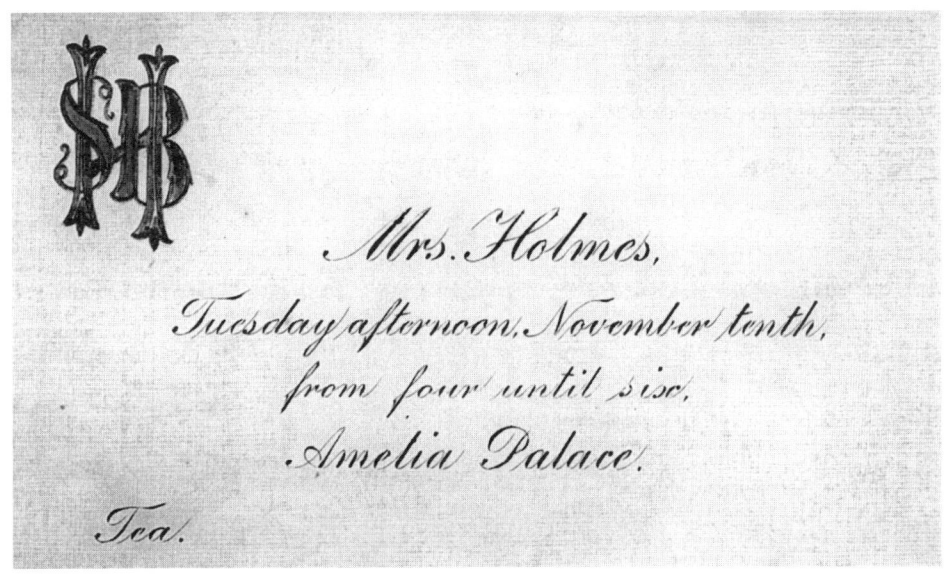

An invitation to one of Susie's teas at "Amelia Palace." Courtesy of James Ivers.

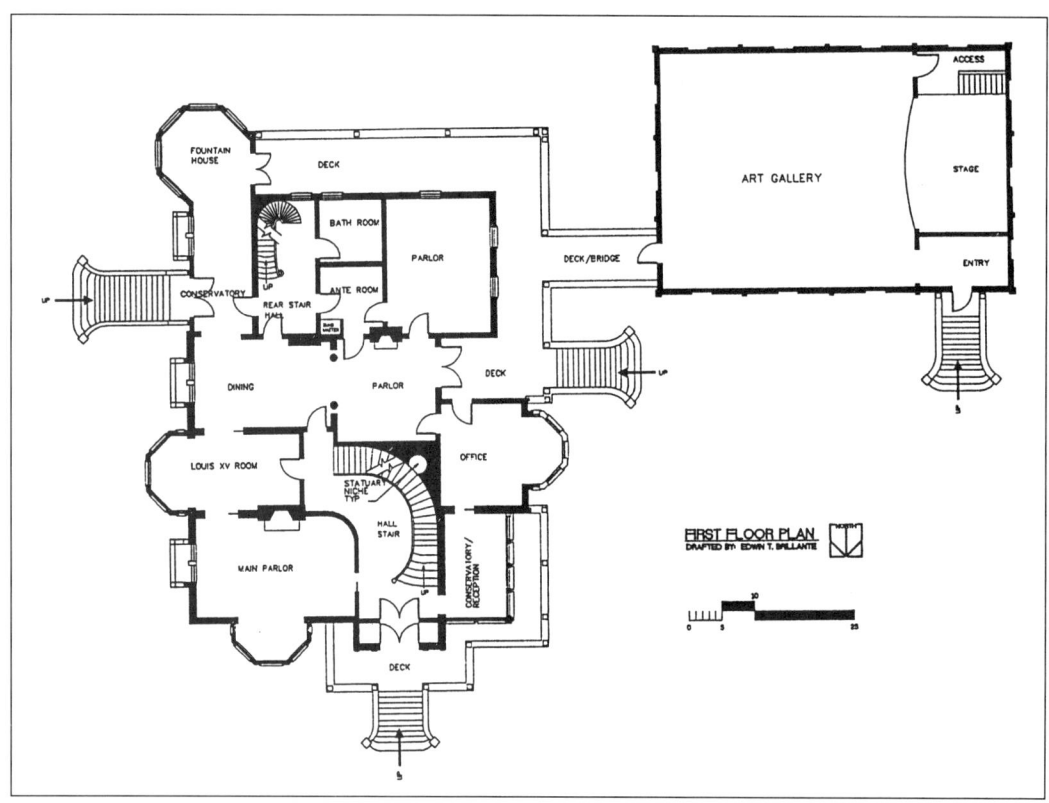

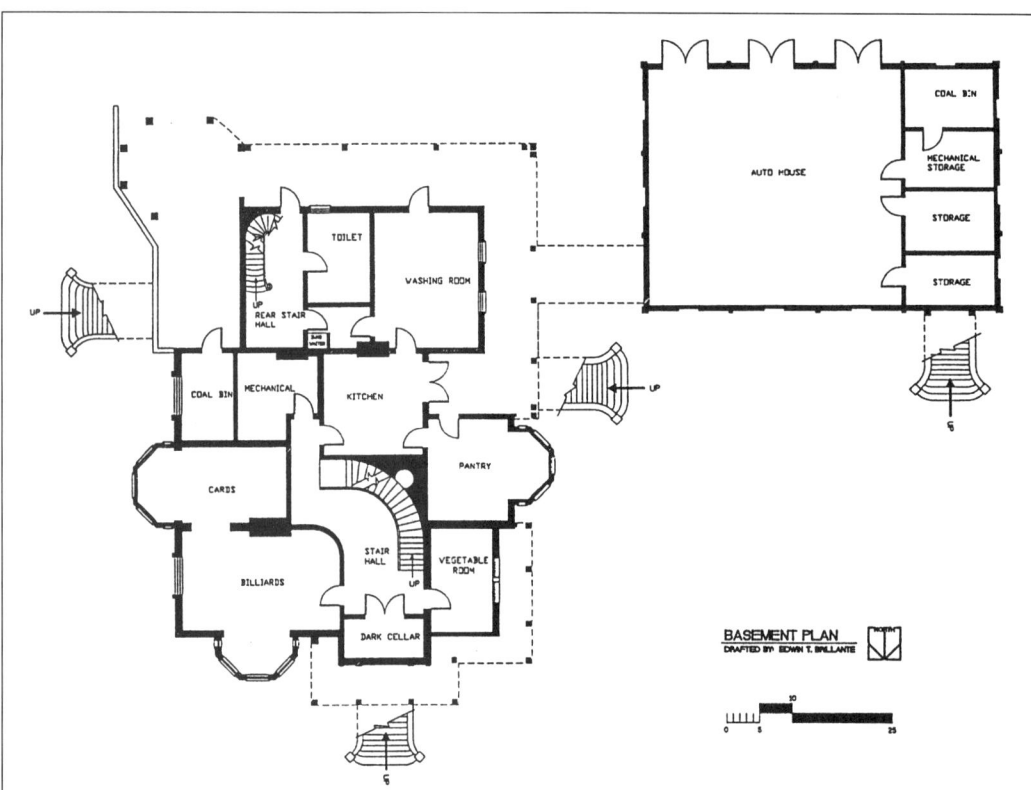

Mark Curtis, who has studied the Gardo House extensively, recreated these floor plans from the period when Susie owned the home. They demonstrate several of the useful features of the house, such as the rear stairway for family and servants to move from floor to floor without encountering guests and the dumbwaiter that could carry food from the kitchen in the basement to the dining rooms on the main floor, insuring that meals would be served hot.

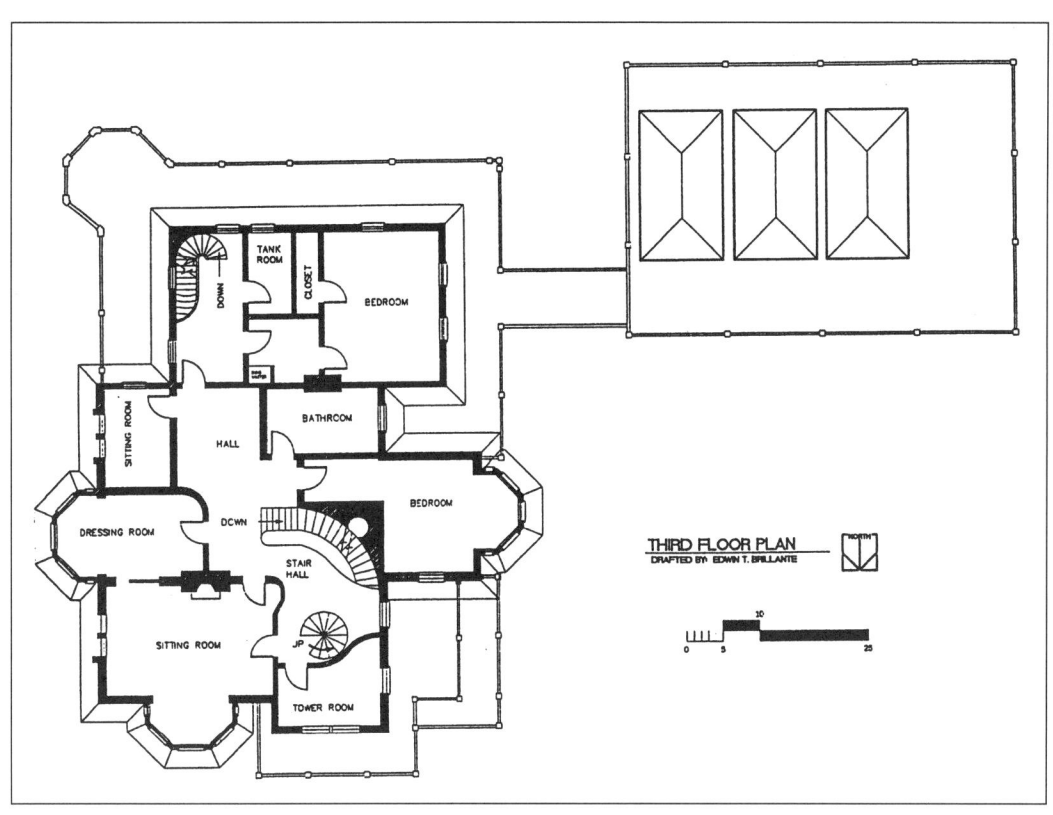

THIRD FLOOR PLAN
DRAFTED BY: EDWIN T. BRILLANTE

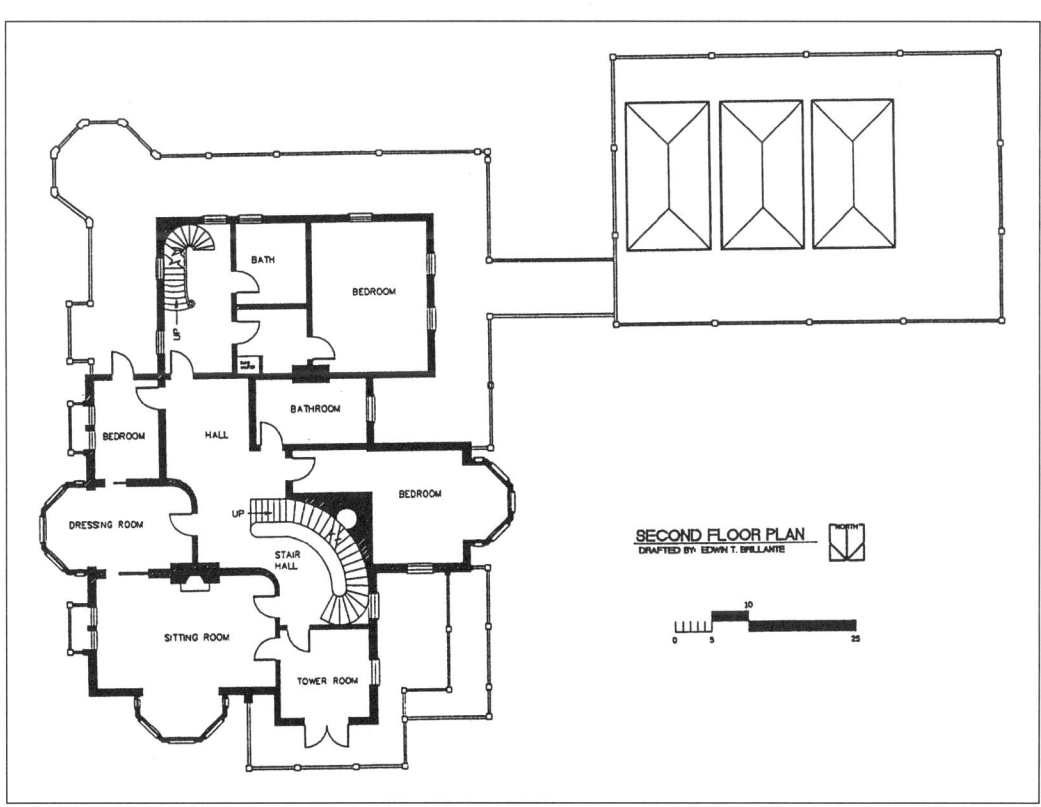

SECOND FLOOR PLAN
DRAFTED BY: EDWIN T. BRILLANTE

The double doors could be opened to allow easy entrance and exit for large crowds. Following Susie's death, her niece, Susanna Hartman, donated a photo album of the Gardo House to the Utah State Historical Society. This and all following pictures from the society are copied from that book. Used by permission, Utah State Historical Society, all rights reserved.

The front entry and main staircase were deliberately made large enough to accommodate a great many people. Susie frequently entertained over one hundred people at dinners or receptions. Used by permission, Utah State Historical Society, all rights reserved.

The main floor salon became a focal point for future parties and receptions. Its walls were decorated in a rich rose satin brocade and woodwork of ivory enamel. The carpet was reseda green and covered in places with Persian silk rugs and some beautiful skins. Much of the furniture was from France's Louis XVI period, except for a few locally purchased pieces of furniture. Used by permission, Utah State Historical Society, all rights reserved.

The main parlor opened onto a series of other rooms to provide easy access for entertaining large groups of people. Used by permission, Utah State Historical Society, all rights reserved.

The dining room was decorated with a Gothic flavor. The furniture, ceiling, and woodwork were made of richly carved Belgian oak. The walls had a dull gold glaze with bronze, dull greens, red, and silver in Gothic designs. The ceiling had a fresco painted above the table and the carpet was a rich red. The draperies were red with appliqués of cloth of gold. Used by permission, Utah State Historical Society, all rights reserved.

The round table was large enough to accommodate more than a dozen diners at a time. Brigham Young was a carpenter by trade and designed the chairs with their extremely high, exquisitely carved backs. Used by permission, Utah State Historical Society, all rights reserved.

Like many wealthy wives during that period, Susie had a suite of rooms separate from her husband the Colonel's bedroom. Susie's room had a fireplace and delicately carved furniture, including a desk, a lounge, and several ornate chairs. The carpet was a floral pattern, and rich draperies with heavy valances covered each window. Used by permission, Utah State Historical Society, all rights reserved.

Susie's bed had its own separate room, as did her gowns. Her dressing room contained up to one hundred dresses. Used by permission, Utah State Historical Society, all rights reserved.

Susie's richly carved, mahogany bedroom set was purchased from Brigham Young's estate. These pieces had been ordered years earlier when Young first commissioned the construction of the Gardo House. Used by permission, Utah State Historical Society, all rights reserved.

In 1904 Susie added an art gallery and ballroom with a stage at one end of the large room above the garage. It easily allowed one hundred people to sit down for dinner. Before it was completed, guests ate at tables scattered throughout the house, and a family member presided in each room. Used by permission, Utah State Historical Society, all rights reserved.

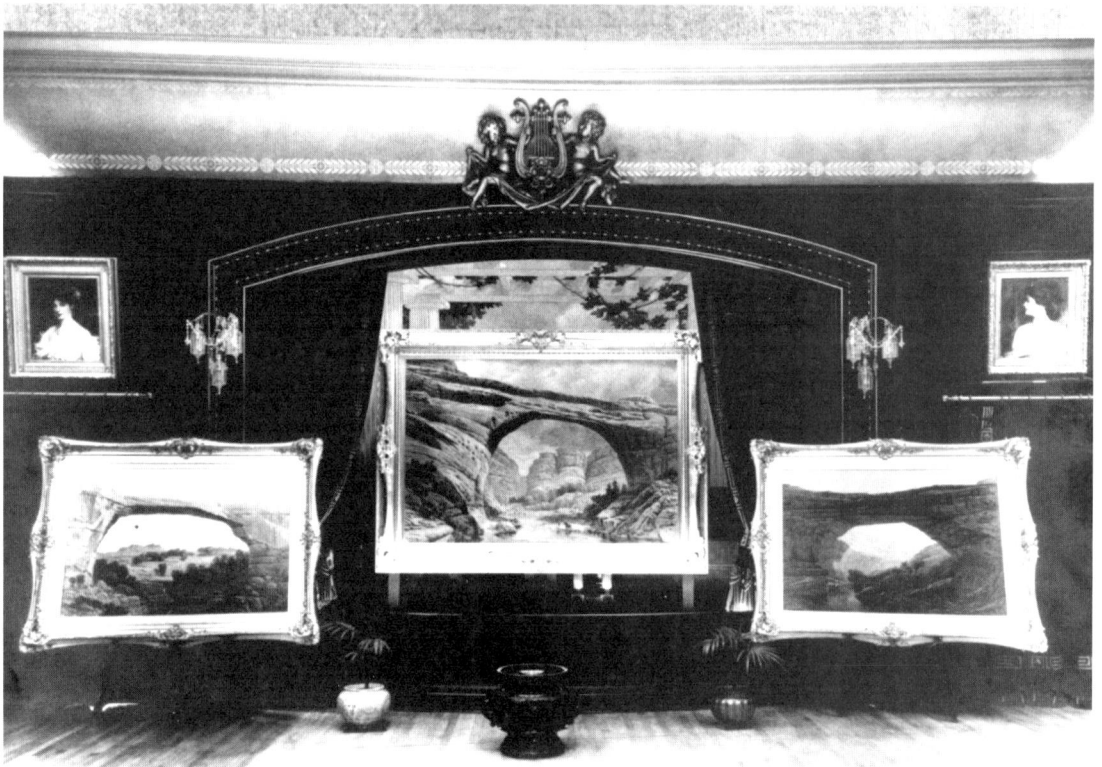

The stage in the art gallery was used for performances of various kinds, but it could also be used to display particularly significant works of art. The painting in the center here is H. L. A. Culmer's *Mystery of the Desert*. Photograph courtesy of Anne Bransford Newhall.

Susie purchased five pianos and scattered them throughout the house. The most impressive was this Steinway, which was painted with scenes from *Aida*. Pianos were a status symbol in the nineteenth century; the shipping bill alone was pricey. Used by permission, Utah State Historical Society, all rights reserved.

The hallway by the second floor stairway featured a gallery of Native Americans. Used by permission, Utah State Historical Society, all rights reserved.

Colonel Holmes used his study frequently. He was concerned with civic problems ranging from the water supply to the prevalence of crime in the city. Used by permission, Utah State Historical Society, all rights reserved.

Colonel Holmes's bedroom was particularly spacious but was simply decorated. Used by permission, Utah State Historical Society, all rights reserved.

Guests who stayed in the Gardo would find themselves housed in one of the many comfortable bedrooms in the house. Used by permission, Utah State Historical Society, all rights reserved.

The kitchen contained the dishes necessary for Susie's lavish parties. She frequently served several-course dinners to large groups of people. The light fixture in this room was designed to operate with gas or electricity. Used by permission, Utah State Historical Society, all rights reserved.

The basement windows were large, allowing plenty of light into the billiard and card rooms. Susie offered her guests dining, dancing, and several alternate forms of entertainment. Used by permission, Utah State Historical Society, all rights reserved.

Originally, the exterior of the Gardo was painted in natural colors, beige with a white trim. Susie had it repainted in the heavy colors favored during the Gilded Age: the walls were a deep Victorian red, and the window frames were white with blue accents. The awnings were red, white, and blue. Used by permission, Utah State Historical Society, all rights reserved.

# 7

# The Progressive Movement

Chroniclers of the Gilded Age have observed that America's wealthy citizens often behaved as though they considered themselves the country's ruling class—and in many ways, they were. In 1880 English diplomat Lord James Brick made the following observation:

> In the new, pushing, industrial United States, the centers of real power lay with these new personages [the wealthy] and not with the shadowy officeholders in Washington. In its huge habitations and extravagant entertainments, this Society celebrated . . . power by imitating court life abroad, and often married . . . its daughters into it.[1]

Gifford Pinchot became the first professional forester in the United States by managing the grounds of George Washington Vanderbilt's Biltmore estate. When he left there to head the U.S. Forest Service, Pinchot commented that not only did Vanderbilt hire more men than he could, "he is spending more money than Congress appropriates for this department."[2]

In Salt Lake City, as it was nationally, the Progressive Movement was spreading the notion that the wealthy had not only power and resources but the obligation to use them to the betterment of society. Accordingly, the two men in Susie's life, her brother, John, and her husband, Colonel Holmes, became two of Utah's leaders at the turn of the century. Elements of the Progressive Movement merged with the values and goals of the elite, so motivations were both pragmatic and altruistic. President Theodore Roosevelt's programs to break big business monopolies, protect the environment, and develop western lands appealed to many Westerners.

The reform movement also coincided with Utah's period of adjustment from prolonged territorial status to statehood. During much of the territorial period, many activities had been communitarian in nature and had been directed through LDS (Mormon) Church leadership. Now the LDS Church tried to stay out of politics, education, and economic development, while encouraging individualism and adjusting to the influx of non-Mormons. But after decades of leadership, church leaders found it hard to sit on the sideline and watch others take over.

By 1900 Salt Lake City was fast becoming an urban center, with more than fifty thousand people.[3] It was not as sophisticated as New York or Chicago, but the city now had many of the conveniences found in the East. While hundreds of small homes and many cultivated fields were found on the outskirts of the city, the downtown area had broad streets crisscrossed with trolley wires and tracks and lined with businesses. In addition to the businesses, Salt Lake had electric lights, sixteen telephone companies, a public library with thirty-one thousand books, an orphanage, ten cigar factories, a theater, an opera house for performances, four daily newspapers, and two hospitals—St. Mark's and Holy Cross. There were full-time police and fire departments, an amusement park called Wandemere, Saltair on the Great Salt Lake, electric street cars, pawnbrokers, dozens of saloons, two museums, sixty-eight realtors, the Keeley Institute to cure drunkenness and drug addiction, and a "well established red light district." There were also twenty gasoline-powered automobiles in the city.[4]

Socially and politically Salt Lake City and Utah were becoming more progressive as well. A section in the state's constitution expressly outlawed polygamy, the Republican and Democratic Parties had replaced the religiously oriented People's and Liberal Parties, state-supported public schools had been mandated by the constitution, and Utah's women again had the right to vote. While many women in the country still could not vote or hold property in their own names, Utah's women first had the right to vote as of 1870 and to hold property and manage their own affairs by 1872. These rights were removed by the federal government in 1887 under the Edmunds-Tucker Act but were restored shortly after Utah became a state in 1896.[5]

Even though some non-Mormon factions doubted the sincerity of the Mormon Church to give up polygamy and its influence in local politics, many Mormons and non-Mormons reached out to one another and tried to put the old bitter disputes behind them. A number of women's and

Susie's brother, John, became a successful businessman and served as mayor of Salt Lake City. Photograph courtesy of Anne Bransford Newhall.

men's clubs were formed in the city to involve Utah's wealthier and better-educated citizens of all religious backgrounds. Upon moving to Utah, Holmes quickly blended into the social fabric of Salt Lake City. Since he had not participated in the acrimonious debate over polygamy and statehood, he now served as a moderating influence. "As to Mormonism, it has come to stay," he said in Detroit in 1903. "They are good people, honest and trustworthy, and polygamy is a matter of ancient history or will soon be such. When this is removed, the great prejudice is removed."[6]

An activist for modernization and change, Holmes was alarmed when he noticed that even though current Eastern fashions, music, and literature had arrived in Utah, several areas of the Salt Lake Valley were filthy. Without a city dump for refuse, some citizens merely tossed their garbage into vacant fields near their homes or burned or buried it. It was nothing for drivers to discard the carcass of a dead horse by the side of the road, and carcasses frequently became very ripe before

In 1893 the Mormon Church built Saltair resort on the southeast shore of the Great Salt Lake. Visitors could swim in the lake, dance in the Moorish Pavilion, and, eventually, enjoy amusement park rides, including a roller coaster. Used by permission, Utah State Historical Society, all rights reserved.

Salt Lake City, viewed here from Capitol Hill, was rapidly becoming a modern metropolis in 1900. Used by permission, Utah State Historical Society, all rights reserved.

someone towed them away. The city had no adequate sewage system and lacked safe, clean water for all of the residents.[7]

Concerned, Holmes and a number of other prominent men organized for change. He joined Salt Lake City's infant Commercial Club and twice served as its president. Forerunner of the Chamber of Commerce, the club's goals were to promote business development and to make the city's environment more desirable. He also joined the Country Club and the Alta Club, which included many of the state's wealthy miners. The one major social club he did not affiliate with was the Masons. This seems surprising because his obituary claims he was a thirty-second degree Mason in the East. Possibly his plate was too full of activities, or maybe he simply didn't want to compete with Albion's reputation as the former grand master of Utah's Masons.[8]

Holmes was motivated by altruism and the desire to be useful and productive, but he also hoped to create a favorable climate for his own business investments. While living in the Great Lakes area he had made millions in the lumber and shipping industries. Following their marriage, he and Susie pooled their finances and expanded his shipping interests. Together they started the Bransford Transfer Company which had three million dollars invested in freighters and facilities. Now in the West, he focused on his mining and agricultural interests. He was one of the principal stockholders in Park City's Anchor Mine and had large farms in Idaho and Utah, where he hoped to plant sugar beets and fruit trees.

Aware that the future of Western agriculture was tied to wise management of its limited water resources, Holmes studied the water problem and hoped to solve it. He used his own money to study the existing canal system in Salt Lake and Utah Counties, traveling, interviewing, and reading. He finally decided the best thing the Wasatch Front could do would be to consolidate the then scattered, independent water and irrigation companies into one entity. That way he hoped to

In addition to his interest in politics and concern for civic betterment, John loved the newfangled automobiles. Photograph courtesy of Vadney and Jean Murray.

bypass regional politics, build more canals, and open more land to cultivation. He realized the individual companies were accustomed to acting independently and would fight to keep their autonomy, but he fervently believed that nothing could be accomplished under the existing system.

As a part of the overall plan, Holmes also hoped to persuade timber and land interests to expand and dredge Utah Lake to store more runoff, making it a reservoir to irrigate central Utah and providing culinary water for the region. This would mean sacrificing good farmland in Utah Valley and diking the lake. It also would entail altering stream flows so the Great Salt Lake would gradually shrink considerably, though that would not occur for many years. He also proposed securing the water rights to all of Salt Lake County's canyons for future development and building reservoirs in most of the canyons to store as much water as possible. All of these proposals would cause major social adjustments and initially be costly, but they seemed to him more sensible than having the water flow into the Great Salt Lake, where it became useless.

Always conscious of world problems and major American issues, Holmes saw the West as a critical resettlement area for the poor. If the West could be developed to support more people, he saw it as a safety valve for the overcrowded Eastern cities. He firmly believed that something had to be done to help the millions who were living there in poverty. As president of the Commercial Club, he advocated a new rail line between Salt Lake City and the Pacific Coast and traveled to California to study the feasibility of the plan. Eventually, Tom Kearns and other investors built the San Pedro, Los Angeles, and Salt Lake Railroad that Holmes and the Commercial Club advocated to improve Utah's commercial ties with California. As Susie and the Colonel traveled, he frequently wrote Utah newspapers about the people and places he visited. When their world tour took them through the Orient and Russia, he wrote at least seven lengthy articles about the problems, strengths, and weaknesses of each country.[9]

The Colonel's sincerity, scientific approach to problems, and inventiveness gained him much respect from the local business community and earned him the presidency of the Twelfth National Irrigation Congress that met in Ogden in 1903. Some Utah farmers were not as impressed, however, and the North Jordan Canal Company refused to cooperate with his plan to bring all the canals under central management. In response, he gave them a cost breakdown and tried to convince them of the logic of the plan. Though the issue was thoroughly debated, the loss of local control was too threatening: the legislature voted the measure down.

Having lost the battle to consolidate the canals, Holmes applied his study of the region's water to the Great Salt Lake. He encouraged mineral exploration and prompted the community not to give up on Saltair, although the lake had receded from its pavilion. He pointed out that studies of the lake predicted it would soon rise again. The area normally cycled through wet and dry periods, and it had been dry for several years; as soon as the wet cycle returned, the lake would fill again. As he reviewed the matter later, the pettiness of the situation made him more disillusioned with Utah politics. While other progressives nationally often sought public office, Holmes believed politics got in the way of solving problems. Some admirers eventually proposed he run for Salt Lake City mayor or governor of Utah, but he turned both suggestions down. Earlier, friends in Michigan and Illinois had also discovered that he was not interested in politics.[10]

The Colonel and John Bransford became capable allies in working for necessary improvements in Salt Lake City. They realized the city's water system, sewage system, and garbage collection were inadequate and often primitive. Telephone and electric services needed to be extended to outlying parts of the city, while crime and prostitution were menaces. John's congenial nature, upright bearing, and honest character quickly impressed others. From his modest start with the Salt Lake Stock Exchange, he became its president. In addition to his floral company, he became director of Utah State Bank, president of Rogers-Evans Insurance Company, a director of Utah Mexican Rubber Company, vice president of Silver King Coalition Mines, director of the Keith O'Brien store, president of several small mining companies, and general contractor for several real estate projects. After he had lived in the area for only three years, the American Party also wanted him to run for mayor of Salt Lake City in 1902. He at first accepted but later declined because he was too busy and could not concentrate on the mayoral duties.

In his stead the American Party, comprising the city's leading non-Mormon businessmen, nominated Ezra Thompson. Thompson was also a popular Park City mining figure and was easily elected. Humorously, a few years later he was forced to resign for "reasons of health," a euphemism for some irregularities in his administration. Two Scottish visitors had been fleeced in a crooked poker game; the investigation into the situation led to the chief of police and, eventually, on to Thompson. While Thompson was not directly involved, he was tarred with accusation and forced to resign because he had appointed the chief of police. American Party leaders again turned to John for help. This time John accepted and finished Thompson's term of office. When election time came around, he ran on his own progressive reform platform and handily beat his opponent.[11]

During his term of office Bransford enacted several civic improvements as promised, but he managed to get entangled in a prostitution scandal that tainted his reputation. Like many elected officials of his time, he felt prostitution was an inevitable problem to be dealt with forthrightly so it could be controlled. Some Mormon and non-Mormon clergy organized the Civic Betterment Union and challenged his idea of moving the prostitutes to a prescribed area and warehousing them. Despite their reservations, John found a location on Second South between Fifth and Sixth West and built a compound with hundreds of small rooms or cribs. He also hired an Ogden madam, Belle London, to run the facility. Under her supervision the women were regularly checked for disease, protected from abuse, assessed fees, and allowed to ply their trade.

When asked why he picked that location, Bransford said it was the best place for the brothel because it was close to the railroad tracks, was not heavily populated, and had many foreigners. A

Despite the amazing number of good things John Bransford accomplished while he was mayor of Salt Lake City, he is best remembered for the controversy surrounding the stockade he built to house legalized prostitution. The *Deseret Evening News* mocked the rival *Salt Lake Tribune*'s endorsement of the plan. Used by permission, Utah State Historical Society, all rights reserved.

number of west side businessmen also enthusiastically lobbied for the stockade, believing it would help the area economically. Later Bransford was criticized when his opponents pointed out that he owned a three-story apartment building near the stockade. Belle also managed two buildings outside the stockade, and one, which leased rooms to prostitutes, had a bar and a cafe. Since both places presumably gained patronage from some of the brothel's customers, this appeared as a conflict of interest. Despite this controversial revelation, the stockade operated for three years before Belle unexpectedly announced to the local press that she was closing it on September 28, 1911, and would not reopen it. A few members of the Civic Betterment Union questioned her resolution, expecting her to quietly start business again, but she kept her word and the brothel stayed closed.[12]

Some claimed that Belle acted on her own to close the stockade, while others believed Bransford closed it because elections were approaching. One way or another the damage to Bransford's reputation was irreparable; he was not reelected despite the numerous good things he had accomplished.

John hired an Ogden madam, Belle London, to manage the business of the prostitutes inside the stockade. She later surprised everyone by closing the place down. Used by permission, Utah State Historical Society, all rights reserved.

During the four year period from 1907 to 1911, John spent six million dollars on public improvements, which is four times the amount spent during the previous fifteen year period. Those improvements included building new water and sewer lines, developing new parks and recreation facilities, hiring additional police and firemen, paving Second West, Broadway, and Ninth East, and adding miles of curb and gutter.[13] Bransford continued to live in Salt Lake City and tended to his business obligations until 1916, when he retired at age sixty. That year he and his wife, Rachel, moved to California to take advantage of the favorable climate. When she died in 1929, he returned to Salt Lake City to be near their children.[14]

All this while Susie was busy as well. One of the great obligations of a society woman was to entertain. It was a weighty responsibility. Alva Vanderbilt said, "I know of no profession, art, or trade that women are working in today, as taxing on mental resource as being a leader of Society."[15] Susie entertained with great gusto. She also joined a number of social and civic clubs. Membership in clubs, like frequent travel and attendance at concerts and museums, gave women a way to extend their education. While some American women were well educated and had attended universities, most women's education was limited; the clubs provided them ways to extend their knowledge and broaden their horizons. Members of the Ladies' Literary Club studied history, art, and similar topics, and then each took a turn presenting information she had researched. Across the country, women in various clubs were engaged in similar activities; consequently, the club movement became a significant element in the suffragette movement as women gained skill and confidence in public speaking.

Susie joined the exclusive Author's Club organized by Dr. Martha Hughes Cannon, in which all of the members were wives of prominent men in Salt Lake City politics, business, or the Mormon Church. Susie also became an associate member of the Ladies' Literary Club, where members took turns presenting information and leading discussions. For Susie, formal public presentations could have been difficult and threatening, since she had little formal education, and some of her letters reveal that her grammar was below traditional standards. As an associate member, she paid

As mayor, John Bransford increased the force of the Salt Lake City Police Department by several more officers and by horses as well. Used by permission, Utah State Historical Society, all rights reserved.

As both a candidate and mayor, John Bransford campaigned for increased fire protection. Used by permission, Utah State Historical Society, all rights reserved.

dues, but she was not required to lead discussions in the meetings.

In addition to providing women with opportunities to educate themselves in literature, history, and current affairs, both clubs held numerous socials and took part in philanthropic projects around the community. Both enthusiastically supported Salt Lake City's library next to the Alta Club and donated books to libraries throughout the state. Projects to help the poor and homeless in the city were launched as well. Susie soon found there was no shortage of groups to help with financial aid. People sponsoring the Orphans Nursery and Day Home, the Salvation Army, and the Red Cross frequently approached her for money. A music lover, she also supported the infant orchestra that eventually developed into the Utah Symphony.

Susie also supported her husband's progressive efforts. She appealed to women to use their newly won right to vote to improve Salt Lake City: "Women with the right to vote have it in their power to . . . advance civic beauty." National candidates also sought her financial backing for their campaigns. Basically a Democrat, Susie supported most of the Democratic candidates, the major exception being her support of Theodore Roosevelt's Republican presidential campaign in 1904. In 1916 one of the Vanderbilt women invited Susie to join a train of Republican women campaigning for Charles Evans Hughes, but Susie declined. She may have simply been a Wilson supporter, or she may have been responding to an earlier rebuff from Eastern society.[16]

She also joined the Salt Lake Country Club, which at that time had no family memberships; each individual joined separately. At the club, women as well as men played golf. One of California's foremost women golfers, Mrs. Jean Bowers, became one of Susie's friends and stayed in the Gardo House. Club members may also have gone horseback riding because Susie had a striking riding habit with matching leather shoes in her wardrobe. However, like Colonel Holmes, she also did not associate with the Masons at this time.[17]

Attending meetings to raise money for worthy causes must have become a routine activity for the Holmeses with all of their many club activities. Sometimes the event would be an enjoyable social with dancing, food, and entertainment. On other occasions an event could be pretty tedious—or even humorous or embarrassing. During a fund-raising meeting for the Salvation Army, Susie's generosity was really tested by General William Booth, the Army's founder. The meeting room was crowded and poorly ventilated. As the evening wore on, the temperature continued to climb, and Susie, sitting in a box near the stage, felt faint. To create a breeze and gain some relief she started to fan herself. She was unaware that the fan bothered General Booth until he suddenly turned in her direction and said, "If you will please dispense with that fan—it is the only one in the house and it goes right through my head—I would be very grateful to you." Embarrassed at the sudden stares from the audience, Susie closed her fan and quickly left the box. In the hallway outside the room, a reporter approached her for her comments on the incident. Still embarrassed, she brushed him off saying she would rather not discuss the issue further. Just the same, the following day one of Salt Lake City's newspapers attacked General Booth and hinted that his behavior might have cost him Susie's future patronage.[18]

The Holmeses' patronage of good causes was typical of the wealthy at the turn of the century. Many civic-minded socialites started sharing their money with the poor and with charitable groups. Prior to that, most of the rich had simply squandered their money on parties and entertainments. Now, as philanthropy became fashionable, some loved the attention it earned them, while others shunned it.[19] Susie did both. On many occasions she avoided boasting of her generosity and donated money or goods anonymously. Six months before her death in 1942, a reporter pressed her about her donations to charity and later commented on their discussion:

> The Princess gives liberally to charitable organizations. "I give what I can, then forget it," she declared. "It irritates me to hear boastings of this and that given to a cause. I think everybody should give according to their ability and let it go at that."

And she did give, generously. She doted on newsboys, contributed to orphanages, and frequently gave shoes or clothes to children. One anonymous Park City resident recalled that she spotted him and his boyhood friends standing barefoot in the road; moments later she sent her chauffeur to take the boys to the shoe store and purchase new shoes for all of them.[20]

Susie's charities ranged from organized events to sudden impulses, and some of them extended over years, giving a great deal back to her. In 1904 or 1905 fate sent Susie an unlikely orphan who would remain close to her for the rest of her life: Lory Snow, the youngest son of

Lory Snow became Susie's business manager, chauffeur, and friend. He was also one of the pioneers of aviation, selling one of his engines to the Wright Brothers. Photograph courtesy of Lelia Armstrong.

In 1904 downtown Salt Lake City was a mix of old and new: wagons shared the streets with trolley cars and automobiles, while utility wires seemed to take over the air. Used by permission, Utah State Historical Society, all rights reserved.

LDS Church President Lorenzo Snow. Both of his parents were now dead; he had been raised by one of his father's plural wives until he turned eighteen, then he struck out on his own. When Susie heard about his situation, she took him under her wing. In time, she educated and sponsored him, then finally announced him as her godson. He filled many roles for her, secretary, confidant, even chauffeur. Although cars were now in vogue, Susie had never learned to drive; women of her social class were expected to have a driver. Consequently, Lory traveled with Susie and her maid or the Holmeses and their servants. Years later, when Susie needed a business manager, Lory filled that position as well. Susie always claimed she handled her own finances, but she was not a good money manager. She lost track of amounts spent on travel, entertainments, and clothes and needed someone to gently keep her in line. She and Lory used a little account book, but she frequently forgot to enter the amounts she spent.

In 1908 Lory and Susie formed a company to manufacture airplane engines. Two years later he traveled to Dayton, Ohio, to sell an engine to the Wright Brothers. They initially turned down his engine but offered him a job on their project if he could help them true up the wheels for their plane. Lacking the needed skill, he rejected their offer, but felt he could have had the job if he had really wanted it.[21] Lory's skills and interest would eventually prove valuable during World War I, when he joined the Air Force. But when Lory first entered Susie's household as a young man, he was simply accepted as part of the family. Lory was near the age of Harold, who at the time attended college in the East but spent most of his free time with his father. When Carleton Holmes and Harold returned home for visits, Lory made it a threesome and the boys became inseparable.

Susie's scrapbooks are full of snapshots taken by Carleton, Lory, and Harold, but Carleton was the truly serious photographer.[22]

Carleton's love of and eventual career in photography were direct outgrowths of one of Colonel Holmes's good works. As a part of his land use studies, he sent Carleton with a scientific expedition to map, photograph, and paint the scenic wonders of southern Utah. The eight-man expedition originally planned to spend six weeks in southeastern Utah in present-day Natural Bridges National Monument, but they returned after just four weeks of roughing it. During that time H. L. A. Culmer, a skilled landscape artist, produced sketches used to paint a large oil painting entitled *Mystery of the Desert*. Holmes hung the painting in the Amelia Palace Art Gallery until Susie sold the house; they then returned it to the artist's family. Two years later, in 1907, Holmes sent a University of Utah professor, Byron Cummings, to explore southern Utah and the Bridges area. Together the men worked hard to have the president designate the area a national monument in 1908. Holmes even sent photos of the area to the National Geographic Society so they could help promote the project.[23]

The expedition had a major impact on southern Utah but also dramatically affected Carleton's life. After working with an expert photographer, Ogden's S. T. Whitaker, he came home smitten with the idea of being a photographer. Years later he moved to Hollywood so he could work professionally in the movie industry. Carleton's passion for photography became so absorbing that he never married, but maintained his freedom so he could travel and take pictures at will.

Neither Susie nor the Colonel overlooked his daughters during these years. One Pasadena newspaper stated that the three girls—Hellen, Harriet, and Olive—were regular visitors to the area, where the Holmeses lived part time. The girls also visited Salt Lake City frequently, and one society page clipping comments that Susie attempted to introduce the younger two to young men on numerous occasions. Matching up the girls, who were tall, very bright, and regarded as homely, must have been frustrating. The oldest daughter married a Canadian widower, Dr. John White, late in her thirties but had no children. The other two girls and Carleton never married. Carleton was outgoing, but his sisters tended to be shy and reclusive. This turn of events must have frustrated Susie, who liked to take care of people. She would have gladly given all of the girls a grand wedding if she could have married them off.[24]

# 8

# The Next Generation

In addition to Grace and the Colonel's children, Susie showed great affection for other members of her family's younger generation. Her motives certainly included family feeling, but, like other Gilded Age aristocrats, she may also have had a penchant to establish a dynasty. In the case of her sister Viola's son, Harold, she considered herself his guardian, a responsibility she proudly accepted. She saw to it that he was well cared for and educated.

Harold stayed in school long enough to attend two years of college but dropped out before graduation. He proved to be a natural athlete, and, like Susie, he enjoyed tennis, horseback riding, and other sports, especially golf, which he wanted to play constantly. Impressed by his abilities and aware that the wealthy were not necessarily required to work, Susie encouraged him where others might have chided him to study and stay in school.[1]

In 1912 Harold married a young Texas beauty named Grizzelle Houston. Grizzelle came from a wealthy, well-educated family with an impressive pedigree. Harold found a job as a landscape architect for Ware & Treganza and worked on several small projects as he learned the trade. Thrilled for his happiness, Susie decided to give him an allowance to supplement his income so he could continue to live in the style he had always known, but Harold worked hard, too. Eventually he became a partner in the firm and the name was changed to Treganza and Lamb. The next year Susie gave him and his bride a beautiful home on Michigan Avenue. The large, two-story home sat on a small canyon three blocks south of Mt. Olivet Cemetery and resembled a prairie-style house designed by Frank Lloyd Wright. The young couple lived there comfortably for several years and started their family in that house. They eventually had three children, Joe, Susan, and Harold Jr., the latter nicknamed Hal. Susie

Harold V. Lamb, Susie's foster son and nephew, became a landscape architect and an avid golfer, winning several golf championships. Photograph courtesy of Harold Lamb.

Harold's wife, Grizzelle Houston Lamb, and their three children, Joe, Susie, and Harold Jr. Photograph courtesy of Harold Lamb.

Susie purchased this home on Michigan Avenue for Harold and Grizzelle when they married in 1912. Photograph by Judy Dykman.

enjoyed the Lamb children and celebrated birthdays and Christmas with them when she was in town. Typically each received fifty dollars to spend on these occasions.

But Susie looked beyond her own nieces and nephews for people to assist. Like other wealthy women, she enjoyed sponsoring young women into society or helping them meet young men. Promoting a successful protégée was considered a significant accomplishment and was an additional mark of social status. William Randolph Hearst's mother, Phoebe, for example, sponsored and raised a young niece, Anna Apperson, giving her a place to live and taking pride in her accomplishments. When Susie visited Chicago, newspapers reported she and Mrs. Palmer Potter entertained together, an indication that Susie was a protégée of the famous Mrs. Potter. Eager to emulate the Eastern socialites, Susie also helped young artists, athletes, orphans, and relatives. It was a heady experience to catapult them to fame or claim partial responsibility for their success.[2]

Her favorite and best-known protégée was actually the niece of her brother, John, and his wife, Rachel. Rachel's brother, Ira Blood, and his wife, Frances, lived in a small home near the heart of San Francisco with their only child, Adele. Susie first met Ira Blood when they were young children growing up in Indian Valley. The Bloods and Bransfords were like family, especially after John married Rachel. Adele was Grace's age, but unlike Grace, Adele was fun loving and outgoing, like Susie.

When Adele was barely six years old, Ira suddenly died, leaving Frances to support the little girl as best she could. Even so, they lived in extreme poverty for several years. While still in her teens, Adele went to work to help her mother pay the bills. She sang in the church choir and was an old hand at waiting on tables and singing in small cafes. As time passed she received a few roles in a number of local theatricals, but even minor roles in San Francisco could be considered significant.[3]

By 1900 San Francisco had a third of a million people and was the ninth largest city in the United States. It had come a long way from the Gold Rush days, when most of its buildings were constructed of wood, and its dirt roads were deeply rutted by wagon wheels. By the turn of the century most of its wooden structures had been replaced with brick and stone buildings, and many of the streets were paved and equipped with lights. In its harbor were many ocean-going vessels, as the city now had well-established commercial connections with several countries around the Pacific Rim. The town also had its wealthy class, composed of millionaires such as Mark Hopkins, Charles Crocker, Leland Stanford, James Flood, and George Hearst. These and many other aristocrats built lovely mansions overlooking the city and bay on fashionable Nob Hill and shared a rich social life that could rival any found in New York City or Washington, D.C.

Susie claimed to know them all on a first name basis, especially Phoebe Hearst. Unlike some of her playful boasts, this was probably true, for in later years she lived in Pasadena and in 1935 the *San Francisco Chronicle* devoted a full page, not just a few columns, to her and referred to her as America's Silver Queen. Such a tribute implies prominence and social acceptance. However, as important as San Francisco society was, the city was about to experience something much bigger.

On April 18, 1906, an earthquake registering 6.6 on the Richter Scale hit San Francisco, wiping out most of the inner city. Over three thousand acres of land were devastated by a series of violent jolts and then by numerous aftershocks. Californians had grown accustomed to experiencing several small quakes each year, but this was the first time a major population center had been seriously hit. They were not prepared. Bad as the tremors were, the worst damage came from fires that erupted moments after the rumbling stopped, as sparks ignited gas leaking from ruptured lines. Whole sections of the city instantly burst into flames, the acrid smell of burning wood and debris filling the air for several days. Water mains that supplied the city's fire hydrants also ruptured, and the water that might have stopped the fires flowed down the streets instead of through fire hoses. Some of the taller buildings toppled immediately; others caved in over the next several days because of the aftershocks. The fires burned unchecked for many hours, and over the next several days five hundred people died. One source claims that the earthquake itself caused twenty million dollars in damage, but that the fire which followed caused

Adele Blood, John's and Rachel's niece, became Susie's protégée. She was famous on Broadway and did many vaudeville shows, including a tour of the Orient. A publicity photograph using backlighting shows Adele's trademark blond hair, which earned her the title "America's most beautiful blond." Photograph courtesy of Vadney and Jean Murray.

William Randolph Hearst was the only child of George and Phoebe Hearst. Using the fortune he inherited from his parents, he built an influential media empire. He was thirty-one when his lifelong friend, Orrin Peck, painted this portrait in 1894. Photograph courtesy of Hearst Castle™/Hearst San Simeon State Historical Monument.™

Hearst Castle™ perched 1600 feet above sea level in the Santa Lucia Mountains overlooks the Pacific Ocean from amid 127 acres of gardens, terraces, pools, and walkways. Though construction on this complex was begun about 1920 and the estate has 165 rooms, it is still unfinished. It is open to the public with tours daily and offers interesting insights into the Gilded Age. Photograph courtesy of Hearst Castle™/Hearst San Simeon State Historical Monument.™

another forty million.[4] Thousands of people lost everything. They had no place to stay and no means of making a livelihood. Relief organizations and individuals helped as much as they could, but the disaster was overwhelming.[5]

When the fires were out, Frances and Adele returned to their home to find it had been destroyed with most of the surrounding buildings. It was time to leave town. Realizing they needed help, an anonymous friend came to their rescue. While no record remains of the friend's name, there is a high probability that it was Susie. She certainly had the funds to do it, and it was typical of her behavior to help her friends in need. In addition, over the next few years, she openly and generously helped Adele. Susie was impressed with her relative by marriage and was glad to claim her as a protégée when Adele decided to pursue a stage career. With her mellow, clear voice, good looks, and thick, long, blond hair, she seemed a natural for a stage career. Susie provided her with traveling money, money to live on, and money for clothes until she could make it on her own. Later, when Adele's mother wanted to visit, Susie sent her east as well in one of the Holmeses' cars.

Adele initially was turned down by many casting directors, but she took bit parts in off-Broadway productions and worked odd jobs between acting stints. One afternoon she finally got her big break: the director of a Broadway show listened to her sing because he thought she was a beautiful blond. When she finished the song he told her candidly that good voices and good looks were common in New York City, but her blond hair was so unusual that he would give her a chance. From that time on, Adele's career on the stage was assured. She had a natural grace in front of an audience and belted out show tunes like a real trooper. She played the lead in the musical *Every Woman* on Broadway for five years and soon earned the title of "the world's most beautiful blond." Ironically, it could be said that the San Francisco earthquake literally launched her career while destroying the livelihood of so many others.

In the meantime, Adele's pastor, Reverend Edward Cader Davis, decided to go to New York to take care of her. Adele was startled when he appeared at the door of her dressing room and even more startled when he offered to marry her and manage her stage career. Davis was charming and good looking, with a presence that was hard to ignore, so Adele agreed to marry him. For a few years they appeared to be happy. He promptly gave up preaching the gospel and turned to acting while he promoted Adele's career.[6] One of the gimmicks he used to publicize Adele was to insure her ankle-length hair for fifty thousand dollars. A womanizer, he found it hard to be faithful to Adele and was embroiled in several torrid affairs before she filed for divorce. Davis counterfiled and vengefully accused her of adultery with several prominent politicians. News of the suits for divorce made major headlines in 1914, since Adele had become a prominent star by this time. Fortunately for her, the judge heard both sides and in 1914 quickly granted her divorce petition. Davis's star faded, but Adele continued to perform in several Broadway productions, including *The Picture of Dorian Gray*. She and Susie remained close friends for the rest of Adele's life.[7]

Much as she may have enjoyed helping all of these people, Susie's greatest concern still lay with her daughter, Grace. As she had matured, Grace appeared to have fewer bouts of anxiety, but her relationship with her mother improved little and normal communication between the two was difficult despite Susie's efforts to find a common ground. Grace still agonized about why her mother traveled without her or sent her to distant boarding schools. Sadly, she was too emotionally distressed to recognize that Susie treated her as most wealthy parents treated their children. While much of the blame for their problem lies with Susie, Grace's periods of anxiety and depression were also aggravated by the normal patterns of puberty.

By the time Grace was in her late teens, the differences between the women were more dramatic. Susie accepted the life of a nouveau riche without questioning it, while Grace wanted a quieter lifestyle. Like many of the other Bransfords, Grace preferred solitary pursuits, like reading and doing handwork, or outdoor activities with only a few close friends.[8]

To her credit, Susie did try a variety of approaches to reach Grace. During 1902 Susie arranged to take sixteen-year-old Grace to Europe to finish her education. Her grades at the National Park Seminary had been disappointing, but Susie was determined that her daughter would acquire the culture and poise needed to compete with the other girls in society. Grace could mingle informally during her travels, learn from what she saw, and develop some social graces. Most of the time the trip went well. On occasion tensions mounted when Susie could not interest Grace in the museums and sites they visited. However, while they were traveling they actually got along better than they had for several years. Susie noticed Grace's maturity and was proud of her. Now that Grace was nearly an adult, Susie wanted to take her to parties, travel, and spend time with her.

When Grace became bored with Europe, Susie arranged for her to stay with the Baroness Prou and her several teenage children in the Chateau St. Rodegonde near Paris. After dropping Grace off at the Baroness's home, Susie and the Colonel traveled to the Middle East. Grace was relieved to be left behind; the Baroness was very warm and welcoming. When Susie returned to the United States several months later, she was shocked to receive a letter from the Baroness proposing the marriage of Grace to one of her sons. Susie called Grace home immediately. She felt that, at sixteen, Grace was too young, and, besides, Susie had even bigger plans for Grace's future. John met Grace in New York and brought her back to Salt Lake City.

As Grace neared her eighteenth birthday, Susie tried to interest her in planning a grand coming out party in Utah. Before the Civil War, coming out parties had been quiet affairs for family and friends, but the nouveaux riches managed to turn them into yet another excuse for competitive excess. Debutantes spent countless hours planning spectacular parties for their introductions into society. By the time the decorations, food, clothes, invitations, servers, flowers, and music were paid for, the event could cost many thousands of dollars.

Eastern families competed to see who could get the most media coverage and dazzle their friends. In 1909 George Jay Gould spent two hundred thousand dollars for his daughter's party. For Alice Whitehouse's coming out, her parents hired warships from the U.S. Navy to moor off Newport and shine searchlights on the shore. James Paul of Philadelphia created an absolute disaster for his daughter in his attempt at novelty: He had thousands of monarch butterflies captured and stored in net bags on the ceiling of their ballroom. As his daughter made her grand entrance that evening, Paul planned to release the butterflies to fill the air with a sense of magic. Unfortunately, his timing was poor; by the time his daughter arrived, the butterflies were all dead, smothered in the excessive heat. As the poor girl made her grand entrance, thousands of dead insects fell on her in a clump. As silly as this extravagance sounds, parties were thought to be failures if they were not exciting and different.[9]

Although coming out parties were *de rigueur* in the East in the early 1900s, Utahns were not providing them for their daughters, and Susie was anxious to introduce this idea to her wealthy Salt Lake friends. As she talked of giving Grace an elaborate party, she hoped her daughter would become enthusiastic about the upcoming festivities. In planning an elaborate party, however, Susie was not just being frivolous. Like many women of her class, Susie hoped Grace would marry well. In an age when women could not be employed and retain social status, security lay in a husband who could provide well.

Given a chance to arrange Grace's marriage to a proper young man, Susie would have paired her with a member of the Swedish royal family. This scheme sounds pretentious and ridiculous, but from 1870 to 1914 there were about five hundred transatlantic marriages between monied Americans and members of Europe's royal families, usually of wealthy women to titled men. Two of the best-known marriages were those of Consuelo Vanderbilt to the Duke of Marlborough and Jennie Jerome to Lord Randolph Churchill. Phoebe Hearst broke up a few of William Randolph's relationships in hopes of influencing his choice for a bride. When he eventually married Millicent Wilson, Phoebe was heartbroken. She had hoped he would marry someone of his class or a member of Europe's nobility.[10]

What Susie did not realize was that Grace was not interested in meeting anyone, and she resented her mother trying to plan her future. In fact, Grace had already fallen in love and chosen her future husband. After meeting John's son, Wallace, three years earlier, Grace had been writing to him on a regular basis. During the years when she had been warring with her mother and was bitter about being ignored, she confided her

Louise Grace Emery at about the time of her marriage. Photograph courtesy of Vadney and Jean Murray.

John's son, Wallace Bransford, at about the time of his marriage to Grace. Photograph courtesy of Anne Bransford Newhall.

feelings to Wallace in lengthy letters. At first Wallace felt nothing for her—she was just an awkward little cousin to be pacified—but as Grace blossomed into young womanhood, Wallace realized he was also falling in love. True, he was five years older and studying business at Berkeley during the courtship, but Grace's immaturity and lack of education were not an issue. He enjoyed her dependence on him, and her total devotion flattered his ego. When they were home from school, they spent many hours together, walking, talking, hiking with friends, and playing games. As time passed and the relationship developed into a serious romance, Grace wisely kept her feelings for Wallace a secret from her mother. Wallace's family soon guessed they were serious about each other, but they, too, kept the relationship a secret from Susie, who they all knew would not approve of Grace's plan to marry Wallace.[11]

When Grace celebrated her eighteenth birthday on May 1, 1904, she confronted Susie. Wallace had told her she was a wealthy woman in her own right: the probate had divided Albion's property between Susie and Grace. Now that she had reached legal age, Grace wanted her share so she could go her own way. Susie refused, claiming she should continue to manage Grace's money for her and put the money into investments so it could draw interest. Susie had always planned to leave Grace the money in her will, but *she* wanted to be the one who gave it to her. This angered Grace and she bitterly complained; she also announced that she intended to marry Wallace immediately. Susie told her it was inappropriate to marry a first cousin. The proscription against cousins marrying was of course based on potential genetic problems for their children; Susie knew this issue was invalid in the case of Grace and Wallace because the girl had been adopted—a fact she had still never shared with Grace. But Grace did not care about social taboos or genetics, so Susie tried another argument. She said Grace should marry someone who had money to take care of her; Wallace was not even employed full time. He managed his father's floral company or worked temporarily in the Silver King Mine when he was home from school. Still, the more Susie objected, the more determined Grace became to marry Wallace.

The problem was exacerbated when Wallace naively made several offhand comments about Susie to J. B. Feldman, an employee at the floral shop, who repeated them to Susie. Wallace said he was lucky to be engaged to Utah's wealthiest young heiress. He also criticized his aunt's intelligence and spending practices, intimating that she was silly and wasteful. Many probably shared this view, but they were not marrying her daughter. When Susie heard these comments, she was understandably hurt and angry. However, looking through her own narcissistic filter, Susie may have magnified Wallace's boyish criticisms and given them more significance than they deserved. Wallace was exactly the kind of person the insecure members of the newly rich feared: he was extremely bright and, like many people of very high intelligence, had little patience with people with less education. He came from a secure social background—his father, after all, eventually became Salt Lake City's mayor. He also had the easygoing poise and self-confidence that comes from that background. Beyond her concern with

Wallace himself, Susie also had to wonder if Wallace wasn't repeating his father's views on her lifestyle, because John managed her money. If that were the case, how much could she trust John? Wallace apparently did care for Grace, but her money made their relationship even more attractive. When Grace first proposed marriage, he turned her down because he had nothing to bring to the relationship. He suggested they wait a few years to marry until he had a job and had saved some money. Grace refused to listen and insisted they marry immediately. Why wait when she already had money? Besides, she wanted to be independent of Susie as soon as possible.[12]

Susie appealed to John to step in and stop their children's marriage plans before they went any further, but he surprised her by refusing to take her side. He and Rachel loved Grace, knew the couple were not genetic cousins, and so saw no reason the children should not marry. When Susie angrily reminded John that Wallace had no money or job to support a wife, John gave his son several thousand dollars from his family bank account. Desperate to stop the marriage, Susie next threatened to disinherit Grace if she would not call off the wedding, though legally the money already belonged to Grace—Susie's guardianship had ended on Grace's eighteenth birthday.

After many heated discussions, Susie finally caved in to Grace's demands and gave her half of their money and real estate holdings, but she charged Grace's estate with the legal fees needed to separate their monies. Triumphantly Grace made plans to marry on September 6, 1904, but Susie refused to give her a big society wedding and reception. There was no engagement announcement; friends were not encouraged to give Grace parties, and Susie refused to pay for a church ceremony or a wedding dress. Family friends undoubtedly compared Nellie's wedding four years earlier to the small ceremony hosted at the Gardo House for Grace. When Nellie married, Susie had spent lavishly to make the event a spectacular success; now she offered Grace nothing. Grace was probably devastated by Susie's attitude toward Wallace and her refusal to give her a large wedding. Grace had been a flower girl at Nellie's ceremony and remembered the splendid food, decorations, clothing, and music. Still, regardless of Susie's threats and demands, Grace would not change her mind.

On September 6 the *Deseret News* and *Salt Lake Tribune* printed full descriptions of Grace's private ceremony performed by a judge in the Gardo House. Grace was married in a stylish brown dress trimmed in blue with a matching hat. The house was decked in flowers, and Wallace covered his car with thousands of flowers for the occasion. No guests outside of the immediate family were invited, and a small formal dinner was served after the brief ceremony. John and Susie served as witnesses on the marriage license but had little to say to one another. Susie gave Grace a beautiful tea service made from Park City's silver. The Colonel was a gracious host but wisely avoided getting in his wife's way. A loving father to his own children, he probably had mixed emotions about Grace's marriage. After the dinner the newlyweds quickly left for the train station in Wallace's car. Wallace seemed happy, but Grace was ecstatic. Later she told friends it was the first time she had really experienced affection from anyone in her life. During their extended honeymoon they traveled to several of America's largest cities and spent many days sight-seeing at each stop.[13]

Shortly after they entered their private car on the train, Wallace told Grace she was not Susie's natural daughter. Wallace had wanted to tell Grace the story of her adoption for several years, but John had insisted he keep Susie's secret until he married Grace. The news was startling at

This car, elaborately decorated with flowers, may be the one Wallace decorated for his wedding to Grace in 1904. Used by permission, Utah State Historical Society, all rights reserved.

first but not unexpected. Grace had wondered for many years how two people could be related and yet be so very different. At first Grace was thrilled to finally know the truth; somehow the information reassured her that she was a good person in her own right. But as the days went by, new issues shattered her peace of mind. Why had she been abandoned by her birth mother in Boston? Was the woman alive? Did she have brothers and sisters? Could she find her biological family, if she had one? Would any of them even want to see her? When Grace returned from her honeymoon she had little to say to Susie. She was angry with her on many counts: first, for her coolness to her when she was a child; then, for her need to control Grace's life and money; and now, for concealing her true identity from her. Grace wanted to ask Susie why she had been so selfish, but she could not find the courage.

Grace and Wallace immediately moved into one of the apartments in the Emery-Holmes Apartments, part of her legacy. The building offered all of the latest amenities to wealthy renters, including an elevator, electricity, running hot and cold water, and telephone service. Grace decided to put her money in a joint banking account which Wallace would manage for them. Wallace also assumed responsibility for renting and maintaining the apartment complex, which they renamed the Bransford Apartments. Meanwhile, Grace happily set up housekeeping and furnished their apartment. She was very artistic and loved to decorate with things she made herself: pictures she drew or painted and doilies she crocheted for the arms of their sofa and chairs. Friends who knew her well reported that she had four hobbies: pleasing Wallace, reading current fiction, crocheting, and housekeeping. Outwardly, at least, she appeared the picture of domesticity and happiness.[14]

Despite the fact that the apartments were just across the street from the Gardo, Grace infrequently visited there and always brought Wallace or his sister, Stella, with her. It was as though Grace felt she needed support to talk to her mother and was uncomfortable seeing her alone. For Susie's part, she remained very upset with Grace for marrying Wallace. She could tell by Grace's aloofness that Wallace had told her about the adoption and that Grace resented her mother's years of concealment. Both women shed bitter tears over their estrangement, but neither was willing to discuss the problem and they began to avoid each other. Susie confided in her mother, while Grace confided in Rachel and Wallace about what she saw as a return to Susie's early cruelty.

But Grace was not Susie's only problem. Sarah's health was deteriorating rapidly, and the Colonel's arthritis was becoming more severe. Anxious to help both of them escape Utah's winter cold, Susie purchased a second home in sunny Pasadena. Constructed of shake shingles, it had three floors including the rooms in the attic. From its vantage point on the edge of the arroyo, it had a wonderful view. When Utah became too cold and the Colonel's arthritis started to bother him, they moved to their Southern California home, which they called El Roble for the large oak tree in the front yard. When they traveled to California, they took Sarah with them. Like the Colonel, her health problems were alleviated by the warmer weather in the winter. They developed a regular schedule: Pasadena in the winter and Salt Lake City in the summer.

Like the Gardo in Salt Lake, El Roble became a gathering place for both friends and family. Harold's son, Hal, was particularly fond of his great aunt and took advantage of every opportunity to be with her. He was impressed that she always seemed to be in control of any situation. He recalls one Christmas when the whole family visited Susie in Pasadena. Susie had the chauffeur drive her big, yellow Rolls Royce in the Tournament of Roses parade because she knew this would delight Hal. No record exists of Susie having an official title in this particular parade, but both the rules and the people were much more relaxed then, and individuals frequently joined the parade at will in their cars. As Hal watched, the bleachers in a section along the route collapsed, seriously injuring many onlookers. As rescue vehicles rushed to help the injured, traffic snarled, and some of the motorists lost their tempers. But Hal remembers Susie was serenely cool during the incident. Unflappable, she kept her nephew entertained while the car was stuck in the traffic jam.[15]

El Roble solved their winter problems, but summer along the Wasatch Front can be grindingly hot, and the city was hot even in the days before most of the streets were paved with

The Bransford Apartments were part of Grace's inheritance. The Bransford was built from 1902 to 1903 for $150,000. It stood on the northeast corner of State Street and South Temple in Salt Lake City. The structure had forty suites, some with kitchens. The tenants who did not have a kitchen took their meals in a spacious cafeteria on the ground floor. Each apartment had a telephone and electricity. The building had two elevators and was considered one of the most modern apartment buildings in the state. Used by permission, Utah State Historical Society, all rights reserved.

The Louise Grace Emery Apartments were another part of Grace's property. They stood on the corner of State Street and North Temple. The area has recently been turned into a park. Used by permission, Utah State Historical Society, all rights reserved.

asphalt. The heat seems to hover above the center of the valley, and breezes offer relief only in the early morning or evening. One hundred years ago, the average person found relief in carriage rides into the canyons and trips to the Great Salt Lake or to some other resort. Wealthy families, by contrast, had other options, such as moving to summer homes or traveling to a cooler climate. Like their Eastern counterparts, Susie and several of Utah's wealthy families, the Hogles, Walkers, Bambergers, Judges, and Browns, had summer homes in the Cottonwoods or East Millcreek south of the city.

Susie purchased the land for her summer home, Oakwood, in 1904. The Neff family had first settled the property on Evergreen Avenue in 1848. John Neff built a flour mill and a home and planted several acres of crops. Two decades later, electricity made the water-powered mill obsolete, so his sons sold the property to William H. Spafford, a wealthy Salt Lake City councilman. Spafford razed most of the mill but converted part of it into a dance pavilion for outdoor entertaining. Seven years later he sold the property to Edward H. Airis, who in turn sold it to Susie in 1904.[16]

After purchasing the six-acre property, Susie remodeled the home into a two-story structure with several bedrooms and a huge attic. Following the changes it was painted yellow and roofed with red shingles. Frequent breezes from the canyon cooled the house and grounds in the early morning and evening hours, making it a comfortable summer retreat. It was a comfortable place to stay when the Colonel was busy in the city with civic affairs. Sometimes Susie visited the house alone with her servants; other times family came with her—Harold, the Holmes children, and even Grace. Susie's brother, John, and sister, Nellie, also loved the retreat and frequently visited.[17]

Even today deer wander down the creek to nibble on the bushes and young trees, and more than a dozen varieties of birds live in the trees. When Susie lived there, other animals were plentiful as well but were seldom a problem. If they did become an issue, William Hyte, the grounds keeper and gardener, eliminated them. West of the house Susie and William planted several varieties of fragrant flowers. Tulips were a favorite, and she sometimes sold dozens to Huddart Floral. Susie's attitude toward Hyte demonstrates her relationship with her servants and employees. He had young children whom she enjoyed spoiling. One year, just prior to Mother's Day, five-year-old Sue picked a handful of Susie's early spring flowers and gave them to her. Some might have been annoyed that the little girl picked the flowers when they had just bloomed, but Susie accepted them graciously; then, ever sentimental and spontaneous in showing her appreciation for little kindnesses, she sent the chauffeur to buy each of the Hyte children a new set of clothes. She was very loyal to her help and treated them well. In return they showed her much devotion over the years; several stayed with her for their entire lives.[18]

Idyllic as Oakwood may have been, one of its important purposes was to entertain and impress society—and Susie did this with a flourish. News clippings report she held several delightful parties at Oakwood. One summer evening she and the Colonel invited the officers and their wives from Fort Douglas to join them for a dance and refreshments. Typical of her style of entertaining, the house was filled with flowers, and tables in the backyard were piled high with elegant, cool treats for the dancers when they wanted a rest. Lights illuminated the dance pavilion and slightly swayed in the evening breezes that followed the creek bed. Susie was constantly on the lookout for something to make her parties unusual and distinctive. At her request Adele Blood posed as a clairvoyant and read palms on occasions when she was in Salt Lake City. Eventually, Susie hired two of the state's outstanding photographers, Bill and Harry Shipler, to attend some of her parties and photograph the guests for their amusement.[19]

Sarah had little time to enjoy Oakwood, but Susie encouraged her to stay there as much as possible. Susie spent many hours with her mother trying to comfort her. When Sarah died April 7, 1905, John, Susie, and Nellie arranged a lovely funeral and had her buried near their father on the land Susie had purchased in Mt. Olivet Cemetery. Susie was devastated to lose Sarah's company; they had been very close during the last ten years since each had lost a husband. Sarah had been Susie's confidante and was a steadying influence in her life. Without her Susie felt very lost. Colonel Holmes did everything he could to comfort her,

Oakwood in East Millcreek, Utah, was Susie's summer home. East Millcreek ran in back of the house. When Susie redesigned the grounds she put a bridge across the creek so they could visit the property on the south side of the stream. Family members recall that the house was at least five to ten degrees cooler than downtown Salt Lake City. This and all of the following pictures of Oakwood were taken by Bill and Harry Shipler and are from the Shipler collection of glass negatives at the Utah State Historical Society. Photograph courtesy of Harold Lamb.

Oakwood was two stories tall with yellow wood siding and a steep red roof. The home's charm attracted guests like these to Susie's parties at the turn of the century, and it still attracts people today. It has been a setting for the TV version of Stephen King's *The Stand*, episodes of several television series, and many local commercials. Shipler photograph courtesy of Harold Lamb.

Part of this avenue of trees leading from the street to the house was destroyed in storms several years after this picture was taken. In addition to trees, Susie loved flowers and grew many varieties. Occasionally, visitors to the retreat commented that they could smell Oakwood's flowers before they could see the gate to the property. Shipler photograph courtesy of Harold Lamb.

Oakwood was one of the few East Millcreek residences to use Millcreek's current to produce its own electricity, but eventually, like its neighbors, it also purchased power from Utah Power and Light. Shipler photograph courtesy of Harold Lamb.

Inside or outside the house, Susie always served magnificent meals properly, with tablecloths and the correct settings. Shipler photograph courtesy of Harold Lamb.

This picture of the family visiting on the porch at Oakwood was probably taken by Carleton Holmes or Lory Snow, who became the family photographers. At the left is Harold, sitting on the swing next to Nellie; behind them is a cousin, Laura Bransford. Susie is sitting on the right, and Grace is standing next to the pillar. Identification of the other two women is uncertain, but they are likely Colonel Holmes's daughters, Olive at the back in the shadows and Harriett seated next to Susie. Photograph courtesy of Harold Lamb.

but the next few years were very hard for Susie. Instinctively, she turned to Nellie and worked to develop a close relationship with her.

Nellie was past the point of resenting her sister's interference in her life and welcomed the closeness. She had also had her share of heartaches. She had lost two babies since her marriage in 1900: one was a miscarriage and the other lived almost to term before arriving prematurely. Susie could well understand Nellie's frustrations at being childless. Susie was now well beyond childbearing age, but Nellie was still in her prime and could not understand why she was unable to have a healthy child.

Finally, two years after Sarah's death, Nellie announced her third pregnancy. The sisters celebrated her good fortune. Nellie and Jay had moved to California and settled not far from El Roble so they could spend more time with Susie and the Colonel. When the baby was born, Nellie was thrilled to have a healthy son and named him Bransford Harris. The following year she became pregnant a fourth time. Susie stepped in to mother her through this pregnancy, too, and the baby was born in Susie's bedroom at El Roble. Happy and relieved that she had a healthy daughter, Nellie named her Susanna after Susie. A few days later Susie startled Nellie by begging her to give Susie one of her children. Now that Nellie had a son and a daughter, could she raise Susanna? That way both of them would have a child to love and raise. Understandably, Nellie refused, but she did allow Susie to help care for her daughter and spend time with her.

Susie delighted in holding her infant namesake, Susanna. As the little girl grew older, Nellie occasionally consented to let Susanna stay with Susie in the Gardo and at Oakwood overnight. Susie's staff of servants also enjoyed the precocious little girl who delighted in tormenting her older brother and then feigning innocence. The cook allowed her to help pick the menu for the meals if she didn't request corn chowder too frequently. Everyone also looked the other way when she slid down the large banister in the main hall of the Gardo and knocked the large finial on the floor. When the door to the art gallery-ballroom was unlocked, Susanna also enjoyed sneaking into the large room in her stocking feet and sliding on the polished floors. If Susie caught her, she pretended to scold the little girl but could seldom keep a straight face for very long. On warm summer evenings Susie and the Colonel took Susanna for rides in their car so she could enjoy the cool breeze. As she grew older, Susanna sometimes stayed with her aunt at El Roble. Susie gave her the small room next to her own so she could go to her in the night if necessary. Susanna remembers the walls of the room were covered with a dull red linoleum, which Susie thought was particularly attractive, and that she had many toys and plenty of clothes at her aunt's home. Susie delighted in dressing her niece.[20]

Susanna also learned that, in addition to indulging her, her aunt could also tease. Once, while Susanna sat spellbound watching Susie brush her hair in front of the mirror, she suddenly asked her aunt if she were also beautiful. Susie

Susie asked her sister Nellie if she could raise her daughter, Susanna. Photograph courtesy of Susanna Hartman.

Oakwood was a favorite gathering place for the family in the summer. Here John and Nellie are sitting on the front porch that Susie added along the west side of the house. Shipler photograph, used by permission, Utah State Historical Society, all rights reserved.

paused, took the child by the shoulders, turned her from side to side, and then said she would do. The response was not what Susanna expected to hear from her doting aunt. She stood speechless. Susie smiled at her in the mirror to show her approval and to reassure the child. Susanna eventually learned to tell when her aunt was teasing, but for a long time she really did believe her story that the song "Oh Susanna" was written just for her.[21]

Susie's delight in her namesake offered still more evidence that she was grieving inwardly over her estrangement from Grace and wished she could undo some of her past mistakes; however, she could never approach her to make peace, and Grace seemed equally unable to reach out to her mother.

# 9

## A House Divided Against Itself

Despite the strains in their relationships, the next several years were basically quiet for the Bransford family. John continued to work for Susie and capably managed her money, but he had little to say to her most of the time. He must have been badly hurt when Susie tried to prevent the marriage of their children. He was always very proud of Wallace. Nellie became a go-between for her brother and sister during the tense times when neither could talk to the other directly. One incident illustrates the division between them: on one occasion when John was very ill, Susie contacted Nellie to find out how he was doing instead of calling on him personally. She swore Nellie to secrecy but said she would help if he needed anything, regardless of the cost. Possibly she feared he would not accept the help if he knew she was the one to offer it. And so it went for most of the next thirty years.[1]

As the years passed, Susie and Grace also remained estranged. Wallace and Grace appeared to be happy together though disappointed that she was sickly and did not become pregnant. Grace's friends claimed she wanted a family very badly but seemed incapable of having a child.[2] Whenever a friend would visit with a baby, she was captivated and wanted to hold it. Wallace also wanted a child but wisely did not make an issue of it. It would not help Grace's frame of mind if he complained. Otherwise they seemed a contented couple. Their only major problem occurred in 1908 when Grace developed a severe case of rheumatic fever. She was bedridden for several months and sank to the depths of depression as the illness wore on. Once, several friends visited her and clowned around for the camera to amuse her, but she failed to rally and remained morose. She seemed to feel as if a dark cloud were always on the horizon. In reality she was right.

After Grace's rheumatic fever ran its course, she recovered but was frequently exhausted. The disease sapped the little energy she had and severely damaged her heart. She would have enjoyed a visit from Susie while she convalesced

In 1908 Grace suffered from rheumatic fever, which left her with a badly impaired heart. While she was recuperating in her bed, her friends often visited. Photograph courtesy of Harold Lamb.

While Susie loved parties and crowds, Grace seemed happiest outdoors alone or with a few good friends. Photograph courtesy of Harold Lamb.

in bed, but Susie claimed she did not learn about her illness until it was nearly over. While there was initially little love lost between Wallace and Susie, each developed a real dislike for the other as time went on. He did not feel comfortable calling her to report on Grace's illness until it was really serious. When she finally did hear that Grace was ill, Susie pushed past his family to see Grace and spend time with her.

During these years Susie and the Colonel spent many months each year traveling or living in Pasadena because his arthritis was very painful and debilitating. From 1904 to 1919 they spent less than six months a year in Utah, always avoiding the cold weather. When she was in town later and Grace had recovered, Susie seldom asked her to help entertain company at Oakwood or the Gardo. Instead she invited Adele Blood to visit and entertain friends by reading their palms. Susie may have felt that Grace was not interested or was too shy to be a good hostess because she had resented her mother's efforts to help her socially when she was younger. But from Grace's perspective this was just one more example of Susie's rejection since her marriage to Wallace. Most of the time Susie seemed to ignore her or treated her more like a guest than a member of the family. As a result Grace began to worry about her real mother and wondered if she were alive. Possibly she even made an effort to find her mother through the orphanage in Boston.[3]

It is hard to know what was going on in Susie's mind at this time. She may not have understood why she felt warmer toward Grace on some occasions than at others. Wallace later reported that at one point in 1910 he visited Susie to beg her to be kinder to Grace. He explained that she was extremely depressed and needed her mother's love and reassurance. He later claimed that Susie promised to make up with Grace but never did. Instead she continued her travels with the Colonel and her socialite friends. From Susie's point of view, Wallace was an open wound to be avoided as much as possible. His presence was intolerable, in part because she heard so often of his negative, caustic comments about her. It was as though he were taunting her, and she could not abide it. John's and Rachel's coolness also upset her, and she resented their judgmental behavior. Possibly Susie very humanly allowed her resentment of these individuals to keep her from rebuilding her relationship with her daughter.

As the years passed, Grace seemed to age quickly and grow steadily weaker. She loved to socialize with her friends and frequently played bridge with them, but she and Wallace seldom traveled far from Salt Lake City. It was hard to leave the apartment complexes for someone else to manage for even a few days. Wallace handled most of the renter complaints, arranged for needed repairs, and collected the rents. However, they did travel together occasionally, and in 1916 they visited a friend in Nevada who advised them to make a will to simplify the settlement of their estate. Grace eagerly acted on his suggestion. When they returned to Salt Lake City, she promptly found an attorney to draw up a will.

In her will Grace made provisions for Susie and Albion's three sisters, but she left the bulk of her property to Wallace. Wallace also drew up a will that left everything currently held in both

This picture of the Bransford family was taken in Los Angeles, California, shortly before Grace's death in 1917. Grace is seated at the far left wearing a fashionable hat with a feather; Wallace is next to her. The young girls are Stella's daughters, Stella and Rachel Evans. Wallace's sister, Stella (in the white blouse), stands next to her husband, Levis Evans. John and Rachel Bransford are standing at the far right. Photograph courtesy of Stella Evans Inge.

their names, such as their bank account, to Grace. Neither dreamed that her will would soon be needed. In May 1917 Grace's health became so bad that doctors recommended she travel to California to recover her strength. The experience must have been an ominous one for Grace, who remembered that over twenty years earlier her father was also advised to take a similar trip for his health. Like her father, Grace did the best she could to make the last weeks and days with her loved ones pleasant. At their request she agreed to pose in a family portrait and spent many days with her in-laws at John's home in Los Angeles. Rachel had become a mother figure in her life, and Grace was very fond of Wallace's sister, Stella, and of Stella's two young girls.

Even though doctors had warned Wallace that Grace could have a heart attack at any time, when the end came, he was not prepared for it. Wallace and Grace firmly believed she would recover if she did not overexert herself. To their amazement, five days after arriving in Los Angeles, she collapsed at her father-in-law's home. The day had started out normally, and she did not seem unusually tired or weak, but at 3:45 P.M. she suddenly dropped to the floor and died before help could be summoned. Wallace was completely overcome and openly wept. He would be in shock for several days following the funeral. After several minutes of grieving, someone contacted the rest of the family in Salt Lake City.[4]

Susie was in Hot Springs, Virginia, with the Colonel, his three single children, and Adele Blood, the family friend and actress, when her family finally located her with the bad news. When Susie received the telegram that Grace had died in California, she ran to the bedroom of their suite and threw herself onto the bed. She cried uncontrollably for several minutes and would not allow the Colonel or Adele to comfort her. Her anguish was particularly terrible because she felt guilty about her estrangement with

Grace. Now that it was too late, she would give anything for a last opportunity to make things right between them.⁵

As upset as she was about Grace's death, Susie did not go to the funeral. Upon receipt of the telegram, she sent Wallace a cable to tell him the Colonel was recuperating from an illness and she could not leave him. This statement could have been an excuse to avoid confronting Wallace or it could have been entirely true. Tourists generally visited the springs to soak their sore arthritic joints and muscles in the warm mineral water, believing it to be therapeutic. Many well-known Americans, including a few former presidents and their spouses, used them to treat a number of illnesses, including arthritis, rheumatism, and even polio. The Colonel had suffered from arthritis for several years, making Susie's excuse very reasonable. But she may simply have chosen not to attend because she did not feel comfortable around Wallace or his family. The chasm between them was so wide that nothing, not even death, could bridge it. Possibly she feared they would criticize her for neglecting Grace or for not taking the initiative to solve their problems.

In either case, when Wallace received the telegram, he was furious that Susie was not planning to attend the funeral. She did not even send flowers. In her own defense she later said she felt it was in poor taste for a mother to send flowers to her own child's funeral. In reality, she may have reasoned that the flowers would mean nothing to Grace; they would only benefit Wallace—and she'd be damned if she'd benefit Wallace. In retribution, Wallace purchased a plot in Mt. Olivet Cemetery across the street from the Emery and Bransford area where Albion, Milford, and Sarah were all buried. He wanted to be sure Grace would not be buried near her mother when Susie later died. When Susie heard that he had refused to use the plot she had reserved for Grace, she was very angry. As far as she was concerned, he had just added salt to an earlier wound.⁶

A few days after the funeral, Grace's attorney read her will to the members of the Bransford family who were in town. As expected, Wallace received the lion's share of her estate and Susie and Albion's three sisters received a token amount. The will set forty thousand dollars aside for the four women to divide among themselves. Despite the tension between her and Grace, Susie was still upset when she discovered Grace had given away most of the property that had formerly been hers. After all she had gone through when her father and Albion died, had experienced during the Chambers trial, had done to help Albion earn the money in the first place, she felt entitled to the entire estate. She had always resented the probate court's decision to arbitrarily divide it between her and her daughter.

Susie also had her husband to consider. Colonel Holmes was nearly seventy-four years old and needed a warmer climate year-round, so they decided to sell the Gardo House and permanently live in southern California. They dickered with several possible offers before they finally decided that, instead of selling the house, they should allow the Red Cross to use it as headquarters during World War I. When the United States entered the war against Germany, the Red Cross became more active in campaigning to raise funds for war relief, working to make bandages and socks for the U.S. troops, and recruiting medical staff to aid the wounded. The organization really did need a large building. To celebrate her gift to the Red Cross, Susie did what she did best: she threw a party. The state acknowledged the

Before she turned the Gardo House over to the Red Cross in 1917, Susie held a party. Over two hundred guests attended and a former governor spoke. The building in the background is the Alta Club. Used by permission, Utah State Historical Society, all rights reserved.

Holmeses for their generosity in a number of speeches that day and made arrangements to help the Red Cross move into its new quarters. But all the praise and good press Susie received was drowned out by criticism a few months later when she announced a lawsuit.[7]

There had been strains in Susie's relationships with John and Wallace for the last ten years, but after Grace's will was read, any bonds that remained were completely unraveled. Susie brooded for several weeks before she had her attorneys serve Wallace notice that she was suing him to claim half of Grace's money. As soon as Wallace received the paperwork for the lawsuit, he contacted an attorney and the story hit Utah's newspapers. The first report of the lawsuit appeared in a Utah newspaper in January 1918, but it would be eight months before the trial actually got under way in mid-September.[8]

During those eight months Susie, in a display of incredibly bad timing, publicly announced that she had decided to make Adele Blood her heir. Adele and Susie had become very close friends over the years, and Adele openly welcomed the security the arrangement provided her. By this time she had endured the bitter, messy divorce from Cader Davis and was beginning to tire of life on the stage. To reassure Adele, Susie gave her costly gifts and money. The two were much alike, and it pleased Susie to share the spotlight with a well-known celebrity who shared her interests.

When Susie started to refer to Adele as the "Silver Princess" and openly talked of suing Wallace to reclaim half of Grace's estate, the newspapers had a heyday. Newspapers across the country talked of how Adele had become the heir to the Silver Queen's millions because Susie needed someone now that Grace was dead. Family and friends were shocked by her behavior and many thought her hardhearted to name a new heir so soon after Grace's death. Unfortunately, the critics did not see the whole issue; they only heard or saw what Wallace and his family felt about the situation. Susie was in California, and Wallace, his family, and probably his attorneys fed stories to the newspapers. Susie's name was sullied; she was called cruel, selfish, unfeeling. In reality it is hard to understand her behavior unless we assume that she was vengefully reacting to Grace and especially to Wallace. She wanted to hurt the man who had injured her and spoiled her plans for Grace. Once again her behavior was typical of many of the nouveaux riches, the old guard, and Europe's royalty. The Vanderbilt clan, for example, was almost as well known for its competitions and jealousies as it was for its extravagant homes. The Commodore openly feuded with at least one of his children during his lifetime. Today, gossip magazines and even respectable news organizations regularly air the disagreements in the Kennedy families and House of Windsor.[9]

Susie hired several attorneys to represent her and to plan the challenge to Grace's will; included were her former attorney in the Chambers trial, Judge W. H. Dickson, and Judge John A. Marshall. For Wallace's part, he hired Athol R. and Joseph L. Rawlins of the firm of Rawlins, Ray, and Rawlins. Both sides tried to find the best legal talent in Utah to battle this potentially vicious case; Susie used former judges, and one of Wallace's attorneys was a former state senator. Susie alleged that Grace could not have been in her right mind or free of undue influence to overlook her in the will. Wallace had weakened the bond between mother and daughter, but he could not totally sever it. Through her attorneys she charged Wallace with maliciously manipulating a slow-minded, poorly educated, and sickly woman to get her wealth. Wallace countered with witnesses who could swear that Grace was a capable, happy woman with above-average intelligence. Grace cut Susie out of her will because she believed her mother had been cruel to her.

The trial opened in the Salt Lake County Court House, now the City and County Building, but within weeks a nationwide epidemic of Spanish influenza hit Salt Lake City, complicating the whole affair. As people began to sicken by the hundreds across the country and then across the state, public gatherings of all kinds were banned if at all possible—the risk of exposure was too great. In the midst of the chaos, Susie's business partner and friend, former Senator Thomas Kearns, died, and his public funeral had to be cancelled because of the epidemic. He was laid to rest with a small family service instead of the public mass the family had planned. In view of the crisis, Judge Harold Stephens, on advice of the Board of Health, barred spectators from attending the trial, hoping to minimize the number of people who would get the disease and also to keep the witnesses and attorneys healthy. Despite their efforts, the disease slowed the pace of the trial as several witnesses, one of the attorneys, and Mr. Rawlins's young daughter became very ill with pneumonia-like symptoms. As a result the trial dragged out nearly five months, into January 1919. If the influenza had not come along to slow things down, the matter of Grace's will might have been resolved before Thanksgiving of 1918. Instead, tempers flared as the disease frustrated the judge, attorneys, and witnesses. Many were afraid they would be exposed and become ill if the trial were not concluded quickly.[10]

Despite the public ban on attending the trial, news reporters were there every day to keep the public informed of the proceedings. Susie's lawyers called her to the witness stand first. Following her account of Grace's adoption, troubled youth, subsequent marriage to Wallace, and their period of estrangement, Wallace was called to tell his side of the story. After each side examined and cross-examined Susie and Wallace, Susie's attorneys presented a string of individuals to support her claim that Grace was feebleminded and under Wallace's control. The principal of Rowland Hall, former neighbors, Susie's maid, her florist, and friends were paraded before the court. The witness who had the greatest potential to help her, however, was Adele Blood. With the attorney carefully guiding her, Adele recounted the day in Virginia when Susie received the cable

The *Emery-Holmes v. Bransford* trial was held in the Salt Lake County Court House, today the City and County Building. Used by permission, Utah State Historical Society, all rights reserved.

that Grace had died. She emphasized how devastated and inconsolable Susie had been. Adele said Susie had been very upset to have to choose between leaving her husband who needed her and traveling to her daughter's funeral. Moving from Susie to Grace, Adele claimed that Grace told her she was unhappy under Wallace's control and wanted a reconciliation with Susie at any cost. She repeated a damaging conversation with Grace at the Bransford Apartments that painted Wallace as miserly and unkind. Assuming the story is true, Grace was obviously upset on the day Adele talked to her, since the couple was usually very happy. Adele was a good witness, and her testimony deeply eroded Wallace's character. To correct the damage, the defense attorneys showed that on the date she said she had visited Grace at the Bransford Apartments, Grace was not in residence there. They further discredited all of her testimony simply by pointing out that as a divorced woman and actress, she could not be trusted to tell the truth. Worse, because Susie had just named Adele as her heir, the young woman was branded a cheap opportunist, a charge that many people accepted.[11]

Shortly after being excused from the witness stand, Adele announced she wanted to leave Utah, fearing the influenza epidemic. Before the trial publicity reports claimed that she would be living in the Gardo House with Susie and the Colonel. Her aunt and uncle, Rachel and John, disowned her because she helped Susie in the trial, and they would not have anything to do with her. When Adele saw how vicious the trial was and how unkind the people in her family had become to one another, she left Utah for California. The newspapers reported she was under contract to a film producer to make a movie and Susie would underwrite the venture.

Adele did make two or three movies, but none were widely released. As "America's most beautiful blond" she succeeded on the stage, but on film she fizzled and faded. Shortly after this she married a theater agent, Waddell Hope. She toured with his troupe of entertainers to the Orient, where she performed brilliantly. Soon after the tour ended, however, Hope died, leaving her with their baby daughter, Dawn, to raise on her own. Adele was still more fortunate than her mother had been in her place years earlier, when

After Grace died, Susie needed a new heir to her fortune. Just as her suit against Wallace was entering the courts, she named Adele Blood, who would also appear as a witness against Wallace. Here Adele and Susie are seen at a garden party at Oakwood. Photograph from the Shipler collection of glass plates, used by permission, Utah State Historical Society, all rights reserved.

she, too, was widowed with a small daughter, since she had some money to live comfortably on. When she was only thirty-five years old, Adele announced she was retiring from the stage, claiming that all actresses should retire before age took too heavy a toll. Saying she was going to devote herself completely to motherhood, she moved to a suite of rooms at the Plaza Hotel and quietly lived there with her daughter for many years.[12]

While Adele may have been viewed as an imported witness, Wallace's attorneys brought a line of prominent local business people and social leaders to the witness stand to testify that each knew Grace was competent and reasonably healthy most of the time. Wallace's and Susie's

A year after Grace died, Wallace married Edna Leonard. They had one son, Wallace Jr. Photograph courtesy of Anne Bransford Newhall.

own testimonies were used to explain that mother and daughter had become estranged and had not resolved their differences before Grace died. Ironically, one of Wallace's chief witnesses was a neighbor in the Bransford Apartments, Justice Joseph E. Frick, of the State Supreme Court, who had witnessed Grace's will. He testified that as far as he could tell Grace was entirely competent and knew what she was doing when she signed the will. After both sides made an impassioned and emotional plea in their closing statements, Judge Harold M. Stephens announced that he wanted to take Christmas and New Year's weekends to think over the issues presented. Once again, Susie spent Christmas waiting for a judge to make a decision.

On January 25, 1919, he called both sides back to court and announced his decision. Neither Susie nor Wallace was present; both were in California. They could both have simply been out of town, but each may have wished to avoid press and friends if the verdict went in favor of the other. The courtroom was full, however, of press representatives and members of Salt Lake society, especially those who had testified in favor of Wallace. The judge not only ruled against Susie, he castigated her in a thirty-one thousand word ruling that took more than two hours to read. The judge was impressed by Wallace's devotion to Grace and believed that Wallace was telling the truth when he said Grace was happy with him. Judge Stephens noted the natural consequence of children growing up away from their parents taking on adult relationships, but also indicated that Susie had done nothing to keep the affections of her daughter. A small part of the ruling explains:

> The court draws the inference from the whole of the record of the lives of the plaintiff and her daughter that while in the early part of the plaintiff's life, before she became wealthy, she perhaps bestowed upon her daughter that singleminded attention and those single personal services which, seemingly insignificant in themselves, are the roots of tender regard. Nevertheless, when great affluence came, the attention of the mother became somewhat divided, somewhat casual. . . . [I]t was travel that kept her [Susie] away, not a scheme or shielding, tepid or casual interest, and infrequency of contact on the part of the mother will normally cause sorrow and wonder to a child, as it plainly did to the deceased. . . . [Susie's] are the actions and words of casual regard, not the marks of that crushing grief which death brings to deep affection. It is with reluctance that the court discusses this phase of the case, it being no pleasant part of a court's duty to set out an analysis of human character.[13]

Judge Stephens said that Grace's will showed her desire "to honor her husband and shower her affections on the man who had given her the first real love she had ever known." At one point Wallace had broken down on the witness stand and sobbed when a lawyer questioned him about his feelings for Grace and her relationship with Susie. The judge discounted Susie at that point because she did not appear visibly moved by her nephew's grief. Her bitterness toward Wallace was evident and made her appear to be only a selfish, self-absorbed woman. Just the idea that a wealthy woman rumored to be worth millions would put her own kinsman through this ordeal to recoup a mere four hundred thousand dollars disgusted the judge.

What he did not know was that Susie was no longer worth millions and probably needed the money for future security. The value of her silver stocks, like many other stocks in America at that point, had dropped dramatically. But Susie's public relations blitz to paint herself as one of America's wealthiest women was too effective for the judge to believe otherwise. In a way Susie had become her own worst enemy.[14]

One of the most significant elements of the ruling, however, had to do less with money than it did with the legal relationship between a husband and a wife. Susie's attorneys tried to shift the burden of proof for Grace's bequest from Susie to Wallace by citing an old English common law. The law held that when the "weaker party" in a relationship granted a gift or bequest to the other member, it was the obligation of the beneficiary to prove that he had not coerced the giver. Judge Stephens "swept away the contention by ruling that the woman was not considered the weaker party in marital relationships in this state. Husband and wife were considered as of equal mental capacities. . . . It was the first decision of this nature made in a Utah court."[15]

Following the conclusion of the trial, a visibly shaken Susie asked her lawyers to appeal the judge's decision to a higher court. Later, on her attorney's counsel, she dropped the issue completely. She had come to realize that public sentiment would be irreversibly turned against her if she pressured Wallace again. While she outwardly feigned indifference, the public outcry against her wounded and embarrassed her more than she was willing to admit. Susie not only lost the battle, she lost the war. The trial bitterly divided the family that had meant so much to her. John and his children would have nothing to do with her again. Nellie tried to stay neutral and support both of her siblings, but it was a difficult juggling act. John and Susie would go to their graves without a reconciliation.[16]

Susie enjoyed parties and socializing, but she also enjoyed the time she spent with her family. Such opportunities were more limited after her court battle with her son-in-law and nephew, Wallace. Photograph courtesy of Harold Lamb.

## 10

## Three, Two, One . . .

In addition to the break with her family and the unpleasant publicity accompanying the verdict, Susie was now saddled with all the court costs, attorney fees, and other expenses of the trial; it totalled many thousands of dollars. This financial burden may have been greater than many people realized. Part of her motivation for the suit had been vengeance against Wallace, but perhaps she also really needed the money. Income tax had been instituted in 1913 and cut into the incomes of all Americans. Only the rich who learned to invest or shelter their money survived the depression with their fortunes intact. Most of the nouveaux riches did not. The Gilded Age was dying, but few recognized it.

As soon as they could, Susie and the Colonel left Salt Lake City for California. During the following months the Colonel and Susie disposed of nearly all of their Utah assets. She gave Oakwood to Harold. It was the perfect place for him to raise his young family with its stream, tall trees, and clean, cool country air. Harold and Grizzelle were delighted with the large gift and promptly sold their home on Michigan Avenue. The large, two-story house Susie had given to Sarah had already gone to Nellie when their mother died.[1]

The Colonel, too, began selling off his property. With the money he made from disposing of some of his assets, he purchased Shelbourne Farm in Batavia, a suburb of Chicago, for his two younger daughters. Realizing at this point that neither was likely to marry, he wanted to be assured of their security after he was gone. As he expected, the girls were pleased. The seven-acre farm was close to the University of Chicago so Harriet, the scientist, could commute to work. Olive, the quiet, shy one, would live with her older sister and keep house. She became known in the neighborhood as "the cat lady" because of her love and gentle care for the animals.[2]

The Gardo House sat empty through most of the next year as Susie debated what to do, but by 1921 the Holmeses knew they were ready to leave Utah forever. Susie's business agent contacted the LDS Church and offered to sell the mansion back to them. The Church jumped at the opportunity to purchase the home and paid full market value, one hundred thousand dollars. Susie removed the things she wanted, made a hefty donation to the Red Cross, and left the mansion behind her. We will never know if she realized the LDS Church would soon demolish the building and sell the property to the federal government for a bank. No doubt it would not have affected her decision if she had, for she felt she now needed a permanent change.[3]

The change was not complete, however, since some of their servants went with them. J. B. Feldman, one of John's employees, had testified for Susie during the trial, and John immediately fired him. Feldman went with the Holmeses to California and became their gardener. He lived in the estate's gatehouse, where he married, raised his family, and eventually died. In a few years Lory Snow would leave the Air Force and move to

Cornelia Snow, pictured here at about twenty years of age, became Susie's close friend and confidante at El Roble in the 1920s and 1930s. Photograph courtesy of Lelia Armstrong.

At age sixty, Susie still looks remarkably youthful. Her secret, according to Lory Snow's daughter, was plastic surgery and a good photographer. According to her daughter, Lory's wife, Cornelia, accompanied Susie to the plastic surgeon for treatments to her hands and face. Harold Lamb, however, thinks this is bunk. Used by permission, Utah State Historical Society, all rights reserved.

Pasadena to be Susie's business manager at El Roble. His wife, Cornelia (Corney), became Susie's closest female friend and confidante despite the difference in their ages. Out of love and appreciation for their companionship, Susie built a two-story home at the base of the estate and gave it to them. A walkway and stairs were added between the two homes so they could easily visit each other, and Susie encouraged the Snow children to visit her often.

Only Corney knew the secret to Susie's apparent eternal youthfulness: she accompanied Susie to the plastic surgeon who injected chicken fat into the backs of her hands to give them a youthful appearance and smoothed the wrinkles out of her face. Corney also sat with Susie when she went outside for a cigarette. Susie was careful to conceal her drinking from the family, but she did not mind being seen with her long, elegant cigarette holder. As she aged, she used the holder as a prop to get attention in the same way many Hollywood personalities did. The rest of her help seemed to be equally loyal. Like the Feldmans and the Snows, the cook and second girl remained with her the entire time she lived at El Roble.[4]

The only things the Holmeses did not sell or give away were their mining properties. The Park City mines were still producing, but at much below their earlier, extremely profitable levels. Most of their art collection and furnishings, except the pieces that were too large, also went to California. Holmes had collected much of the art as an investment when he had plenty of money. Now that much of his mining stock was close to worthless and many of his other investments were either gone or greatly diminished, the art comforted him. Like his daughter, Harriett, who cataloged Batavia's local plants in her spare time, he also immersed himself in wildlife and botanical studies of the birds and flowers around his home. In 1915 Susie surprised him by assembling his notes and some photos in a booklet and having them bound for his seventy-second birthday. This small gesture of devotion delighted him, and he kept the little booklet until his death ten years later.[5]

While Susie and the Colonel were consolidating from three residences to one, Susie was determined to make the best of the situation. It was no major adjustment to make El Roble their sole residence because they had lived in Pasadena during the winter months for fifteen years and they had many good friends there. Susie entertained them all in lavish style and enjoyed outings to the country clubs, mountains, and beaches. Their greatest problem seemed to be the Colonel's arthritis, which continued to severely cripple him, making walking and sitting for prolonged periods uncomfortable. His frail health sometimes made him edgy and depressed as he anxiously watched Susie spend their remaining funds.

But it was hard to live in Pasadena and not keep up appearances. By 1920 Pasadena was the

Colonel Holmes delighted in tracking the birds and flowers found on their estate. Susie compiled his work into a book as a gift for him. Courtesy of Pasadena, California, Public Library.

### Foreword

Written by Edwin Francis Holmes one day in June and arranged in this little book by "Madame," as a surprise for his seventy-second birthday, nineteen hundred and fifteen.

Products catering to America's sweet tooth provided the fortune to build the Wrigley mansion, one of the finest in Pasadena. The building is now the headquarters for the Tournament of Roses. Photograph courtesy of the Pasadena Tournament of Roses Association.

wealthiest city per capita in the United States. It had experienced phenomenal growth during the first two decades of the twentieth century so that it little resembled the agricultural area it had once been. Almost overnight, Orange Grove Avenue became "Millionaire's Row," lined with the homes of multimillionaires such as Busch, Wrigley, Morehouse, Durand, Harkness, McNally, Barnum, Guyer, and Blossom. One historian claimed that by 1915 the city also had more cars per capita than any city in the world and was populated by the "crème of culture, education and refinement of the eastern cities . . . in its midst." Ironically, it was also nicknamed the city of churches because of the many magnificent churches within its boundaries.[6]

The city's residents were some of the country's most affluent citizens and insisted on bringing the finer things from the East with them. Large, upscale homes, stores, banks, libraries, museums, fine gardens, and orchestras seemed to spring up spontaneously to cater to the wealthy who wintered in sunny southern California. The community soon hosted luxury hotels to service those who chose not to buy a residence in the area. One, the Green, had a bridge that spanned the street and was considered to be very elegant. In 1911 Adolph Busch summarized much about the city:

> I selected Pasadena as the winter home of my family because I consider it a veritable paradise, it has no equal in the world, regarding healthful climate, scenery, vegetation, flowers, shrubberies, fruit and general comfort of living. . . . Pasadena is undoubtedly destined to become . . . a most popular American winter residence.[7]

Susie fit in well here. She had a number of good friends and numerous acquaintances whom she invited to her lavish parties. By 1925 she had twice been the cover girl for *California Life* magazine, which reported the following on its first page:

The Maryland Hotel published *California Life*; neither the Hotel nor its magazine exist any longer, but both were important elements of California society in the 1920s. Susie appeared twice on its cover; the first time was this cover in October 1922. Photograph courtesy of Pasadena, California, Public Library.

> We have pictured on the cover of this issue Mrs. Edwin Francis Holmes of Pasadena, popularly known as the "Silver Queen," because of her silver mine holdings in Utah, and also because of her queenly presence in society. . . . Mrs. Holmes is wearing an evening gown and wrap of sumptuous beauty which came from . . . I. Magnin. . . . An individual note . . . is the white wig in bobbed design which she wears over her own abundant tresses, and which lends a Parisian flair to her appearance. Apropos of this allusion to grand dames of France . . . one is reminded that Mrs. Holmes' Grand Avenue residence in Pasadena . . . which is furnished in the period of Grand Monarch, has lately seen the inception of a salon.
>
> Every Sunday in the season Mrs. Holmes entertains at dinner, her guests being notables from near and far—artists, writers, musicians; never too many at one time, but little intimate groups who discuss world affairs and the "Seven Lively Arts." Recently a diplomat from a far country told of the complications of a new regime, while a former prince of an imperial family from a neighboring country met him on amicable grounds. And so it goes.[8]

On March 16, 1916, the *Pasadena Star* had this to say about Colonel Holmes:

> El Roble, his Pasadena winter home on Grand Avenue is one of the show places of the city and betokens good judgment, for its setting is of the finest. . . . Not many men have the natural ability to accomplish even in a very long lifetime what Mr. Holmes has done. He is practically a self-educated man. . . . He is a member of the Loyal Legion and of the G. A. R. and fraternally is a thirty-second degree Mason. In club life he has taken a keen interest and belongs to leading club organizations from the Union League of Chicago to the Annadale Country Club in Pasadena.

Susie's second appearance on the cover of *California Life* emphasized her importance in the world of fashion. Photograph courtesy of Pasadena, California, Public Library.

But Pasadena was more than just a bastion for the wealthy. It attracted scientists and became an art colony for several prominent landscape artists during the 1920s. George Ellery Hale had established Mt. Wilson Observatory, financed by the Carnegie Foundation, on one of the mountain peaks overlooking the city. California Institute of Technology hosted Albert Einstein in 1931–1933. Literary figures such as Upton Sinclair, Robinson Jeffers, and George Wharton James lived in the community.[9]

The Holmeses' decision to buy the house in 1905 was apparently wise. Gertrude Daniels, a wealthy Chicago woman, had built the three-story, twelve-room, shake shingle residence in 1902. 141 North Grand Avenue has a magnificent view of the arroyo below, and Gertrude intended the house to be a winter residence for her parents and family. The Holmeses had been content with the original home during their winter stays, but now that they had just one residence, they wanted to convert it into a splendid showcase for displaying their art and for entertaining.

To refurbish their home, Susie and the Colonel used most of the bric-a-brac they had purchased in their travels. They had spent many months in England over the years and admired the English Tudor homes. So in 1922 Susie decided to remodel the home, its four-car garage, and gatehouse into an English Tudor mansion. She hired the Postle Company, the builders of the Pasadena Playhouse, to draw up the plans for the project, and she spent thirty-seven thousand dollars to alter the estate. Each of the three buildings was given a stucco and brick veneer facade with dark wood accents. Originally, the front of the house overlooked the arroyo, but now the architects restyled the house so the back became an impressive front entrance with a circular drive.

Inside, dark oak paneling and an aeolian organ were installed in the main entry, and lead glass was mounted in some of the windows. The Bransford family crest was displayed in the glass panel in the front door, and a high iron fence was added around the perimeter of the property for greater privacy. All of the flower beds on the spacious ground were enlarged as well, since the couple enjoyed raising their own flowers and had several dozen in their home each day.

Still, the highlight of the property was the large oak tree that gave the estate its name, El Roble. When Susie finished the house, it little resembled the home she had purchased in 1905; instead, it was one of the most impressive residences in Pasadena. If Susie hoped to keep up with the city's elite residents, she now had an impressive home where she could entertain in grand style.[10]

Susie and the Colonel took advantage of El Roble's renovation in 1922 to travel east. Neither of them wanted to stay in the house while the workmen remodeled it; the construction noise and dust were unbearable. They booked a stateroom on the Santa Fe Railroad and headed toward Chicago and New York City. Along the way they stopped in several major cities in Arizona, New Mexico, and Texas before arriving in Batavia to see the Holmes girls. After traveling around the country for several months, the Colonel announced he was tired, needed to rest, and would follow later. In the meantime, he told Susie to go on ahead to see how the house was progressing. Weeks later when Susie arrived in California, a cable from the Colonel was waiting: he had decided to stay with his daughters for a while. The visit had lifted his depression, so he planned to stay longer. No one knows how Susie handled this turn of events. Perhaps she agreed it was better he stay with his daughters as his health was poor, but she probably felt lonely since they had been married for twenty-four years.

Susie now had the freedom to travel with her older socialite friends. Many older women traveled nearly constantly; it became a way of life. Susie was in Europe two years later when Harriet cabled her that the Colonel had died. Susie sent word that she would return as quickly as possible. She booked passage on the next ship headed for the United States; in the meantime Edwin Holmes was buried near his first wife, Jenny Carleton. Months later an attorney negotiated a settlement between the Holmes children and Susie. Originally the Colonel had left his children everything and Susie nothing, but after the Bransford lawsuit, he had deeded her some stocks and had not changed his will to reflect that gift. This adjustment was needed because he had given away the bulk of his estate and was almost penniless in the end. With no money coming in, they only had her investments to live on, and the value of those investments was dropping rapidly.[11]

Susie in one of her stylish outfits. Used by permission, Utah State Historical Society, all rights reserved.

Gertrude Daniels, a wealthy Chicago woman, built this three-story, twelve-room, shake-shingle residence in 1902. The Holmeses bought it in 1905 and stayed there during the winters until 1920, when it became their single permanent residence. Photograph courtesy of Pasadena, California, Public Library.

Originally, the house faced across the arroyo. Susie reversed the entrances and the former front became the back. Below is another post card view of El Roble. Post cards courtesy of Kirk Myers and Pasadena, California, Public Library.

In 1922 Susie's $37,000 remodeling project turned the house into a Tudor mansion. The house is currently for sale and valued at just over $2 million. The back of the house became this impressive front entrance with a circular drive. The giant oak tree (in Spanish, *el roble*), which gave the house its name, used to grow in the flower bed at the right. Photograph by Judy Dykman, courtesy of the current owners, Mr. and Mrs. Marshall Morgan.

A fence and high iron gate were added for privacy. This view of the entrance from the street has become familiar to many Americans because El Roble has appeared frequently as a setting for advertisements, television series, and motion pictures, most recently in *Franklin and Eleanor* and *The Christmas Box*. Photograph courtesy of Mr. and Mrs. Marshall Morgan.

Susie's remodeling included this spacious patio and fountain at the back of the house to take advantage of the view. Photograph courtesy of Harold Lamb.

The four-car garage included its own gas pump and grease pit, where the mechanic could repair the family's cars. Photograph courtesy of Mr. and Mrs. Marshall Morgan.

The interior of the main entry featured dark oak paneling and an Aeolian organ. The organist sat in the basement, but the music reached the upper house through speakers in the staircase. The Bransford family crest was proudly displayed in the glass panel in the front door. Photograph courtesy of Mr. and Mrs. Marshall Morgan.

A stairway with carved banister and rails ascended from the main entry to the second floor, going past beautiful leaded glass on the landing. Photograph courtesy of Mr. and Mrs. Marshall Morgan.

J. B. and Letitia Feldman lived in this gatehouse. Like the other two buildings on the estate, this was given a stucco and brick veneer facade that had dark wood accents. Photograph courtesy of Mr. and Mrs. Marshall Morgan.

Susie built this castle-like gatehouse at El Roble for Lory and Corny Snow and their children. Photograph courtesy of Lelia Armstrong.

Susie moved to New York and lived in the Plaza Hotel, the finest, and certainly the most fashionable, in the city. Adele Blood and her daughter, Dawn, also lived there; by now, Susie regarded them as her heirs. Photograph courtesy of The Plaza Hotel.

## 11

## Hard Times

The Colonel and Susie shared twenty-four good years together before his death in 1925. He had lovingly referred to her as "Madame," and she adored him and catered to his needs. If she had married another man like him, the end of her life may have been very different. After his death it appears that Pasadena held too many memories she preferred not to remember alone. Instead of moving back into El Roble, Susie closed the house and kept traveling with her numerous society friends. When she did eventually settle down, she moved to the Plaza Hotel in New York City to be near Adele and her daughter, Dawn, the new heirs to her fortune. Susie enjoyed Adele's outgoing personality and encouraged her to attend social events with her. Susie also liked having a child around to dote on. Dawn was a pretty, petite blond with a sweet disposition and a desire to please adults.

Susie did, however, face one of the chief problems of single women in the 1920s: any woman, married, widowed, or single, needed a male escort to attend most social activities. Naturally, a group of male escorts developed to take care of the needs of society's single women. In some cases the men may have been the equivalent of call girls hired to meet a multitude of needs. In other cases, the relationship was platonic; the men were just escorts or "walkers." Most of these men were in their twenties or thirties, but some were much older. Some specifically sought out wealthy women, each hoping to convince one to marry him so he could have financial security. When the woman ran out of money, the man moved on to another wealthy woman. Men with an agenda like this are commonly referred to as gigolos.[1]

One such man, Prince Nicholas "Nicki" Engalitcheff, was known as the "melancholy Slav" in New York society. The illegitimate son of a prominent Russian statesman and soldier, Nicki had once been attached to the Russian Consulate in Chicago and sold insurance part time. Sometime in 1927 he spotted Susie and decided to woo her for her reported millions. Nicki had been married twice before. His first marriage in 1898 was to a Chicago heiress, Evelyn Partridge. After nearly twenty years, their marriage ended in a messy and well-publicized divorce stemming from Nicki's numerous affairs and his open assignation with one mistress, Jane Hathaway. Nicki tried to force Evelyn to settle the matter in a Russian court, where he felt he would get a more favorable judgment. Publicity about the trial embarrassed their teenage son, Vladimir, and it may have contributed to his sudden death several years later. Vladamir died on March 7, 1923, at twenty-one, a college graduate with a good job at the time. His obituary suggests a suicide because he had been planning to travel with his mother and had appeared healthy when he suddenly died.[2]

After his first marriage ended, Nicki, like many expatriate Russian princes, was again impoverished and desperate. The only income these men had ever known was swallowed up in the Revolution of 1917. With no income and, in many

Susie at a restaurant in the company of a "walker." Because women were required to have male companions at any public function, many young men became "call boys" or hired escorts. Photograph courtesy of Harold Lamb.

cases, no marketable skills, these princes often turned to wealthy American heiresses to support their lifestyle, offering a title in return. Nicki's second wife, Danise de Bertrand, claimed to be wealthy and socially prominent, but when he found out she was a fraud and could not pay their bills, they quarrelled and she disappeared.[3] He never saw Danise again and assumed she was dead, as he never received any papers for the divorce they had planned. For a time he courted the widow of Oscar Hammerstein, the operatic impresario and grandfather of the lyricist, from whom he received a great deal of money and valuable gifts. Their friendship was interrupted, however, when he met Susie, who was reputedly worth over one hundred million dollars. After being set aside, Mrs. Hammerstein sued Nicki for nine hundred dollars that she had lent him months earlier while they were still presumably friends.

Nicki found that he had competition for Susie's affections from Prince Dadiani of Georgia, another impoverished prince. She was in awe of both men, or, at least, of their titles, and she enjoyed the attention and prominence they offered her. Relatives claim she had long dreamed of marrying a prince and becoming a real princess one day. Despite several warnings from Nellie, Susie enjoyed and encouraged both men. Being pursued by handsome, younger men flattered her.[4]

When Engalitcheff eventually proposed, Susie accepted quickly, unaware that he was still married, and together they planned a grand wedding. Family members insist it was not a love match on either side: he wanted her money and she wanted his title. The title would give her the social legitimacy she had craved for years. The courtship and engagement ran smoothly. They announced the grand event in the New York *Times*, rented a Russian Orthodox church, and even lined up many Russian notables for the ceremony.

Then they went to apply for the marriage license. To their surprise the clerk at New York City's license bureau told them the prince was still legally married and would have to wait at least one more year, until Danise could be declared legally dead. There was no way to get around the mess unless the prince could produce a divorce decree or a death certificate. Since he could manage neither, no license could be issued. Horrified at the embarrassment, Susie called everything off, had an announcement printed in the New York *Times*, and took a trip to Paris to calm her nerves. She wanted to be as far away as she could from the newspapers, which she knew would capitalize on such a story, as indeed they did. One of the great dangers of being a celebrity was the certain savagery of the press if any kind of scandal occurred.[5]

In the months that followed, Susie encountered Dr. Radovan Delitch, a Serbian doctor whom she had previously met in New York society. Delitch was tall, handsome, and very charming. Unlike Engalitcheff, he had a distinguished career in medicine and an income of his own. In addition to his career, he was a decorated veteran of World War I. After he valiantly risked his life to care for six thousand French soldiers, France awarded him the Legion of Honor for his service. In addition to the medals and honors, Rada claimed the French also gave him a small estate in Paris. In his homeland of Serbia he had been the crown prince's personal physician before the war. After the war his homeland gave him the Cross of Danilo. Most of the year he taught at a medical school in Paris, conducted cancer research, and consulted on cancer cases. While visiting in the United States, he spent his time working at the Fifth Avenue Hospital, but he used his spare time to be an international playboy. Rada's attentions caught Susie at a very vulnerable time. She was still wounded from the embarrassment of the debacle with Engalitcheff (and still in need of an escort) when the doctor started calling on her. Apparently it was just a minor flirtation until Susie started to believe his flattery. Then she fell head over heels in love with him. It was a heady experience to have one of New York's most eligible bachelors chasing after her. He was also thirty years younger than she, and that made her feel like a girl, not like a matron of seventy-one. In Rada's defense, it was Susie who proposed marriage, but their May-to-December romance was doomed from the start.[6]

New York society was stunned when they announced their marriage. Susie rationalized that age was insignificant and told everyone she had never known true love before. Nellie, who had known Albion and the Colonel, knew better but was shocked into silence. Susie reasoned that if a man could marry a woman more than ten years his junior, which frequently occurred then as it does now, then a woman should be able to marry a much younger man. After all, she had married Albion, who was at least twelve years older, and the Colonel, who was sixteen years older than she, and in both cases she had been happy. Why couldn't this relationship also work out? Rada also enjoyed the recognition of marrying the famous Silver Queen. People seemed to know her wherever they went. When she suggested he give up medicine so they could travel, he willingly complied. He even invited a six- or seven-year-old nephew to live with them so they could have a semblance of family life. Sadly for both of them, the little boy was afraid to leave British Columbia for France. Susie would have enjoyed raising a second boy, and Rada might have been a good father as well. A common interest might even have saved their relationship.[7]

When it came time to take their vows, Susie joked that she had never been so married! They were first married in a Russian Orthodox church because Rada was an Orthodox. Susie claimed she did not understand a word until the priest called her Suzanne Delitch. Rada and Susie both enjoyed the humor of the situation. Later they married a second time in France on July 20, 1930. Right after the marriage the Delitches left on an extended honeymoon that dropped them back in Pasadena by New Year's Day. They stood on El Roble's balcony overlooking the arroyo, and Rada told reporters they planned to leave for Paris in a few days.

During the next year and a half Susie and Rada traveled back and forth across the continent from Pasadena to New York and then on to Paris. Rada began to drink heavily and complained of boredom. He refused to shave, stayed in his pajamas all day, and cursed at Susie and the servants in Greek, amazing her with his behavior. He also became extremely possessive and got angry when she talked with other men at parties. As his drinking problem worsened, Susie began to go to parties alone. In retaliation he hired detectives to follow her around and report her activities to him.

Dr. Radovan Delitch, a prominent surgeon in Paris and New York City, became Susie's third husband. Photograph courtesy of Harold Lamb.

When Susie and Rada married in 1930, he gave up medicine to be able to travel with her. The decision proved to be disastrous. Photograph courtesy of Harold Lamb.

When he confronted Susie with charges of flirting, she got very angry and left the room.[8]

Whether there was any basis for his jealousy is questionable, but Rada did recognize one area of real trouble. He checked Susie's accounts and discovered she did not have the money she had claimed to have. Although her assets were losing value, she continued to spend recklessly. He ordered her to cut back her lifestyle immediately and to fire some of the servants. Aware that the largest number of unemployed persons in Pasadena during the Depression were the servants of wealthy families, Susie refused. She knew they would not find other jobs. Rada could not understand her loyalty to the servants and grew more surly. He continued to drink and berate her for being irresponsible with money. What he did not recognize was that Susie had always been irresponsible with money. In the past there had been enough money coming in to conceal her bad habits. Now income taxes and a decline in the stock market pushed her dangerously toward bankruptcy.[9]

Finally accepting some level of reality, Susie hired a business manager, Culver Sherrill. He watched her accounts and was probably the one who fired her maid in an effort to economize. In addition to keeping track of her money, he traveled with her, made her social engagements, helped her pack, and acted as her publicist, since he had formerly been a newspaperman. Some would later claim he was also her lover, but that is highly unlikely since Culver preferred men. A small, effeminate man, he was the perfect companion for an older woman, and no threat to her husband.[10]

On September 10, 1932, Susie and Rada were in Salt Lake City, where Susie gave Susanna Hartman, her favorite niece and namesake, an elaborate wedding. Susie and John had each threatened to boycott the wedding if the other attended, but at Susanna's insistence they both came. Susie started drinking heavily to conceal her nervousness; John also drank more than he normally did. While they were both very drunk, they started speaking to one another. By this time even Susie recognized that her financial situation was becoming desperate, and she told her brother she needed his advice. He offered to look into her accounts and help if he could. The following morning John came to the Hotel Utah where she and Rada had a suite of rooms, but Susie, now sober, would not admit him to the apartment. She was too embarrassed to let him see just how bad her finances really were. John tried a few times to talk to her before giving up and going home. Apparently he had still hoped for a reconciliation.

Susie did take advantage of her time in Salt Lake to take care of some other problems, however. She stopped at a local hospital for a checkup, and she summoned James Ivers, one of her business partners at the Silver King Mine, to talk privately about her stocks. While he was there, Ivers made some interesting observations about the relationship between Susie and Rada. He noted that Susie quizzed him for several minutes about the mine before dismissing him; Rada, however, was very quiet and distant. After Ivers left, Susie and Rada quarrelled about money again, and Susie told him to leave. It startled Rada that Susie could kick him out so easily, and he begged to stay, promising to behave. When he failed to move Susie with his pleas, Rada wrote very similar letters to all members of the family begging them to persuade Susie to drop divorce plans. One letter, written from the Santa Fe's California Limited said

> I feel absolutely desperate but as I told you I love Suzy, leaving everything in Her Hand and Heart
> 
> She knows that I never asked nothing for me and I signed all the papers she asked me to sign. . . .
> 
> If she is tired of me as she seems to be—Here I am, alone, going back to my work—and will stay there—Suzy will find in Paris just the same Rada. . . .
> 
> I Beg you Bill, ask Her not to go through. I did not answer I left my fate in Her Hand and Heart. But do I deserve such a hard punishment? I have nobody in the world, but Suzy and for over two years left everything and everybody to follow her.
> 
> Bill, Help me. . . .
> 
> Desperately and gratefully,
> Rada[11]

Days later Rada was headed for France and Susie returned to California. When Rada reached Europe, he realized he had wasted his resources, lost his medical practice, and had nothing left. Despondent, he boarded a ship headed back to America, planning to throw himself at Susie's feet. A few days later, while the entire ship was

Susie carefully maintained her facade of wealth to impress the East Coast social aristocracy though, in fact, the Depression and falling stock values had decimated her assets, as they had those of many others. Used by permission, Utah State Historical Society, all rights reserved.

celebrating Christmas Eve, Rada's depression deepened. He excused himself from the table where all of the other guests were having a great time and returned to his stateroom to drink alone. Sometime that night he gave up all hope of saving his marriage and wrote a suicide note. He pinned the note to his jacket, tied a rope to one of the portholes, and hung himself. The following morning the ship's purser was suspicious when no one answered his knock and broke down the door. There he found Rada dead and immediately arranged for burial at sea.[12]

Days later Susie was having lunch with her niece, Susanna Hartman, when she received a cable telling her that Rada was dead. She paused for a moment, then folded the cable and put it into her pocket. When Susanna asked what the problem was she told her Rada was dead and asked her to order lunch. Years later many people condemned her for appearing to be so cold, but Susie would never let Susanna, or anyone else, see her upset. One of the obligations of the upper crust was to maintain dignity and appear self-possessed at all times. In behavior as well as money, one had to keep up appearances. Besides, she had her pride; when she married Rada, many people had laughed at her, saying the marriage was doomed because of the difference in their ages. When Susanna left later, Susie fell apart in the privacy of her room. Her new business manager took charge of the situation and paid for Rada's burial expenses. The Gilded Age was over, but its social obligations lingered on.[13]

Susie stayed away from friends and family for several weeks. Within days of Rada's death she hired George Fisher and Sons to auction off her El Roble estate, Rolls Royce, art and statuary, and some of her furnishings. The auction made headlines in California as more than twenty-five thousand people from near and far came to buy the famous Silver Queen's things—at rock bottom prices. January 1933 was the depths of the Depression. After the auction, the house, furnishings, art, clothes, jewels, car, and everything else netted Susie just one hundred thousand dollars. Some appraisers feel she should have made more than a million dollars, but she was in too much of a hurry to sell. When asked why she sold El Roble, she simply said it was full of too many memories, but it was also too expensive to maintain. Susie quietly took the money and moved into a hotel in Pasadena. During the next several years she would move back and forth from the Maryland to the Green Hotel, to the east coast, to Europe, and back to Pasadena. It appears reality was too painful, so she avoided it. She denied that Rada committed suicide and claimed they would have reconciled and mended their relationship. According to Susie, he had become violently ill on shipboard that night; he had not hung himself from a porthole.[14]

Amazingly, instead of conserving money, Susie continued to spend it, pretending that all was well. And she was not alone. The Great Depression had finally killed the Gilded Age, but many people continued to live by its standards, even though some now lacked the resources to do it.[15]

# 12

## Here Comes the Prince, Again

Susie had little time to mend her wounded ego and regain her perspective before Prince Nicholas Engalitcheff came courting a second time. His wife had now been missing long enough to be declared legally dead, so he was free to marry. When he once again asked Susie if she would marry him, she happily agreed. At last she would be a real princess, and New York's stuffy aristocrats would have to accept her. In retrospect, some family members wonder whether Susie actually proposed to him as she had to Rada.[1]

Once again, there would be two ceremonies. The first was held in the New York City Municipal Building and was performed by a justice of the peace. A month later they pledged their vows a second time in the Russian Orthodox church so their marriage would be blessed by God. The civil wedding went smoothly enough, but the somber church service had a moment of slapstick: when the gold marriage crown was placed on the prince's very small head, it fell down over his forehead and slipped over one eye.

And, once again, Susie's engagement and marriage made headlines. The aging Silver Queen was marrying a younger man, but at least this time he was a prince. Nicki was fifty-nine, while Susie was now seventy-four. One newspaper reported that she gave her age as fifty-eight, but noted that "when she was married to Dr. Delitch in Paris in 1930 dispatches said she was 71." Despite that snide observation, Susie still retained a remarkably youthful appearance; her hair was snowy white, but her skin and face looked flawless, thanks to a gifted plastic surgeon. She was still a beauty who would turn heads in any restaurant. This fact was not lost on Susie, and she began making grand entrances to see how people reacted. Frequently she was well rewarded for her efforts as some would stop eating with their forks in the air and stare as she entered a restaurant or a party. She was not unusual in this, however. Society people in general attracted much attention from the public and coverage from the media: they were America's royals. When they gave their spectacular parties, police were required to hold back the crowds that came to watch the arrivals; it was a lot like Oscar night in Hollywood. Mary Cable points to photographs to support her assertion that "top-drawer weddings invariably clogged the streets with spectators."[2]

There is no record of Susie's height, but judging by the clothes she gave to the Daughters of Utah Pioneers, she was over five-feet-eight. Nicki was about six inches shorter, had white hair and a mustache, and smoked cigarettes or cigars constantly. The day they left for their honeymoon cruise to England, Nellie and her husband, Jay Harris, and their daughter, Susanna, came to the boat to say goodbye. Nicki was sitting in a overstuffed chair, wrapped in a sable robe, with a drink in one hand and a long cigarette holder in the other. The cigarette smoke was so dense that both Nellie and Susanna had to leave the room to breathe. The prince nonchalantly invited Jay to join him for a drink. Then they discussed "manly" topics: the Depression, foreign affairs, and politics.

RUSSIAN ROYALTY RE-WED—Ceremonial royal crowns are placed on Prince Nicholas Engalitcheff and the former Mrs. Suzanne Delitch in elaborate re-wedding at Russian Cathedral, No. 105 Houston St. First wedding was Oct. 18.

On October 18, 1933, Susie married Nicholas (Nicki) Engalitcheff, becoming Her Royal Highness and assuring her acceptance by Eastern society. However, by 1933, income tax and the Depression had essentially ended the Gilded Age, leaving many society figures impoverished. Newspaper clipping from unidentified newspaper courtesy of Harold Lamb.

While she listened, Susie was waiting on the prince. She seemed spellbound by him and quickly fetched things he asked for or fluffed up his pillows.[3]

Despite appearances of happiness, the prince soon tired of Susie and reverted to the pattern of his first marriage: he went looking for a younger woman. He did not have to look far. He had complained about having a bad heart, so Susie arranged for a nurse to care for him. The nurse had a good figure and was half Susie's age. Within a few weeks the prince was seducing the nurse whenever Susie left them alone. By the time they arrived in England, Susie had guessed what was happening. The prince was quiet and distant and made no effort to be good company. But beyond leaving those subtle clues, he charged a necklace for the nurse to Susie's shipboard account, providing written proof of his infidelity. Susie was crushed, embarrassed, and angry. The nurse was immediately dismissed, and she moved to Denver to find work.

Sometime later, when Susie asked Nicki what he was thinking about and where he would like to be at that moment, he answered without pausing or turning away from the window: he wanted to be in Denver. Showing amazing control, Susie asked Culver, her business manager, to make travel arrangements for the prince and left. Several weeks later in Denver, the prince was chagrined to find the nurse was not interested in him any longer, since he no longer had access to vast sums of money. She wouldn't take his calls or see him even though he sent her dozens of flowers.[4]

Susie was distressed at the turn of events, but divorce was unthinkable. Like many other women, she was determined that no one would know her secrets or feelings. Years earlier, when the newspapers had announced her divorce from Rada, she lost credibility in society; a second divorce would make her an outcast! When the prince left Denver and returned to New York, Susie moved back to the Green Hotel in Pasadena. When her family or friends asked where he was, she told them he preferred to live in New York so they had separated. Rather than face criticism from society's matrons, she quietly supported him until he died two years later.

Ironically, just before the Prince's death, a news reporter asked him if he were divorcing Susie. He feigned love for her and said they were "great pals" and would never part permanently.

The same reporter contacted Susie, but she would not give him a straight answer. An article on both of them took up an entire page in the *San Francisco Chronicle*. The reporter added photos of Susie in her beautiful clothes and good-naturedly poked fun at both of them. Susie apparently did not let a little negative press upset her. Like many society figures, she seems to have survived barbs from the press by developing a hide as tough as an elephant's. She nonchalantly laughed and passed it off as cheap publicity for the prince. She continued to live in California or travel to Europe to

Prince Nicholas V. Engalitcheff was one of the many members of the Russian nobility dispossessed by the Russian Revolution. Photograph courtesy of Susanna Hartman.

join her wealthy friends at fashionable retreats, but she avoided New York completely.[5]

When the prince eventually died of a stroke in 1935, Susie turned it into a joke, telling one of the fabulous fabrications that has become a part of her public persona. Despite the fact that California, New York, and Utah newspapers reported Nicki had died and was buried in New York City, Susie told some friends and family that he died while they were taking a cruise on the Mediterranean Sea. She explained that because the boat did not have a freezer large enough to hold his body, it was necessary to put him in a packing crate and stop in Naples to store him while she and her friends continued their cruise. After she made the rounds of all of the fashionable places, she planned to pick his body up and take it back to New York for burial. Now on a roll, she added that when Stalin's government got wind of her plans from a news release, she was told to bury the prince immediately and to follow protocol in doing it. Engalitcheff may have been a minor royal, but he was Russian nobility and should be treated with deference. Not wanting to bother with Nicki further, Susie claimed she arranged for a funeral, hired a Russian battleship, and then paid a woman to impersonate her. The woman was to wear her clothes and a veil while marching behind the coffin at the funeral, showing proper grief. Meanwhile, Susie attended a card party with friends on the luxury liner.[6]

Though the story is ridiculous, it illustrates how bitterly Susie hated him. He had publicly embarrassed her, and then, to avoid more scandal, she had been forced to support him—in style. With Susie's allowance, he could afford to live in the Hotel Barclay, have friends over for drinks, and see other women. Some said he even rented a limousine to drive him to his weekly manicures. For the prince, life was good to the very end.[7]

Soon after the prince's death, Suzanne faced a far more tragic situation involving her protégée, heir, and friend, Adele Blood. For months after the trial over Grace's will, she had promoted Adele as a movie star and spent nearly a million dollars financing her in two or three films. When none of these ventures succeeded, an embarrassed and humiliated Adele moved back to New York and

At age seventy-five, Susie still rated a full-page story on the front page of the Sunday magazine section of the *San Francisco Chronicle*. Newspaper clipping courtesy of Stella Inge.

rented a suite in the Plaza Hotel. When Susie was in New York, she, too, lived in the Plaza and the two women maintained a close relationship. Adele generally kept a low profile, although she tried some advertising work to support herself. She spent most of her time doting on her only child; Dawn had become a little beauty. The girl was given violin, dancing, singing, and acting lessons.

In 1936 Adele suddenly decided to come out of retirement and return to the stage as a writer, producer, and star. She moved with Dawn to the neighborhood of the exclusive Westchester Country Club in New York and rented the high school auditorium to perform several plays she had written. She hired well-known actors, paid good money to promote the plays, and personally acted in them. She hoped the plays would launch Dawn as a Broadway star and revitalize her own stage career. She expected the local socialites to support her at the box office because she had been a popular guest in the area during the previous few summers, but no one attended. When she failed, she was both humiliated and financially distressed. It was the first time she had not succeeded on the stage, and she now had many debts to pay. She began drinking heavily. Friends worried that she was becoming very unstable, and some tried to reassure her. She had impoverished herself, yet she was too proud to ask anyone, especially Susie, for money. She may have known that by 1936 Susie was having money problems of her own, but she also made the comment that Susie's help now came with too many strings, expectations, or demands. Susie appeared to be using her money to control Adele as she had once used it to try to control Grace.[8]

One night Adele and Dawn invited Dawn's violin teacher, a well-known musician, to dinner, but Adele had been drinking and soon became nauseated. Dawn took her mother home and helped her to bed before hurriedly driving their guests to the train station. When the young woman returned less than an hour later, she found that her mother had shot herself. The tragedy was even greater for Dawn because she had attempted to hide the gun from Adele, then finally gave it to her mother when she promised not to use it. Dawn called for an ambulance and rushed Adele to the hospital, but three hours later she died from a gunshot wound to the head. Dawn was just seventeen.

Dawn bravely auctioned off all of her family's possessions, including the family dog, to pay her mother's bills. Then, shattered by her mother's death, she collapsed and was bedridden for weeks. Emotionally, she never completely recovered. She had been a child prodigy on the violin and had a promising career in music. At one time her violin teacher had arranged a recital at Carnegie Hall to launch her musical career, but after her mother's suicide Dawn could not play any longer.

Less than a year later she married a handsome young band leader, Herbert James Noel. Whether the marriage was happy or even stable is not clear, but it ended in yet another tragedy. The couple moved to North Hollywood, not far from Susie, and rented a home. One day in 1938, as a lark, Dawn and Herbert decided to go to a nudist colony. They stayed two days before Herbert abruptly took them away. Apparently Dawn, a beautiful young woman, had attracted too much attention. When they returned home, Herbert called one of the men who had fussed over his young wife's shapely silhouette and exchanged rude words. Mortified by his behavior, Dawn tried to disconnect the phone or hang it up, but Herbert refused to cooperate. Finally, embarrassed

Adele's daughter, Dawn Hope, was an accomplished violinist. Crushed by her mother's suicide and her husband's jealousy, she killed herself two years after her mother's death. Drawing by Jana Whitley.

DENVER, COLORADO, SUNDAY MORNING, FEBRUARY 3, 1918 — MAGAZINE SECTION

# Why Adele Blood Deserted the Stage

## The Aladdin-Like Romance of "America's Most Beautiful Blonde" Who Will Have the Millions of Utah's "Silver Queen" and Live in the Palace of Twenty-Sixth Wife

covered the relationship.

Mrs. Holmes, herself once had been a poor girl—helper in a dressmaking shop in a Utah mining town. It was there she was found and courted by A. B. Emery, a descendant of Brigham Young, who had inherited from the Mormon prophet many mining claims. Soon after they were married the mining claims left by Brigham Young gave up great hoards of silver, and the dressmaker's assistant became the mistress of a fortune. This fortune and the mines became hers alone when her husband died, hardly a year after their marriage.

The young widow married Edwin Holmes, a capitalist, two years after her first husband's death. As a mark of the regard held for her by the Mormon Church officials as the former wife of a member of their one-time "prophet's" family, Mrs. Holmes was allowed to purchase from the church the "Amelia Palace," which had never been opened since the death of the favorite wife for whom it had been built. No other building ever owned by any Mormon official has been allowed to go out of the church possession. Mrs. Holmes's silver mines increased until they made her the richest woman in the West.

When Mrs. Holmes discovered that the noted actress was a cousin of whom she had lost track when Miss Blood still was a child, there was no thought that the star of "Everywoman" might ever become her heiress.

During the first night Mrs. Holmes spent in the "Amelia Palace," a desperate mother left on the doorstep, a little bundle in which was found a girl baby scarcely three months old. Mr. and Mrs. Holmes adopted the child and raised her as their own. They named her Louise Grace Holmes, and it was to her the millions of Mrs. Holmes were destined.

Two months ago this adopted daughter died. She had been married to a young business man of Salt Lake City. Her wedding gift from her foster mother was a check for $5,000,000. Mrs. Holmes has now asked her son-in-law to return this amount to her, that it might be restored to the Holmes fortune.

The death of her adopted daughter was a tragic blow to Mrs. Holmes. She could not bear to return to the Amelia Palace without some one to take her daughter's place. She had not even an heir to whom she cared to look for the future guardianship of her fortune. It was then she remembered that Adele Blood, her almost forgotten cousin was almost the same age as the daughter she had lost.

Adele Blood, the Actress Famous as the Star of "Everywoman" and Often Said to be the "World's Most Beautiful Blonde," Who Has Become a "Silver Princess." An Almost Forgotten Cousin, Mrs. Edwin Holmes, "Silver Queen of the West," Discovered Miss Blood Was Her Cousin and Made Her Her Heiress.

to search through Europe for rare art treasures, including costly vases and famous paintings, that he might furnish Amelia palace to suit the whims

Queen's millions

Adele Blood, Susie's protégée and heir, had been a successful Broadway actress. Distraught over an unsuccessful comeback attempt, she shot herself in 1936. Newspaper clipping from unidentified newspaper courtesy of Stella Inge.

and humiliated, she ran to their bedroom, locked the door, and, like her mother, used a gun to kill herself. She had survived Adele by only two years and was just nineteen when she died.[9]

For Susie, the deaths were overwhelming. By this time she was estranged from most of her family, so she treasured her relationship with Adele and her daughter. She had planned to leave them her estate, but in 1939, with both of them dead, she revised her will, now leaving the bulk of her estate to her servants. When she was later asked why she had left her nieces and nephews nothing, she explained that money was the root of all evil, and she planned to spend it all so they would have nothing to fight over after her death. Until the day she died, she claimed money had destroyed her family relationships.[10]

Some family members might have agreed with her. In the years that followed her last two marriages, younger members of the family criticized Susie, saying her behavior was foolish and even an embarrassment. Even though she had been very generous to many of them, paid for the weddings of two of her nieces, and financed the college educations of several family members, only Susanna Harris Hartman stayed close, and she saw Susie only infrequently during the late 1930s and early 1940s. While Susie had sought out her wealthy friends, the younger members of her family chose instead to live quiet lives away from the artificiality of society life and the glitter of Hollywood.

Nellie's husband, Jay Harris, had allowed their daughter, Susanna, to stay with her Aunt Susie at El Roble, in the Gardo, and at Oakwood as a child. Prior to her marriage to Gage Hartman, Susanna had often visited with her aunt. But her father refused to let Susanna become Susie's protégée. Susie had introduced the girl to several Hollywood personalities, including Rex Bell, Marie Windsor, and Cecil B. DeMille, who visited at El Roble, thinking this would please her. She may also have been grooming her for a Hollywood career as she had Adele. To make sure Susanna had a stunning dress to wear at any occasion, Susie purchased several for her to pick from whenever she threw a party for her niece. Later, after the dinners concluded, Susie would leave her niece with the men so they could get acquainted. When Jay heard about these parties, he put an

When Susanna Harris was in her late teens, she often stayed at El Roble, but her father refused to let her become Susie's protégée. Photograph courtesy of Susanna Hartman.

end to the nonsense; he would not give Susie a chance to mold his daughter any further. Though he had previously indulged his sister-in-law in her affection for his daughter, he now limited Susanna's visits to her aunt's home and constantly pointed out Susie's flaws.

When Susanna grew old enough to travel to Europe with Susie, he again refused to give his permission. He worried that Susanna would not find happiness if she followed Susie's lifestyle. He frequently reminded both of his children that wealth could be a curse or a blessing depending on how it was used. Like Susie, some of his own relatives had great wealth, but he considered them wastrels. He wanted a more secure life for his daughter. Susie was hurt when she heard of his criticisms, but she pretended not to notice or care. At such times she hid behind a nonchalant facade to protect her pride. In response to her family's criticism, she began avoiding many of them even more than she had previously. She had struggled for years to become part of the social set she admired; now her fashionable friends in cafe society were her life. They accepted her and provided the companionship she needed. She would finish her life as did so many women who had outlived the Gilded Age—in near-constant travel, worrying that their money would not last, but doing nothing to economize so that it would.[11]

By the end of her life, Susie was replacing her fabulous jewels with paste imitations to get enough money to maintain her facade of wealth. Photograph courtesy of Angelo Boncoraglio.

# 13

## "To you, my dear Sherrie, I say good bye"

Freed from caring for her El Roble estate, the Gardo House, or Oakwood, or from being concerned about a staff of servants, Susie had greater freedom to come and go at will in the last years of her life, but she was also lonely at times. Occasionally she visited Susanna Hartman and her two boys, Harris and Chris. She also visited Nellie but saw little of other family members and nothing of Wallace and John.

Now Culver Sherrill was the principal man in her life: he arranged for boats, trains, and hotels as she wandered back and forth across the continent between Florida, New York, and California, occasionally going to Europe to meet this or that group of friends. In May 1938 she returned to Salt Lake City to check on her mining stock and visit the Park City mines where her wealth had started. She stayed in her favorite suite of rooms in the Hotel Utah, on the southeast corner of the ninth floor. From that vantage point she could look toward the mountains and Park City as well as south toward Oakwood.

On the afternoon of May 11, two reporters and their photographers, representing the *Deseret News* and the *Salt Lake Tribune*, came for an interview, as reporters regularly did when she was in town. They knew they would be guaranteed an entertaining interview and a lively story—Susie was known for her wit as well as for her clothes and travels. On one occasion she playfully stunned them by saying she "regretted the passing of the era when the elite could live as they were accustomed to without offending the proletariat."[1]

As she expected, the reporters began the interview by asking why she had returned to Utah. At moments like this she knew what the reporters were waiting for: her trademark statement, "Why live life if you can't enjoy it?" Everyone expected her to say something that would get the readers' attention, so she started with, "Florida was too cold, New York too hot, California too shadow crowded with memories, New Port too banal, and Maine was too monotonous so she had come home to Salt Lake City which had always been like her hometown." In the next forty-five minutes she modeled a new piece of jewelry and a quaint hat from Paris, discussed finding a bootlegger in Manhattan, reminisced about the gay 1890s, and finished by singing F.D.R.'s praises. She also included a comment many people found painfully true: "I am unfortunate in keeping husbands." The newspapermen seemed pleased with her efforts to entertain them, so she was pleased as well.[2]

After they left she finished unpacking her suitcases and slumped into a chair to call the desk for a manicurist. Her nails needed work, and even if she were down to her last dollar, she would keep up appearances. Moments later a charming young girl knocked at the door. Culver showed her in and then went out for a while. As the girl worked quickly and passed the time with her in pleasantries, Susie was struck by how much she missed having Harold, Adele, Dawn, and even Grace around. It was hard to believe all of them were dead. Spontaneously she asked the girl if she had

Culver Sherrill became Susie's business manager, escort, and companion during the last years of her life. Photograph courtesy of Frances Darger.

been to Europe. The girl looked up at her in amazement. A young woman of her modest means could never hope to travel and see the world as this well-traveled cosmopolite had.

When Susie could see the girl was speechless, she asked her more directly, "Would you like to go to Europe with me? I could show you the cities, palaces, museums, and things too wonderful to describe!" The young blond laughed with embarrassment, not knowing how to respond. What girl in her right mind could turn down that offer if it was sincere? But she knew she would; her parents would not approve, and they needed her at home. When Susie had been younger, she would never have asked a stranger for company, and now this girl had turned her down. How times had changed in fifty years!3

But a melancholy mood would not last long. Culver was used to cheering Susie up when she was down in the dumps. They would go down to dinner in the hotel's dining room in a few minutes, and she would make one of her grand entrances and soon be smiling again. Tomorrow they would visit the bank to see how her accounts looked, and then they would head for Park City. Culver knew if her accounts looked too dismal she would give him one of her pieces of jewelry—a necklace, bracelet, ring, something—to sell. Deftly he would take out the gem, pawn it at a jewelry store, and replace it with a paste stone. This stopgap measure would provide money to travel on for a few more months.

In the five years he had worked for her, they had both accepted the fact that the Depression had depleted her stocks, bonds, and any savings she might have had. Now she was living off the sale of her fabulous jewelry and hoping she would not run out of money before she ran out of life. Some might have suggested she live more frugally, but that would mean admitting she was no longer part of the social elite. Some might turn to relatives if such a disaster occurred, but Culver knew Susie could never do that. Most of her family had been warning her for years that she was living beyond her means. Heaven forbid that she would need to ask John, the mayor, for help. Culver remembered hearing that John had once come to this very room to look at her accounts but Susie had not let him in because she was embarrassed at how bad they looked. John had been willing to help then, but she had rebuffed him. There was no reason to imagine he would take care of the aging Silver Queen now that she had frittered away her millions.4

Still, for the moment things were not desperate, so the charade continued. After a pleasant visit in Salt Lake City, Susie and Culver headed back to Pasadena and her rooms in the Green Hotel. Occasionally when she was in Pasadena, Susie would call Susanna to see how she was doing or see Lory Snow. If she missed them, she would catch one or both on her next visit to California. She would spend a few months in California with some of her friends, and then she would be off for another destination on the east coast or in Europe. She would be in England for the Ascot races, then on to Vienna for the opera season, Madrid for Easter, Monte Carlo for a few nights at the casinos, New Orleans for Mardi

Susie spent the last years of her life in constant travel, California to New York to Florida to Europe, with occasional stops in Utah. Photograph courtesy of Harold Lamb.

Gras, or Newport for the yacht races. Anyone not accustomed to this routine of constant travel and little crises would find it distressing, but "it was part of the pattern of keeping up with 'who's who' in society. The participants in the game didn't dare drop out; if they did, they would certainly soon be forgotten."[5]

By the early 1940s Susie considered writing a biography to replenish her funds. From time to time people had jokingly suggested her life would make a good read with so many soap opera characters and incredible events. Each time someone had mentioned the idea, she had considered it but not followed through. At one time O. N. Malmquist, a writer for the *Salt Lake Tribune*, started to interview her with the idea of compiling a book. After an hour on a hot afternoon in his small office in the Tribune Building, Susie asked for a rain check. The next time she came to town, he was too busy to meet, so the book stayed on hold.

Culver asked several friends for the names of writers who could write a good dramatic biography, and he finally found a Louisville reporter, James M. Ross. Susie was elated and wanted to start right away. A few phone calls were exchanged, then a few letters, then she mailed him her scrapbooks and a manuscript she had started on her own. Weeks passed, and Ross published an article in his newspaper about the fabulous Silver Queen, whose life had encompassed so much, including her observation that "when crossing the country by airplane I could look down and see the country which it took six months for my parents to cross . . . in a covered wagon." The article was a trial balloon to see if there was any public interest in the subject, but it prompted only a few calls. At that time it seemed there was little interest in a book that did not deal with Hitler, the bombing of Britain, the struggles of the Depression, or Mr. Roosevelt's New Deal.

When she heard from Ross that it might be best to wait until the war in Europe ended, Susie gave up on the project. Ironically, her lawyer in California, Lloyd W. Brooks, had told her the same thing years earlier. Immersed in the daily current events, most people were more worried about the United States going to war than about an aging socialite, no matter how zany her life had been. Perhaps when Hitler was out of the way, public interest might change.[6]

In the midst of these concerns, Nellie called to say that John had died May 23, 1941. Susie wept bitter tears as she realized that once again she had waited too long to take care of mending fences. She realized Wallace and Stella and their families would not appreciate her presence at the funeral, so Nellie represented them both. Six months later, in November, Susie was glad to learn that John's estate left his children almost one million dollars to split. He had done well since she had introduced him to Salt Lake City's society forty-two years earlier.[7]

By January of 1942 America was involved in the war in both Europe and the Pacific. Any thoughts of a book deal were definitely postponed. Quietly Susie made a trip to Salt Lake City to see the officers of Tracy Collins Bank. At one time her name on a piece of paper had been worth something; maybe they would still consider giving her a loan. To her surprise, they were willing to allow her to borrow against her estate. As a charitable measure, several banks across the country had helped wealthy elderly people who needed cash to live on by allowing them to borrow against their homes or other assets, recognizing the bank could be reimbursed later out of the probate settlement.

Thanks to Tracy Collins, Susie now had a few thousand dollars. She reacted to each "withdrawal" in typical fashion: she hosted a party. She invited some old friends and a few members of the family who still lived in the area to her suite at the Hotel Utah. Nellie and her husband, Jay, who were living at the Bransford Apartments down the street, attended. Wallace was still managing the Bransford Apartments, and he and his second wife, Edna, could have walked the distance to the Hotel Utah in less than ten minutes, but they did not bother. After all that had happened between them in the last forty years, he could not bring himself to talk to Susie for any reason.[8]

Harold Lamb had died many years earlier, and Grizzelle had remarried to William O'Conner. With Harold dead and her children grown and gone, she and Susie no longer had anyone in common, so she was unlikely to attend. When her son Harold "Hal" Jr. was in town, he dutifully visited, but during the war he was in the service or in medical school. The other Lamb children, Susie and Joe, had long since married and moved away.

Three generations of Bransford men: John, the mayor, is seated in the center with his son, Wallace, on the right, and Wallace Jr. on the left. Photograph courtesy of Anne Bransford Newhall.

In his later years Wallace was generally highly regarded by his peers in Salt Lake City, and he left his heirs a healthy legacy. Used by permission, Utah State Historical Society, all rights reserved.

There just were not many people around to celebrate Susie's good fortune. A little sad, Susie still went ahead with her plans for a grand evening.9

But the loans only helped for a time. By July 1942 Susie was desperate for money again. In six months she had "withdrawn" twenty thousand dollars and felt she had reached her limit. She wrote Nellie that she was very afraid, but would not elaborate. Nellie tried to soothe her in the letter she mailed back, but Susie was nearly hysterical. It pained Culver to see her haunted by old ghosts, burdened by regrets, and living in constant fear of poverty. He managed to get tranquilizers for her since she occasionally broke down in tears, and he found some sleeping pills for her frequent sleepless nights. They moved from the Plaza into cheaper lodging in late July, which saved a little, but soon even those rooms would be too costly. By the first week of August, sensing that Culver was also frightened, Susie contacted some friends in Norwalk, Connecticut, and planned to visit them.

Three days later in a room in a small hotel above a garage in Norwalk, Susie took some sedatives just before dinner to calm her nerves and didn't wake up. When she did not come down to eat, the manager went to wake her, fearing she would miss the last meal of the day, and found her dead. A few hours later Culver arrived. As she had done on other occasions when she was afraid she would die, Susie had left him a letter with instructions. The envelope said simply, "Mr Culver M Sherrill not to be opened until I die." In it she reminded him where her things were stored, told him where he would find two hundred dollars she left him for immediate expenses, and gave him a phone number. Part of that letter also expressed her feelings for him:

> August 1, 1942
> Dear Sherrie:
> If I should die as I feel at times that I might, don't worry. You have been for years thinking of my happiness and never causing me a moment's worry. I want you to have a happy life as long as you like. Being happy will be to you doing the things you want to do! I have never known a man like you, because there isn't one.... You are the best! I hope you will always be able to live in the way that gives you the most happiness.... So to you, my dear Sherrie, I say good bye, not knowing when the hour will come, but feeling that my time is short. So I bid you farewell with my love,
> Suzanne

Culver arranged to ship the body to Salt Lake City's Evans and Early Mortuary, and then he cabled the family. He contacted Nellie first, then Grizzelle and Wallace. When she received the news from her mother, Susanna Hartman left California immediately. With Culver's help she found the dress Susie wanted to be buried in, wrote the obituary, and arranged for a markedly simple funeral.10

At her death in August 1942, Susie was still regarded as a beautiful, regal member of the upper crust. Newspaper clipping from unidentified newspaper courtesy of Harold Lamb.

This large monument marks the Emery-Bransford section in the Mt. Olivet Cemetery in Salt Lake City. Albion, Susie, and her parents, Milford and Sarah, are buried here. Susie had hoped to have all of the Bransfords buried in this plot, but Wallace, in a vengeful gesture, chose to bury Grace across the street in a separate section. The small stone on the far left may mark Susie's grave, but then again, it may not. One of the cemetery's main water lines runs through the Bransford graves, occasionally necessitating the removal of the headstones to repair the sprinklers. This situation would have amused Susie, who enjoyed creating uncertainty about her life. Photograph by Judy Dykman.

Susie married Albion Emery in 1884; she was twenty-five and he thirty-eight. Used by permission, Utah State Historical Society, all rights reserved.

She married Colonel Edwin Holmes in 1899; she was forty and he fifty-six. Used by permission, Utah State Historical Society, all rights reserved.

Suzanne Egera Bransford Emery Holmes Delitch Engalitcheff, Utah's Silver Queen. Photograph courtesy of Harold Lamb.

She married Radovan Delitch in 1930; she was seventy-one and he forty-one. Photograph courtesy of Harold Lamb.

She married Prince Nicholas Engalitcheff in 1933; she was seventy-four and he fifty-nine. Photograph courtesy of Susanna Hartman.

# Epilogue

After the funeral the family had much to discuss. Culver made arrangements for the will to be read, and he passed out mementos and keepsakes to the nieces, nephews, and Nellie. When Nellie and Jay asked about her mother, Sarah's, beautiful jewelry, they were shocked to hear it had been sold years earlier for living expenses. Other members of the family were also surprised when they heard other heirlooms were missing.

When Susie's lawyer, Lloyd W. Brooks, arrived in Utah, he arranged to meet as many of the will's beneficiaries as possible. Susie had listed only a few: Nellie, her only surviving sibling; the Lamb children, Joe, Susie, and Hal; the Bransfords, Wallace and Stella; and her closest staff members, Culver, J. B. Feldman, and his wife Letitia. For a variety of reasons, primarily the war, only half of the beneficiaries could attend. Culver represented himself and the Feldmans, who by now were very elderly.

After a few hours of legal mumbo jumbo, the atmosphere in the room became very tense because the will came down to this: the family did not get a dime, and what little Susie had left went to the Feldmans and Culver. There remained about sixty-five thousand dollars in stocks, bonds, and miscellaneous items, but the fact was that many of the stocks were worthless; moreover, accumulated legal fees, bills, and estate taxes zeroed out the account. Worried for the Feldmans' security, Susie had directed Mr. Brooks to take four thousand dollars off the top and set up a trust fund. She hoped this would provide them an allowance of one hundred dollars per month for life. In the meantime, Culver inherited some stocks and her personal property, which an appraiser valued at less than five hundred dollars.

The family members looked at one another. Could these figures be right? How could she wipe out her fortune so completely? Had there been fraud? Someone quipped that she had said she would spend it all so there would be nothing to fight over. Now they could see she had meant it![1]

During the following weeks the family discovered that Susie, like Colonel Holmes, had simply given some things away before her death so they would not be probated. Three years earlier she had given Culver the Richmond Apartments so he would have a monthly allowance for life. She had surprised the Lambs and Susanna with a few things that had survived the El Roble auction: pieces of furniture, some Russian goblets and plates, and a little jewelry. But there were still many other items that could not be accounted for. Had she given those to Adele and Dawn, or the Snows, or did Culver also get those items as gifts? Nellie particularly distrusted Culver and wondered if he had the jewelry locked up in a vault in California or Europe.[2]

Tempers flared and some family members talked of suing Culver for everything he had received from Susie. A few even questioned whether Culver had killed her or tricked her into giving him her money or property. Realistically,

Susie was the matron of honor for Susanna's wedding to Gage Hartman. Newspaper clipping from unidentified newspaper courtesy of Harold Lamb.

some members of the family knew she had behaved strangely in recent years. Each of them could recount stories of some of the funny things she did as she aged, like the story Susanna Hartman shared. In 1932, when Susie's marriage to Rada was unraveling, Susanna had invited her aunt to be her matron of honor. Susie was thrilled to be included and excited about picking the perfect dress for the occasion. Later that day she and Susanna went through the clothes Susie brought with her to find something that would blend in with the bridesmaids' lavender dresses. After much discussion, Susanna picked a striking silver and lavender outfit and told Susie she would arrange for flowers to match it. On the day of the wedding Susie arrived at the church in a bright red dress with jewels tucked in the folds of her hair. When Susanna saw Susie walking down the aisle broadly smiling, she nearly burst into tears.

Talking it over later, Nellie and Susanna initially could not decide whether Susie had intentionally picked the wrong dress or if, with her many personal problems, she had simply forgotten the earlier agreement. As far as Susie was concerned, the dress offset her beautiful white hair; it never occurred to her that it also upstaged the bride and was not appropriate for the occasion.[3]

Later the family recalled still more examples of Susie's failing memory or possible senility. Some of her last letters were almost unintelligible. Could this be attributed to sleeping pills, tranquilizers, an aging mind, or just anxiety? As time passed and as Culver repeatedly assured the family he would show them his records, tempers cooled and all talk of a lawsuit was dropped. Nellie even pointed out that since Culver had been Susie's closest companion at the end, maybe it was fitting he get something for his kindness to her. At Brooks's suggestion, the Tracy Collins Bank and Hogle Investments held on to the stocks instead of disposing of them immediately; if they should become valuable again in the future, they would nullify Susie's debts to those companies.[4]

After making the rounds to the family one last time, Culver left for California. Then it hit. Two weeks later, Culver released a story to the media that his former employer, "Utah's Silver Queen," had left him four million dollars. Shock waves resounded throughout Utah. Creditors and family alike were ready to tear him limb from limb! But even this incident blew over in a few days. Those who knew Culver joked that the great publicist was just trying to get a little attention from his own family and friends. Besides, if he were a crook, he had outfoxed them all: how could anyone *prove* anything against him?[5]

By 1950 the problems of Susie's will had finally been resolved; the stocks had been sold and the other issues were settled. As she had promised many years earlier, Susie left no money for the family to fight over. Anything that could be salvaged went to pay taxes, legal fees, and creditors. By this time, Culver was also tired of being a landlord at the Sherrill Apartments (formerly the Richmond Apartments) and hoped to get away to a warmer climate. When the LDS Church approached him about buying the apartments for future church expansion, he agreed to discuss a sale price. Several figures were suggested, but

Culver always wanted more. Finally a church lawyer made him the deal of a lifetime: How would he like sixty dollars per day tax free for the rest of his life? After a few minutes for some arithmetic, Culver agreed. If he lived thirty more years, that would be over a half-million dollars, and tax free![6]

In the years that followed Culver moved to Taormina, Sicily, and rented a villa. He remodeled the home, adding a swimming pool, gardens, and big bay windows to take advantage of the impressive view. Like Susie years earlier, he also hired a business manager, a good-looking Italian gentleman addressed only as Johnny, and a cook and butler, Angelo Boncoraglio. Life was good; he had friends, entertained, was respected by his neighbors in Taormina, traveled to homes in Berlin and England, and toured the world at least once. Occasionally he also went home to Pasadena to visit his sister, Eleanor Boyd, and his nieces and nephews.[7]

But by the mid-1970s, even Culver was running out of funds. Angelo was his closest friend, and with his help Culver decided to write a book, hoping it would bring in some money. He pulled out his personal scrapbooks and tried to find some stories to record in the autobiography. With Angelo taking it all down in long hand, Culver began to dictate his story. In some places he took many liberties; in other areas he skipped years altogether. When he came to the part about Susie, he paused. How much should he tell? What should he leave out? Finally, after months of work, he contacted a friend in the publishing business for a favor. Would he publish the book?

The publisher assigned an editor to rework it. Then there was the problem of a catchy title: it had to attract people's interest. After much debate, the publisher and a ghostwriter settled on *Crimes Without Punishment*. Culver was contacted. Did the title suit him? He paused for a moment. What crimes were they talking about? He was no criminal. The editor laughed—Culver didn't understand that the title was just a hook to pull the reader in.

Culver was given a chance to read his book before it was published. It made him look pretty good, and it had not exaggerated too much, though it was not as kind to Susie. In places it actually made her look foolish. Culver contacted

Like Susie, Culver cultivated a facade of wealth by maintaining a villa in Taormina, Sicily. Here he entertained his friends on the balcony, with Roman ruins in the background. In his book *Crimes without Punishment*, he claims to have entertained royalty here. Photograph courtesy of Angelo Boncoraglio.

the editor, but after a few minutes he was won over. Since when did an autobiography have to be absolutely truthful? Besides, history was a subjective thing. The picture Culver's book presented of Susie has contributed to the folklore that has shadowed the real woman ever since.

When the book was published, a friend, Temple Fielding, gave it rave reviews, but the literary critics panned it. Sales lagged, and the publisher decided to cut his losses; there was no reprint. Culver's royalty check was minuscule, almost insulting. The book he had counted on to support him in his last years had failed miserably. Even more tragic, the little money he had left had been spent to induce the publisher to publish it.

Angelo and Culver closed the villa and sold many of the furnishings to pay back bills. Culver's days as a big promoter were over. Instinctively he headed for California, hoping his sister would take him in; if she did not he would be lost. By 1977 Eleanor was ailing herself, but she made room in her home for him because she said that when he did have money, he had been kind to her. However, she was puzzled. What had become of his money from the LDS Church? He had twenty-four thousand dollars per year tax free. Culver laughed. That had been spent years ago; the money now went directly from a bank account to his creditors.[8]

The following year Eleanor died and Culver was homeless again. At Eleanor's request two of his nephews had promised to care for him, but the state welfare system paid his medical bills. His last days were spent in a Santa Barbara hospital where he lingered for weeks in a coma-like state. It was a tragic end for a little man who had wanted to appear important and impress family and friends. By now all had guessed that he had been bluffing when he boasted that Susie had left him the four million dollars. Certainly if she had left him that much money, he was a fool who had wasted her fortune. Either way he had not come off as the big man he had wanted to be.

In his last months in Taormina, Culver was so short of cash that he was not paying his staff. Afraid to admit he was broke, Culver had promised Angelo he would be a beneficiary in his will, and Angelo, who had a family to support, had been willing to overlook the lost wages with the hope that the will would reimburse him later, perhaps very well. His wife and children had even taken odd jobs to support themselves during the years he served as Culver's butler. When Culver's death was imminent, they thought their financial worries were over, but after the funeral, no one contacted Angelo. Finally, after waiting patiently for several months, Angelo wrote to one of Culver's nephews. When were they going to probate the will? Several more months passed with Angelo still hoping to recoup his back wages, but nothing came. Finally he wrote a friend of Culver's and asked for help. Two weeks later he got a reply: there was no will, no money, just bills to pay. Culver's family had been too embarrassed to tell Angelo the truth.[9]

The Silver Queen's incredible story might have ended with Culver's death, but it does not. The property the LDS Church purchased from Culver is now the site of a twenty-six story church office complex. While Susie had no direct descendants, her great nieces and nephews and their families are still living and all are doing very well. She may not have left the family any money at her death, but throughout her life she had been generous with all of them on many occasions: she paid for weddings, financed college, started businesses, provided homes, and supported some when they were impoverished or orphaned.

Susie's relatives were and are intelligent, competent, talented people, and Susie followed the family's tradition by giving them seed money. They also followed family tradition and made the most of their opportunities and talents. Susanna Hartman is now eighty-nine and has many grandchildren and great grandchildren. Only Hal Lamb survives from the Lamb children, and he is now a retired but distinguished physician. The younger members of the Lamb family have likewise become successful and accomplished. Susie may have introduced John, the mayor, to Salt Lake society, but he made significant contributions of his own. John was subsequently able to help his children and their families. A year after Grace's death, Wallace married Edna Leonard, who gave him his only child, Wallace Jr. The money Wallace inherited from Grace has been wisely invested by his heirs. If Wallace Jr.'s three daughters have their way, eventually there will be a commemorative chapel atop Deer Valley for their loved ones. Stella's two granddaughters, Stella and Sue, have a number of well-educated, hardworking descendants scattered along the Pacific Coast and in Colorado. And so the tradition continues: family has helped family for many generations, and they expect to continue to do so. Along the way they have also helped the communities in which they have lived, and that, too, is a family tradition.[10]

And what of Susie herself? If people live in the retelling of their stories, she is alive and well. She was not perfect and did not claim to be, but she was also not the strange, flighty creature she has sometimes been portrayed as being. Nor is it fair to compare her to the average man or woman of the late nineteenth and early twentieth centuries. Susie was part of an extraordinary social class in an exceptional period of time. Like most other nouveaux riches, she wanted to be accepted by the east coast social aristocracy and knew she would have to follow their rules and meet their standards to do it. Most people in the late twentieth century find those rules restrictive and those standards artificial, but all across the country, people who suddenly found themselves very wealthy realized they would have to conform, at least to some degree, to survive in business and society. Few wealthy American families emerged from the Gilded Age unscathed. The tragedies, passions, and foibles of the Vanderbilts, Astors, Rockefellers, and even the Kennedys were reflected in many lesser-known families across the country.

If Susie is compared to other wealthy Westerners of the Gilded Age, she appears to be fairly typical. She spent enormous amounts of money on clothes, jewels, parties, and houses, but like other wealthy socialites, she also gave liberally to charities and organizations and, most of all in her case, to individuals. Consequently, her gifts may not be as easy to recognize as those of some others. In Utah some individuals and families donated large sums of money or gave buildings and whole institutions to the community. The Kearns family left the Roman Catholic Church a great legacy by donating to the Cathedral of the Madeleine and by creating St. Ann's Orphanage. The Judges donated to the Cathedral of the Madeleine and the YMCA, and they opened a mining hospital that later became Judge Memorial High School. Mont Ferry endowed Westminster College and the miner's hospital in Park City. Thomas Weir and David Keith contributed money toward the construction of the First Presbyterian church on South Temple. The Hogle family contributed to the YMCA and endowed a zoo which remains one of the most highly attended places in the community.

Susie contributed to similar charities, but far more often she gave unobserved: to her family, the Lory Snow family, Adele and Dawn, the local newsboys, her servants, and many other anonymous beneficiaries on numerous occasions. A newspaper story during her lifetime reported that Susie gave away thousands of dollars and had many private charities that she "is averse to having mentioned in any way."[11] Her remaining legacy lives on in the descendants of the people she loved and helped.

Susie, her parents, and her siblings would be pleased to see that their descendants have bridged the gap that divided the family for so many years. In 1995 the extended Bransford family gathered in Utah to see the Park City exhibit on Susie and to become acquainted with each other. For some it was the first time they had actually met their cousins. For all, it was a time to heal.

The descendants of Milford and Sarah Bransford gathered for a family reunion in Salt Lake City in 1994. This was the first time some of them had met because of the deep division in the family. Photograph courtesy of the Bransford family.

# Bransford Family Tree
## (slightly pruned)

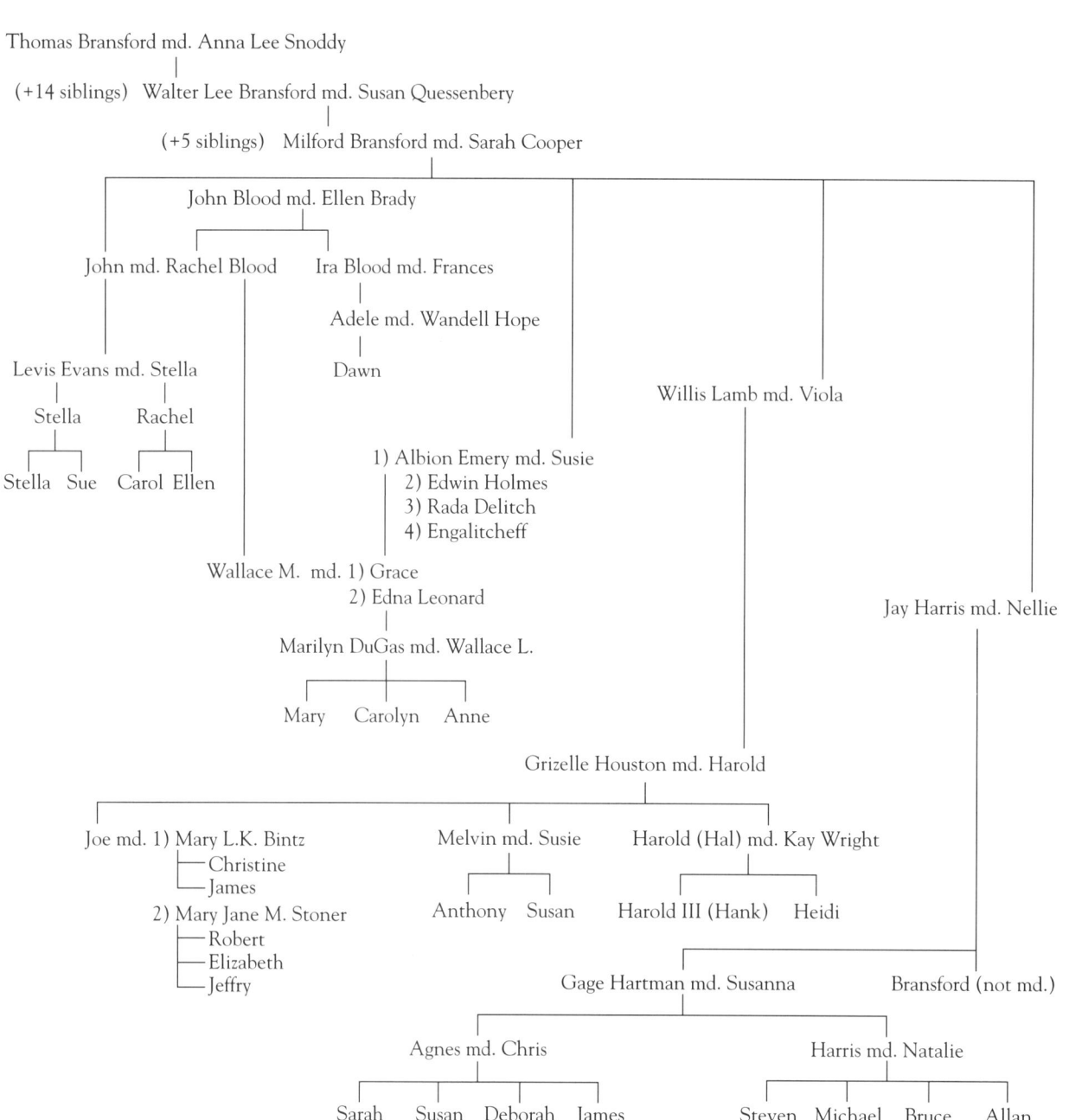

# Notes

## Prologue

1. With so many marriages, Susie's surname obviously changed at various points in her life. In addition, she used variants of her first name—Suzy, Susie, Susan, Susanna, Suzanne—during different periods. To avoid confusion, in the text she will consistently be called Susie, the name she and her family used most commonly. In notes, however, the surname under which a given source is filed will be retained, as "Bransford's autograph book."
2. Susanna Hartman (Suzanne Bransford's niece), interviews by Judy Dykman, 1993–1997; "Rites Planned Saturday for 'Silver Queen,'" *Salt Lake Tribune*, 6 August 1942; Laura Crouch, interview by Judy Dykman, 1997. Laura's friend attended the funeral and substantiated the silver dollar story.
3. Hartman, interviews; Harold Lamb (Suzanne Bransford's great-nephew), interviews by Judy Dykman, 1994–1997; Margaret Godfrey, "The Silver Queen," *Salt Lake City*, September/October 1993, 33–34; Margaret Lester, *Brigham Street* (Salt Lake City: Utah State Historical Society, 1979), 220–21; George A. Thompson and Fraser Buck, *Treasure Mountain Home, Park City Revisited* (Salt Lake City: Dream Garden Press, 1993), 53–58; Raye C. Ringholz, *Diggins and Doings in Park City* (Park City, Utah: by author, 1983), 60–64.

## Chapter 1

1. Walter Lee married Susan after his first wife, Virginia P. Settles, died during childbirth. From that marriage he had four children. He and Susan had five children.
2. John A. Shiver, *Bransford Family History* (Kentucky: McDowell Publishing Company, 1981), 35–41, 135–37; Milford Bransford family Bible, list of births and deaths, in possession of Harold Lamb; James M. Ross, "From Old Kentucky," *Louisville Courier Journal*, 8 March 1942; "Crossing the Plains," unpublished article about the Bransford family, in possession of Stella Inge; A. S. Colyar, "Reminiscences of Distinguished Men, No. 10," n.d., newspaper clipping, Suzanne Bransford Scrapbook, Ms B332, Utah State Historical Society (hereafter cited as Bransford Scrapbook); John B. Brownlow, "Thos. L. Bransford and Col. Colyar's Sketches," 19 December 1903, newspaper clipping, Bransford Scrapbook.
3. Bureau of Census, Ray County, Missouri, 1850; *History of Ray County, Mo.* (St. Louis: Missouri Historical Company, 1881), 386; Shiver; Milford Bransford family Bible; Sarah Cooper's will, copy in possession of Harold Lamb.
4. Price capitalized on local anger when a small army of Confederates was captured by Union Brigadier General Nathaniel Lyon. Days later, as Lyon's troops marched these men through St. Louis, a riot broke out. Bystanders watching the spectacle pelted the soldiers with sticks and stones. The terrified Union troops fired into the crowd, killing twenty-eight bystanders, including a baby. Countless spectators were wounded as the troops struggled to regain control. A few days later a second group of sympathizers tried to free

the prisoners and a second massacre occurred. Only four civilians and two soldiers died this time, but emotions in the area rose to a fever pitch. As word of the massacres spread, no Missourian loyal to the South could resist joining Price's army.

5. Sarah Cooper's will; Milford Bransford family Bible; *Encyclopedia Americana*, 1992, s.v. "Missouri"; James M. McPherson, *Battle Cry of Freedom* (New York and Oxford: Oxford University Press, 1988), 291–92, 350–54, 404.

6. "Milford Bransford," obituary, *Plumas (Calif.) Independent*, 26 May 1894; "Crossing the Plains"; *Richmond, Ray County, after the Civil War* (Missouri: Ray County Historical Society, 1990), 89; McPherson, 350–54, 404; Eugene Parson, "The Striking Career of Thomas F. Walsh," *The Mining American*, 18 November 1916, 8; *Encyclopedia Americana*, s.v. "Missouri."

7. Minnie was the daughter of Milford's sister Albina.

8. "Crossing the Plains"; "John Bransford," obituary, *Salt Lake Tribune*, 24 May 1941.

9. Linda Brennan and Scott Lawson (of the Plumas County Museum and Historical Society), interviews by Judy Dykman, 1993–1995; Scott Lawson to Judy Dykman, 1997; *Plumas (Calif.) National Bulletin*, 11 January 1868; Farriss and Smith, *History of Plumas County, California, 1882* (1979; Burbank, Calif.: Howell-North Press, 1988), 133, 137, 140–42, 232–33, 240; *Encyclopedia Americana*, s.v. "Missouri."

10. Milford Bransford to A. C. Ellis, March 1865 and 24 May 1867; Farriss and Smith, 138–39; Ross; *History of Ray County*, 383–87; Brennan, interviews; Hartman, interviews; Joan S. Reiter, *The Women* (Alexandria, Va.: Time-Life Books, 1979), 79; Carpenter, *History of Mendocino County and Lake County* (1914; Mendocino Historical Society, 1994), 561, 627; "Crossing the Plains"; *State Resources* (Oakland, Calif.: 1890), 267–95.

11. Leonard Arrington, *Great Basin Kingdom* (Lincoln: University of Nebraska Press, 1966), 201; S. George Ellsworth, *Utah's Heritage* (Salt Lake City: Peregrine Smith, 1977), 222; Richard D. Poll, ed., *Utah's History* (Provo, Utah: Brigham Young University Press, 1978), 204, 247, 329, 363.

12. M. Bransford to Ellis; "John Bransford," *Plumas (Calif.) National Bulletin*, 10 January 1895; *State Resources*, 292–93; Plumas County tax records, 1867–1887, Plumas County Museum and Historical Society; Milford Bransford family Bible; Lamb, interviews.

13. Plumas County tax records, 1867–1887; Floralee Millsaps (Utah Heritage Foundation guide), interviews by Judy Dykman, 1993–1995; Hartman, interviews; John Bransford, brief autobiography, in possession of Vadney Murray (a descendant of the Blood family of Quincy, California); *Elite Magazine*, 15 March 1902, in Bransford Scrapbook; Susie E. Bransford's autograph book (hereafter cited as Bransford's autograph book), in possession of Susanna Hartman. A number of autographs in Susie's autograph book indicate she was very popular with the men.

## Chapter 2

1. Plumas County tax records, 1867–1887; *Greenville (Calif.) Bulletin*, 25 April 1881; Ross; *Elite Magazine*, 15 March 1902; Bransford's autograph book; Farriss and Smith, 295–98, 313–15; *State Resources*, 279–93; Reiter, 131, 161–89. Susie continued collecting autographs as an adult and by 1886 she had over five dozen entries.

2. *San Francisco Blue Book, 1875–78*, microfilm copy, LDS Family History Library, Salt Lake City, Utah; "Utah's Own 'Silver Queen' Arrives for Summer Visit in Salt Lake City," *Salt Lake Tribune*, 12 May 1938; Jean Murray (relative to the Blood family by marriage), interviews by Judy Dykman, 1994–1997; Ross; Shiver, 137.

3. The records are not clear about the demise of the store; it either burned down or went out of business in 1874. See Plumas County tax records, 1886–1887; Plumas County deed books for 1870s; Bransford File, Plumas County Museum, Quincy, California.

4. The road is no longer in use; the present road now runs below an old railroad grade. Lawson to Dykman; Farriss and Smith, 227, 235, 279.

5. This mine changed hands and names several times; for simplicity, the same name will be used consistently in this book.

6. Plumas County tax records, 1867–1887; Farriss and Smith, 227, 235, 279; *Greenville (Calif.) Bulletin*, 1881–1886; O. N. Malmquist, *The First One Hundred Years: A History of the Salt Lake Tribune* (Salt Lake City: Utah State Historical Society, 1971), 211.

7. Farriss and Smith, 240–41; Plumas County voting records, 1886–1887; Plumas County deed books for 1870s, xerox copies of deed transfers, in possession of Scott Lawson; *Greenville (Calif.) Bulletin*, 4 June 1884; "Milford Bransford," obituary, *Park Record*, 26 May 1894; Hartman, interviews.

8. Laura Wells (Utah Heritage Foundation tour guide and speaker), interview by Judy Dykman, 1994; Sarah Cooper's will; Bureau of Census, Ray County, Missouri, 1850; Mulholland autograph in Bransford's autograph book; *Greenville (Calif.) Bulletin*, 13 April 1881, 14 September 1881, 13 December 1882, 18 April 1883; *Plumas (Calif.) National Bulletin*, 21 May 1868, 29 December 1868, 16 March 1887, 6 April 1887.
9. Jane Rogers, "Rogers Family History," *Plumas Memories*, 51 (June 1986): 27.
10. Here and following unless otherwise cited, quotations from Bransford's autograph book. A check of Plumas County history and records shows that Holz subsequently disappeared from the area.
11. Researchers at University of California at San Francisco in 1994 confirmed that Susie was not treated under that name in 1882; however, there were listings for two other women (one a seamstress), both of whom claimed to be married and gave birth on the day of Sheets's entry. Either one could be Susie using a different name.
12. Hartman and Lamb, interviews; Marc McCutcheon, *The Writer's Guide to Everyday Life in the 1800s* (Cincinnati: Writer's Digest Books, 1993), 203–9; autograph from Maggie Flournoy's autograph book, in possession of Judy Dykman; Vadney Murray, interviews by Judy Dykman, 1993–1997.
13. "John Hayward Sheets," *Journal of the American Medical Association*, 5 May 1928, 1493; *Directory of Deceased Physicians*, photocopy of page 1400, medical library, University of California at San Francisco.

## Chapter 3

1. Bransford's autograph book; Milford Bransford family Bible; *Greenville (Calif.) Bulletin*, 19 March 1884, 4 June 1884, 7 January 1885; Hartman, interviews.
2. Malmquist, 211; Farriss and Smith, 240; "John Bransford," *Salt Lake Tribune*; Union Pacific Depot Museum, Ogden, Utah, telephone interview by Judy Dykman, 1994; Ellsworth, 258; Stephen L. Carr, *Utah's Ghost Rails* (Salt Lake City: Western Epics, 1989), 100–101.
3. Thompson and Buck, 13, 20, 23–24; Ringholz, *Diggins and Doings*, 42–51; Pat A. M. Chretien, interview by Judy Dykman, 1994; Jeffrey R. M. Kunz, *The American Medical Association Family Medical Guide* (New York: Random House, 1982), 563–64.
4. Two of her relatives once asked Susie about writing her memoirs. One, a young girl, offered to write the story, but Susie gently declined her offer, saying it would be too big a project and would take many volumes to tell it all. Then Susie sent the girl an autographed picture of herself. The other was a Southern clergyman who was trying to collect her story for a family history. Susie thought about it and wrote a brief sketch, saying someday she might share more of her story but probably not. Ironically, a few years before her death, she worked on a biography with a reporter for the *Louisville Courier* that was never finished. Susanna Hartman reported that Susie asked her to destroy her letters and diaries after she died, and she says she did.
5. "Romantic Story of Utah's Famous 'Silver Queen,'" newspaper clipping, Bransford Scrapbook; Ringholz, *Diggins and Doings*, 45–48, 61; Lester, 111; Lawson, interviews; "Albion Bernard Emery," *Biographical Record of Salt Lake City and Vicinity* (Chicago: National Historic Record Company, 1902), 211–12; "Death of Albion B. Emery," *Salt Lake Herald*, 14 June 1894; "Honorable Albion Bernard Emery," *Proceedings of the Grand Lodge Free and Accepted Mason of Utah* (Salt Lake City: Utah Masonic Lodge, 1896), 95–98; "Albion B. Emery," *Tullidge's Quarterly Magazine*, 1902, 502–3; "Death of Hon. A. B. Emery," *Park Record*, 16 June 1894; "Personal Mention," *Park Record*, 15 November 1884; *Greenville (Calif.) Bulletin*, 8 December 1886.
6. Alan Spriggs (Summit County clerk), interview by Judy Dykman, 1993; Sally Elliott (of the Utah Heritage Foundation), interview by Judy Dykman, 1993; Mary Ann Cone (curator of the Park City Museum), interview by Judy Dykman, 1996. The Park City Historical Society lobbied to keep the house. Spriggs believes the original house was destroyed by fire in 1898, and the current structure was built to replace it. However, both Elliott and Cone believe the present building is the original house. The bridge plan was abandoned in 1990.
7. Raye C. Ringholz to Judy Dykman, 1993; photograph of interior of Emerys' Park City home, Park City Museum; Thompson and Buck, 83; Ringholz, *Diggins and Doings*, 61.
8. *Greenville (Calif.) Bulletin*, 4 February 1885, 1 July 1885, 15 July 1885, 24 November 1886, 8 December 1886; Lamb, interviews; V. Murray, interviews; "Mrs. Holmes Takes Stand as Witness," *Salt Lake Tribune*, 3 October 1918; Louise Grace Emery Bransford, probate case

9207, 1918, Third Circuit Court, Third Judicial District, Salt Lake County, Utah, in Utah State Archives, Salt Lake City.

9. "Honorable Albion Bernard Emery," 95–98; "Men and Events Linked with Great Mines of Park City," *Park Record*, 5 June 1931; Malmquist, 211–12; Anne Newhall (granddaughter of Wallace Bransford), interviews by Judy Dykman, 1993–1997; Thompson and Buck, 51–54.

10. *Salt Lake City Blue Book*, 1894–1899 (Salt Lake City: Salt Lake Lithographing Co.); *Polk Directory for Salt Lake City* (Kansas City, Mo: R. L. Polk and Company, 1894); Sanborn Map Company, *Salt Lake City, Utah* (New York: The Company, 1890, 1894); *Utah at the World's Columbian Exposition* (Salt Lake City: Salt Lake Lithographing Co., 1894), picture of five women: Susie, Mrs. G. B. Hamilton, Margaret Blaine Salisbury, Mrs. T. A. Whalen, and Miss Maggie Keogh; "A Big Fortune at Stake," *Salt Lake Tribune*, 18 December 1894.

11. Milton Meltzer, *Bread—and Roses* (New York, New American Library, 1967), 53; "Andrew Carnegie," "Milton Hershey," "The Rockefellers," "The Vanderbilts," *Biography*, Arts and Entertainment Channel, 1994–1995; *Encyclopedia Americana*, 1992, s.v. "Andrew Carnegie"; Judith Robinson, *The Hearsts, An American Dynasty* (New York: Avon Books, 1991), 381; Mary Cable (social historian), telephone interview by Judy Dykman, 1996. Wharton's *The Age of Innocence* was released as a film in 1994 and portrays well the glittering elegance of the period.

12. Dr. Robert Burgoyne, a psychiatrist with LDS Hospital in Salt Lake City, has reviewed materials on Susie, including Judy Dykman's chapter on her in *Worth Their Salt* and Susie's letters to Culver Sherrill. He has diagnosed Susie as narcissistic and histrionic. Robert M. Burgoyne, interview by Judy Dykman, 1996; Mary Cable to Judy Dykman, 1996.

13. Mary Cable, *Top Drawer American High Society from the Gilded Age to the Roaring Twenties* (New York: Anteneum, 1984), 20–22. Cable, in her telephone interview with Dykman, observed that one of the chief characteristics of the age was its narcissism, in terms of the group as a whole and of individuals within it.

14. Albion B. Emery, probate case 102, 1894, Summit County, Utah Territory, in Utah State Archives, Salt Lake City; "Death of Hon. Albion Emery"; "Honorable Albion Bernard Emery."

15. Albion B. Emery, probate case 102; "Honorable Albion Bernard Emery"; "Albion Emery" (obituary and editorial), *Park Record*, 16 June 1894; "Milford Bransford," *Park Record*; "Milford Bransford" (obituary), *Salt Lake Tribune*, 26 May 1894; "Milford Bransford," *Plumas (Calif.) Independent*; Hartman, interviews.

## Chapter 4

1. "Men and Events Linked with Great Mines of Park City"; Thompson and Buck, 13; "Pioneer Miner Dies Suddenly," newspaper clipping, provided by Plumas County Museum, 1995; "Death of Honorable R. C. Chambers," *The Mining Review*, Salt Lake City, 15 April 1901.

2. Ringholz, *Diggins and Doings*, 59–60; Carr, 101; Thompson and Buck, 20. Chambers's unethical behavior extended beyond his business dealings. His wife's will, read after her suicide, left all of her own money, one and one-half million dollars, to her two small nieces. Chambers seized control of her assets, and the nieces sued him for their inheritance. The courts eventually granted the girls two-thirds of the money their aunt had left them. See "Action to Recover," *Plumas (Calif.) National Bulletin*, 28 November 1901.

3. "Legal Record," *Argus*, 29 December 1894.

4. Many people were aware that Haggin and Hearst had an agreement with Chambers to split the money from any of his investments in exchange for their financial backing. Yet testimony in the trial suggested Chambers had used their money and entered into secret agreements with M. S. Aschheim and John Daly to bankroll their businesses, but then occasionally failed to share the profits with his partners.

5. Albion B. Emery, probate case 102; "A Big Fortune Involved," *Salt Lake Tribune*, 22 September 1894; "For a Fortune," *Park Record*, 22 September 1894; "A Big Fortune at Stake"; "Chambers on the Stand," *Salt Lake Tribune*, 19 December 1894; "Submitted to Court," *Salt Lake Tribune*, 20 December 1894; "Chambers Loses the Suit," *Salt Lake Tribune*, 21 January 1895; Thompson and Buck, 11, 13, 35, 54; Hartman, interviews; "Men and Events Linked with Great Mines of Park City"; "Chambers vs. Emery," *Pacific Reporter* (Salt Lake City: Utah State Law Library), 45:192–200.

6. "Mrs. Holmes Takes Stand as Witness"; "Mrs. Holmes Again on Witness Stand," *Salt Lake Tribune*, 4 October 1918; Louis Grace Emery Bransford, probate case 9027.

7. "The Vanderbilts: An American Dynasty," Arts and Entertainment Channel, 1995.

8. Stephen Birmingham, *America's Secret Aristocracy* (Boston: Little, Brown, and Company, 1987), 282–85.
9. Jack Gallivan (former publisher of the *Salt Lake Tribune*), interview by Judy Dykman, 1997; Millsaps, interviews.
10. "Defense Loses in Will Case Decision," *Salt Lake Tribune*, 1 October 1918; "Mrs. Holmes Takes Stand as a Witness"; "Holmes-Bransford Trial Halted by Court," *Deseret News*, 3 October 1918; "Husband Weeps as He Testifies in Trial," *Deseret News*, 15 October 1918; Wallace Bransford's affidavit in Louise Grace Emery Bransford, probate case 9207.

## Chapter 5

1. Harvey Green, *The Light of the Home* (New York: Pantheon Books, 1983), 165–66, 170–72.
2. Green, 166; Ellsworth, 204; Thomas Alexander and James Allen, *Mormons and Gentiles, A History of Salt Lake City* (Boulder, Colo.: Pruett Publishing Company, 1984), 110.
3. Hartman, interviews.
4. "For Love and Affection," *Deseret News*, 20 October 1899; *Salt Lake City Blue Book*, 1894–1899.
5. Hotel Utah file, Western Americana Collection, Marriott Library, University of Utah, Salt Lake City; A. R. Mortensen (director of the Utah State Historical Society) to Mrs. A. W. Naegle, 15 December 1950; *Salt Lake Blue Book*, 1899–1901.
6. Hartman, interviews.
7. "Mrs. Holmes Takes Stand as Witness"; Wallace Bransford's affidavit in Louise Grace Emery Bransford, probate case 9207.
8. Another account claims Susie and the Colonel met in 1899.
9. Hartman, interviews; Lester, 111; *Biographical Record of Salt Lake City and Vicinity* (Chicago: National Historic Records Company, 1902), 211.
10. Lamb, interviews.
11. "Defense Loses in Will Case Decision"; Wallace Bransford's affidavit in Louise Grace Emery Bransford, probate case 9207.
12. Wallace Bransford's affidavit in Louise Grace Emery Bransford, probate case 9207; Plumas County death records, 1867–1900, Plumas County Courthouse, Quincy, California.
13. "Early Mayor of Salt Lake City Dies," *Salt Lake Tribune*, 22 May 1941; "John Bransford," short biographical sketch written for family members, in possession of Vadney Murray; "Leaders Laud Bransford at Final Rites," *Salt Lake Tribune*, 24 May 1941.
14. Ada Patterson ("A Romance Underground," newspaper clipping, in Bransford Scrapbook) hints at the truth of this story, but Susanna Hartman thinks it is bunk.
15. "Mrs. Emery Comes Here to Wed," n.d., unidentified New York newspaper, in possession of Stella Inge; "Mrs. Emery Married," newspaper clipping, in Bransford family scrapbook, in possession of Stella Inge; "Edwin Francis Holmes," *Pasadena Star News*, 16 March 1916; "Former Utahn Answers the Call," *Park Record*, 2 October 1925; Edwin F. Holmes, probate case 14118–14132, 1926, Kane County, Illinois, inventory 799; numerous small, untitled, undated articles about Holmes in Bransford Scrapbook; Frances Steiner (current owner of the home in Batavia, Illinois) to Judy Dykman, 29 July 1994; Marilyn Robinson (who is writing a book about Batavia) to Judy Dykman, July 1994.
16. Hartman, interviews; Edwin F. Holmes, "Birds and Flowers at El Roble," unpublished pamphlet. Bransford Scrapbook includes several small notices about the Holmes children visiting in Salt Lake City. It also includes a note about the family vacation to Yellowstone prior to Grace's marriage.
17. Lester, 112; "Mrs. Emery Comes Here to Wed"; "Mrs. Emery Married."
18. Malmquist, 212; *Biographical Record of Salt Lake City and Vicinity*, 211–12.
19. Hartman, interviews; Ross.
20. "Death Plucks at the Crown of Britain's King," *Salt Lake Herald*, 25 June 1902. Susie later talked about attending a coronation, and many people have assumed that because an invitation to Edward VII's ceremony appears in her scrapbook she was referring to that event. However, she had later connections with the British royal family that may indicate she actually attended the coronation of George VI in 1936. In 1938 his brother, Edward, who had abdicated to marry Wallace Simpson, approached her for money for one of his peace-making missions, and Susie apparently gave Wallace a tea set made from Park City silver. Ross; Lee Armstrong (daughter of Susie's adopted godson, Lory Snow), interview by Judy Dykman, 1996; "Florida Too Cold, New York Too Hot, and California Too Sad, So Globe Trotting Princess Comes Back Home," *Salt Lake Telegram*, 11 May 1938.
21. "Holmes-Bransford Trial Halted By Court."
22. Ross; "Mrs. Holmes Takes Stand as Witness"; *National Park Seminary* (Thompson-Ellis Co.,

1936), 19–25; roster of students in 1903 yearbook for National Park Seminary.
23. "Mrs. Holmes Takes Stand as Witness"; "Mrs. Holmes Ends Testimony in Trial," *Salt Lake Tribune*, 5 October 1918.
24. Kathryn A. Jacob, "High Society in Washington during the Gilded Age: Three Distrinct Aristocracies" (Ph.D. diss., Johns Hopkins University, 1986), 240–66; "Out of the West," *Buffalo Courier*, 17 February 1903; Cable, *Top Drawer American High Society*, xi, 29; "Utah's 'Silver Queen' Has Dazzled Washington," *Boston Globe*, 21 April 1902; and several other newspaper clippings in Bransford Scrapbook.
25. "'Silver Queen' of Utah Would Conquer Society," *New York Herald*, 2 January 1903.
26. Shiver reports that each family descended from a different son of Edward III, the Bransfords from Lionel and the Quessenburys from John of Gaunt.
27. Ross; Cable, *Top Drawer American High Society*, viii; "Genealogy and Arms of Well Known Salt Lake Families," in Bransford Scrapbook.

## Chapter 6

1. "Society Bud of Yesterday Holds Prestige Today," *Salt Lake Tribune*, 11 October 1925; "J. T. Harris, Arrow Press Manager, Dies" newspaper clipping, in possession of Richard L. Stevens; Richard L. Stevens, *Snow Hill Remembered* (Bowie, Md.: Heritage Books Inc., 1994), 110–13.
2. Mark Curtis (who has studied the Gardo extensively and is writing a book on the subject), interviews by Judy Dykman, 1994–1997. Curtis's interviews provided the background information on the Gardo and all stories about it not otherwise noted. One story claims its odd name came from a comment by one of the Young children, who observed that the house seemed to loom above the Beehive and Lion Houses as though it were guarding them. Another suggests Brigham simply named the house as he named the Beehive and Lion Houses.
3. Some believe Brigham had been dissatisfied with the plans and mocked the building during its construction, referring to it as his tabernacle organ.
4. Lester, 112; Susa Young Gates, "The Gardo House," *Improvement Era*, vol. 20, no. 12 (October 1917): 1099–1105; Joseph Heinerman, "Brigham Young's Grandest Residence, Amelia's Palace," *Montana, The Magazine of History* (winter 1979): 59; Poll, 267, 271; "Col. Holmes Buys Gardo House for $48,000," *Salt Lake Herald*, 5 May 1901; Curtis, interviews.
5. Sandy Brimhall (author of an unpublished manuscript on the Gardo House), interviews by Judy Dykman, 1994–1997; Millsaps, interviews; Gates, 1102–3; Lester, 112–15.
6. Birmingham, 230–31; Joseph J. Thorndike Jr., *The Magnificent Builders and Their Dream Houses* (New York: American Heritage, 1978), 323.
7. Cable, *Top Drawer American High Society*, 17; Thorndike, 320.
8. "The Leader of Society in Salt Lake," *Goodwin's Weekly*, n.d., in Bransford Scrapbook.
9. Brimhall, interviews; *Salt Lake City Blue Book*, 1900–1917. Lester gives a brief biography of many of these families.
10. Untitled newspaper clipping in Bransford Scrapbook.
11. *Salt Lake City Blue Book*, 1899–1901.
12. *Elite Magazine*, 15 March 1902; Lester, 114; "Unique Bedset of Pioneers Put on Show," *Salt Lake Tribune*, 24 July 1953; Brimhall and Curtis, interviews.
13. Observation of newspaper articles of the period reveals that Mormons, often even wealthy Mormons, socialized in their churches, while non-Mormons used their homes and their clubs.
14. Wells, interview; Lester, 44, 93–94, 113–15, 190–91; "Only One of Its Design in the World," newspaper clipping, 12 June 1903, in Bransford Scrapbook; Hartman, interviews. Descriptions of the Keith, Kearns, and Wall mansions are from Floralee Millsaps. To gauge the value of the pianos, an ad in *Argus*, 13 October 1907, listed a secondhand upright piano for 555 dollars and a one-quarter grand for 750 dollars.
15. Untitled articles from *Elite Magazine* in Bransford Scrapbook.
16. Cable, *Top Drawer American High Society*, vii. Bransford Scrapbook contains numerous descriptions of her parties and receptions and some of the affairs she also attended.

## Chapter 7

1. Cable, *Top Drawer American High Society*, viii.
2. Thorndike, 323.
3. Poll, 687.
4. Poll, 687; John McCormack, *Salt Lake City: The Gathering Place* (Woodland Hills, Calif.: Windsor Publications, 1980), 42; Ellsworth, 328, 348, 383–88. Alexander and Allen, 155–59.
5. Thomas Alexander, *Utah the Right Place* (Salt Lake City: Gibb Smith Peregrine Press, 1995),

180; Carol Cornwall Madsen (director of women's studies, Brigham Young University), interview by Judy Dykman, 1997.
6. "The Assouan Dam Won't Be in It," *Detroit Journal*, 14 November 1903.
7. McCormack, *Salt Lake City*, 47, 49.
8. "Former Utahn Answers the Call"; untitled articles in Bransford Scrapbook.
9. Some of Holmes's newspaper articles, undated and with no specific newspaper reference, appear in Bransford Scrapbook: "All Around the Globe," "Colonel Holmes Depicts Siberia," "Trip through Siberia," "Round the World," "Conditions in China," "Los Angeles Booming," "Through Siberia," and "Defends Russia."
10. "Former Utahn Answers the Call"; "Hitch in Canal Plan," *Salt Lake Tribune*, 21 January 1903; the following undated articles from unidentified newspapers are in Bransford Scrapbook: "Work on the National," "Coming Western Metropolis," "A Fine Start Is Made," "Water Question Was Well Aired," "Commercial Club Organizes for Its Water Campaign; Holmes Is to Lead," "Utah Lake Plan Costs $7,750,000," "New President of Commercial Club Has Closely Studied Public Problems," and an article mentioning Holmes's farming interests in Idaho; Floralee Millsaps, "Portrait of a Lovely Lady," manuscript on Jenny Judge Kearns. Millsaps extensively interviewed Jack Gallivan about Jenny.
11. Alexander and Allen, 142; "John Bransford, American Party Candidate," *Argus*, 10 September 1907.
12. John McCormack, "Red Lights in Zion: Salt Lake City's Stockade, 1908–11," *Utah Historical Quarterly* (spring 1982): 168. The Civic Betterment Union is sometimes referred to as the Civic Betterment League.
13. Sometimes it seems citizens simply cannot be satisfied. Samuel C. Park won the election and had a few years of peace until another group of citizens decided his police chief, Brigham F. Grant, Mormon President Heber J. Grant's half-brother, was too tough on crime. The jails were overcrowded with prostitutes and other offenders. One inmate even threatened suicide because of the cramped conditions in his cell. Grant's police were dubbed the "purity squad" and were cited for being too hard on the gamblers, saloons, breweries, racing facilities, and brothels, thus depriving the community of needed outlets for frustrations.
14. Alexander and Allen, 163–66; "Former Mayor Succumbs at 84," unidentified newspaper, May 1941.
15. Thorndike, 320.
16. Malmquist, 213; "Mrs. Emery-Holmes Public Reply to Hughes Supporters," *Salt Lake Tribune*, 9 September 1916; membership records of Ladies' Literary Club; membership records of Author's Club; Patricia Lyn Scott, "Eliza Kirtley Royle," *Worth Their Salt: Notable but Often Unnoted Women of Utah*, ed. Colleen Whitley (Logan: Utah State University Press, 1996), 51–52; Patricia Lyn Scott (archivist for the state of Utah), telephone interview by Colleen Whitley, 1997; Beverly Lund (current historian for the Ladies' Literary Club), telephone interview by Colleen Whitley, 1997; "Beautify Salt Lake City," unidentified newspaper, 27 December 1903; untitled article from unidentified newspaper, in Bransford Scrapbook; Armstrong, interview. Armstrong said her mother, Corney, who became Susie's good friend, was from an Eastern family and had a good education. Corney observed that Susie's grammar was definitely substandard and her vocabulary limited; Corney assumed many of Susie's airs and eccentricities were designed to conceal her inadequacies.
17. Lamb, interviews; Chretien, interview. Susie's riding habit was among the clothes donated to the Daughters of Utah Pioneers. Bransford Scrapbook mentions that a Ms. Bowers, a golfer from California, stayed with her in the Gardo.
18. "Fan Annoyed General," newspaper clipping, and untitled article from *Goodwin's Weekly*, both in Bransford Scrapbook.
19. Cable, *Top Drawer American High Society*, 168–75.
20. Ross; Sue Sellers (the gardener's daughter), interview by Judy Dykman, 1995; Park City Museum staff, interview by Judy Dykman, 1993; *Biographical Record of Salt Lake City*, 211–12.
21. "Lory Snow Dies, U.S. Air Pioneer," *Hartford Times*, 7 May 1954. The Wright brothers did buy one of Lory's engines and used it in subsequent flights. It is now on display at the Smithsonian Institution in Washington, D.C.
22. Armstrong, interview; Mrs. M. C. Gardner (Lory Snow's daughter), interview by Judy Dykman, 1997.
23. Charlie Arsteen, "Natural Bridges of White Canyon: A Diary of H. L. A. Culmer, 1905," *Utah Historical Quarterly*, vol. 40, no. 1 (winter 1972): 55–87; Mark Jenkins (of the National Geographic Society) to Judy Dykman, 1996.
24. Frances Steiner, interview by Judy Dykman, 1997; miscellaneous articles in Bransford Scrapbook; Bureau of Census, Coronado, California (home of Hellen White), 1920; Bureau of Census, Hollywood, California (home

of Carleton Holmes), 1920. The Los Angeles telephone directory on microfilm at the LDS Family History Library also listed Carleton as a photographer.

## Chapter 8

1. Lamb, interviews; untitled newspaper clippings, in Bransford's scrapbook.
2. J. Robinson, 144, 162; Lamb, interviews; "Utah Woman Wed in Paris to Physician," *Salt Lake Tribune*, 20 July 1930.
3. Eugene Francis, "Tragedies of the Stage," *American Weekly*, 8 May 1949, 6–7; "Why Adele Blood Deserted the Stage," *Denver Examiner*, magazine section, 3 February 1918.
4. *Encyclopedia Americana*, s.v. "earthquake" and "San Francisco." *Americana* cites a second source that puts the fire damage at nearly $350 million.
5. *The World Almanac and Book of Facts, 1991*, 444; Ross; "Now the Romantic 'Silver Queen'—Aged 75—May Ditch Her Russian Prince to Marry Boy!" *San Francisco Chronicle*, 10 February 1935; autograph in Bransford's scrapbook signed by Ira Blood; "Personal Mention" *Greenville (Calif.) Bulletin*, 17 May 1882, 6 September 1882, 17 July 1895.
6. Davis starred in several plays and movies, including the silent film version of *King of Kings*.
7. Adele Blood file in Billie Rose Theatre Collection, New York City Public Library for the Performing Arts, Lincoln Center.
8. "Wife's Mental Strength Equal to Husband's, Decides Judge in Bransford Suit," *Salt Lake Herald*, 26 January 1919. Several clippings in Bransford Scrapbook mention Grace during these years.
9. Birmingham, 231–32. Such excesses were often justified as providing employment for caterers, waiters, entertainers, and others who needed jobs. To their credit, some members of the upper class recognized the fallacies in this logic and did something better. In the year of her own coming out party, Mary Harriman, daughter of railroad tycoon Edward Harriman, realized many young women would be holding similar parties and asked, "What can we do to make it a particularly good year, and to show that we recognize an obligation to the community besides having a good time?" She answered her own question by founding the Junior League for the Promotion of Settlement Houses, today known simply as the Junior League.
10. Gallivan, interview; Cable, *Top Drawer American High Society*, 23, 124–26; Birmingham, 282; Hartman, interviews; J. Robinson, 330.
11. "Mrs. Holmes Takes Stand as Witness"; Louise Grace Emery Bransford, probate case 9207; "Bransford Takes Stand," *Salt Lake Tribune*, 11 October 1918; "Husband Weeps as He Testifies in Trial."
12. Louise Grace Emery Bransford, probate case 9207; "Spectators Barred from Bransford Hearing," *Deseret News*, 11 October 1918; "Bransford Adds to His Testimony," *Salt Lake Tribune*, 15 October 1918; "Florist Testifies in Will Contest," *Salt Lake Tribune*, 22 October 1918; "Actress to Testify in Bransford Hearing," *Deseret News*, 10 October 1918.
13. Hartman, interviews; Society columns for *Deseret News* and *Salt Lake Tribune*, 6 September 1904; "Testifies Woman Was above Average Intelligence," *Deseret News*, 1 November 1918. Judy Dykman scanned the newspapers in 1904 looking for an engagement announcement and found only a wedding announcement on September 6.
14. "Spectators Barred from Bransford Hearing"; "Bransford Takes Stand"; "Testified Woman Was above Average Intelligence"; "Actress Testifies in Bransford Case," *Salt Lake Tribune*, 19 October 1918; "Husband Weeps as He Testifies in Trial"; "Magnificent New Apartment House," *Salt Lake Tribune*, 27 July 1902; Suzanne Emery-Holmes's affidavit in Louise Grace Emery Bransford, probate case 9207; "Defense Opens in Fight for Estate," *Salt Lake Tribune*, 2 November 1918; "Holmes Hearing Is Renewed in Court," *Salt Lake Tribune*, 29 October 1918; "Witnesses Defend Mrs. Bransford in Trial," *Deseret News*, 4 November 1918.
15. Hartman and Lamb, interviews.
16. The Clarence Bamberger, Pat Hogle, and Teddy Brown families, interviews by Judy Dykman, 1997; Jack Goodman, "House in the Cottonwoods Splendidly Isolated," *Salt Lake Tribune*, 27 July 1997; Lester, 192–93; Utah Heritage Foundation, walking tour notes, 1995.
17. Lamb, interviews.
18. Sellers, interview.
19. Newspaper clippings in Bransford Scrapbook. The Shiplers eventually donated all of their glass negatives to the Utah State Historical Society.
20. Hartman and Lamb, interviews.
21. Lamb, interviews.

## Chapter 9

1. Hartman, interviews.
2. It is uncertain whether she was incapable of having a baby or whether she and Wallace simply

recognized her heart problems would make a pregnancy dangerous.

3. Wallace Bransford and Suzanne Emery-Holmes's affidavits in Louise Grace Emery Bransford, probate case 9207; "Bransford Takes Stand"; "Bransford Adds to His Testimony."

4. Wallace Bransford and Suzanne Emery-Holmes's affidavits in Louise Grace Emery Bransford, probate case 9207; "Bransford Takes Stand"; "Bransford Adds to His Testimony"; Mrs. Bransford Dies in California," *Salt Lake Tribune*, 25 October 1917.

5. "Actress Testifies in Bransford Case."

6. Wallace Bransford and Suzanne Emery-Holmes's affidavits in Louise Grace Emery Bransford, probate case 9207; proprietors of resort in Hot Springs, Virginia, telephone interview by Judy Dykman, 1996.

7. Shipler photos of Gardo celebration, c. 1917.

8. Suzanne Emery-Holmes's affidavit in Louise Grace Emery Bransford, probate case 9207. The following newspaper articles provide insight into Grace's and Wallace's relationship and the information for the rest of this chapter on the trial. It lasted from September 1918 to January 1919. The headlines themselves tell a great part of the story:

    From the *Salt Lake Tribune*: "Mrs. Holmes Sues Bransford for $400,000," 21 January 1918; "Holmes-Bransford Trial Begins Here," 17 September 1918; "Defense Loses in Will Case Decision"; "Mrs. Holmes Takes Stand as Witness"; "Mrs. Holmes Again on Witness Stand"; "Mrs. Holmes Ends Testimony in Trial"; "Bransford Takes Stand"; "Bransford Adds to His Testimony"; "Attorney's Illness Halts Will Case," 16 October 1918; "Actress Testifies in Bransford Case"; "Florist Testifies in Will Contest"; "Holmes Hearing Is Renewed in Court"; "Mrs. Homes May Finish Case Today," 30 October 1918; "Defense Opens in Fight for Estate," 2 November 1918; "Fight for Estate Still Drags On," 5 November 1918; "Bransford Attorney Will Case Witness," 8 November 1918; "Fight for Estate Nearing the End," 9 November 1918; "Epidemic Delays Bransford Hearing," 13 November 1918; "Bransford Wins Suit for Estate," 26 January 1919.

    From the *Deseret News*: "Mrs. Holmes Tells Story of Adoption of Foster Daughter," 2 October 1918; "Holmes-Bransford Trial Halted by Court"; "Cross Examination of Mrs. Holmes in Trial," 7 October 1918; "Cross Examining of Mrs. Holmes Continues," 8 October 1918; "Actress to Testify in Bransford Hearing," 10 October 1918; "Spectators Barred from Bransford Hearing"; "Wallace Bransford Is Still on Stand," 14 October 1918; "Husband Weeps as He Testifies in Trial," 15 October 1918; "Illness of Attorney Delays Holmes Case," 16 October 1918; "Actress Testifies Mrs. Bransford Felt 'Blue,'" 19 October 1918; "Testifies Woman Was above Average"; "Progress Is Made in Hearing of Will Case," 2 November 1918; "Witnesses Defend Mrs. Bransford in Trial"; "Nevada Solon Takes Witness Stand in Bransford Case," 6 November 1918; "Witnesses Testify that Mrs. Bransford Directed Work Intelligently," 7 November 1918; "Bransford Trial Drawing Near to Close," 8 November 1918; "Illness of Witness Holds Bransford Case," 12 November 1918; "Arguments in Holmes Case Finished," 24 December 1918; "Mrs. Holmes Loses Suit against Bransford," 25 January 1919.

9. Suzanne Emery-Holmes's affidavit in Louise Grace Emery Bransford, probate case 9207; Hartman and Lamb, interviews; "Why Adele Blood Deserted the Stage"; "One Hundred Fifty Years of *Town and Country Magazine*—The Rich in America," Arts and Entertainment Channel, 1996; Thorndike, 314–23.

10. David B. Dee (former circuit court judge), telephone interview by Colleen Whitley, 1997; "Spectators Barred from Bransford Hearing."

11. "Actress Testifies Mrs. Bransford Felt 'Blue.'"

12. "Mrs. Holmes Backs Film Venture, Miss Adele Blood Will Be Star," *Salt Lake Tribune*, 29 January 1918; Francis.

13. "Mrs. Holmes Loses Bransford Case," Salt Lake Telgram, 26 January 1919.

14. "Mrs. Holmes Loses Suit against Bransford"; "Bransford Wins Suit for Estate"; "Mrs. Susanna Holmes Loses in $800,000 Bransford Suit," *Salt Lake Herald*, 26 January 1919.

15. "Mrs. Susanna Holmes Loses in $800,000 Bransford Suit."

16. Hartman and Lamb, interviews.

## Chapter 10

1. Hartman and Lamb, interviews.

2. Marilyn Robinson, interview by Judy Dykman, 1995; Steiner, interview.

3. "Historic Landmark Changes Hands, Amelia's Palace Now Music School," *Salt Lake Herald*, 17 May 1920; Lester, 97; Hartman and Lamb, interviews.

4. Pasadena Centennial Room and clipping file, Pasadena, California, Public Library; "Showcase

of Interior Design, Notes on El Roble Residence," 1975, Pasadena Junior Philharmonic Committee information file, Pasadena, California, Public Library; "Romantic History Adds Glamour to Eleventh Showcase Design," *Pasadena Star*, 17 April 1975; Armstrong, Hartman, and Lamb, interviews.

5. Gallivan, interview; Holmes, "Birds and Flowers."
6. Ann Scheid, *Pasadena, Crown of the Valley* (Northridge, Calif.: Windsor Publications, 1986), 96, 109, 116; "America's 'Silver Queen' Passes through Adelaide," *Salt Lake Tribune*, 25 August 1930. Years later Susie commented that on her honeymoon with her third husband, Rada, he was the only man who appreciated her dozens of dresses and many accessories.
7. "Now the Romantic 'Silver Queen'—Aged 75— May Ditch Her Russian Prince to Marry a Boy!"; Adolph Busch, qtd. in Scheid, 95.
8. *California Life*, 21 March 1925, 1.
9. Scheid, 112, 114, 120, 164.
10. "Showcase of Interior Design, Notes on El Roble Residence."
11. Edwin F. Holmes, probate case 14118–14132; "Col. Holmes, Once of Salt Lake, Dies East," *Salt Lake Tribune*, 2 October 1925.

## Chapter 11

1. Cable, interview. The term "walker" is still in use. A reader of *Parade Magazine* (15 December 1996) asked in "Personality Parade," "Is Maurice Templeton a man of limited means who is only a walker for Jacqueline Onassis?" *Parade* assured the reader that Templeton had plenty of money of his own. The practice is apparently becoming institutionalized; cruise lines are hiring men to provide dancing partners for older women. While walker appears to be a more recent term than gigolo, both practices have apparently been around for a long time. See Korky Vann, "'Gentlemen Hosts' Dance Their Way to Exotic Ports of Call," *Salt Lake Tribune*, 26 October 1997, originally published in the *Hartford Courant*.
2. "Silver Queen Widow Again," *Pasadena Sun News*, 24 March 1935; "Prince & Wife Decide to 'Make Up,'" *New York Times*, 26 August 1915; "Prince Vladimir N. Engalitcheff," *New York Times*, 8 March 1923; "Now the Romantic 'Silver Queen'"; "Asks Russian Divorce Trial," *New York Times*, 2 December 1915; "Utah's 'Silver Queen,' 74, Weds 60 Year Old Prince," *Salt Lake Tribune*, 21 October 1933. Evelyn had her own problems that may have made her a difficult parent. Following her divorce she sent all her society contacts printed cards to tell them she was now available.
3. "Now the Romantic 'Silver Queen.'" As of this writing, Danise has never reappeared, dead or alive.
4. Prince Sherbatoff (of the Russian Nobility Organization), telephone interview by Judy Dykman, 1997; Hartman and Lamb, interviews; "Now the Romantic 'Silver Queen.'"
5. Cable, *Top Drawer American High Society*, 198; "Utah's 'Silver Queen,' 74, Weds 60 Year Old Prince."
6. "Mrs. Emery-Holmes Weds Dr. R. N. Delitch," *New York Times*, 20 July 1930; "Mrs. Emery-Holmes Is Bride of Physician at 71," *Salt Lake Tribune*, 19 July 1930; "Silver King Mine Owner Home with Surgeon Husband," *Pasadena Star News*, 7 October 1930; untitled article, *Pasadena Star News*, 5 February 1933; "Religious Ceremony Seals Nuptials of 'Silver Queen,'" *New York Herald*, n.d.; Radovan Delitch to Radisave (no surname given), 1930, trans. from Serbian by Richard Woodruff.
7. Lamb and Hartman, interviews; Michael Delich to Judy Dykman, January 1997. Michael Delich was the little boy Rada and Susie invited to come with them to Paris. When he learned that Dykman was researching their lives, he asked a local genealogist to put him in touch with her. When she called, he asked, "What would my life be like if I had gone with Rada when I was seven?" The question, while intriguing, is impossible to answer.
8. "Mrs. Emery-Holmes Weds Dr. R. N. Delitch"; "Mrs. Emery-Holmes Is Bride of Physician at 71"; "Silver King Mine Owner Home with Surgeon Husband"; untitled article, *Pasadena Star News*, 5 February 1933; "Religious Ceremony Seals Nuptials of 'Silver Queen'"; "Utah Woman Wed in Paris to Physician"; Hartman, interviews.
9. Scheid, 156; Lamb and Hartman, interviews. Nellie maintained the whole thing was Susie's fault for marrying a foreigner.
10. Culver Sherrill, *Crimes Without Punishment* (Hicksville, New York: Exposition Press, 1977), 14–17; Hartman, interviews; Angelo Boncoraglio (Sherrill's butler) to Judy Dykman, 1996.
11. Radovan Delitch to Bill O'Conner (Grizelle Houston Lamb's second husband), 11 November 1932.
12. "Ended Life at Sea on Christmas Eve," *New York Times*, 1 January 1933; "Former Husband of

'Silver Queen' Dies on Ocean," *Salt Lake Tribune*, 28 December 1932.
13. Hartman, interviews; Cable, *Top Drawer American High Society*, 22.
14. Ross; "America's 'Silver Queen' Passes through Adelaide"; "'Silver Queen' Seeks Divorce," *Salt Lake Telegram*, 1 November 1932; "Drawing Hidden Fortune from Earth Finest Method, Avers 'Silver' Queen," *Salt Lake Telegram*, 6 September 1932; Hartman and Lamb, interviews; Lennox Tierney (retired University of Utah professor), interview by Judy Dykman, 1996. One of the items sold at the El Roble auction was a large, full-length portrait of Susie. Both Ross and Hartman report that the buyer had Susie's face painted over and replaced with her own; Susie apparently found the whole thing very funny.
15. *Capitol Losses: A Cultural History of Washington's Destroyed Buildings* (Washington, D.C.: Smithsonian Institution, 1979), 133, reports that Tom Walsh spent forty thousand dollars on a party for the Russian ambassador prior to World War I. Only forty-eight guests were invited, but Walsh made sure his daughter's home resembled a palace and imported European flowers to decorate it. Tragically, Walsh married his only child, Evalyn, to a man from a prominent family, Edward McLean, a spoiled child who was an alcoholic by age twenty. During the next thirty-five years, Evalyn and her husband wasted their families' combined fortunes, one hundred million dollars, in entertaining. Edward died in an asylum and Evalyn lived in a small home in Georgetown until she died in 1947. If Susie could have lived to see this tragedy, she might have thought of the adage "What goes around, comes around," since it was Walsh who blackballed her with Washington society.

## Chapter 12

1. Hartman, interviews; Zua Cram (a Lamb family friend), interview by Judy Dykman, 1996. By now Susie preferred to be called Suzanne, and the press usually used that name.
2. "Prince Engalitcheff Wed," *New York Times*, 19 October 1933; "One Hundred Fifty Years of *Town and Country Magazine*"; Cable, *Top Drawer American High Society*, 194.
3. Hartman, interviews.
4. Sherrill, 68; Ringholz, *Diggings and Doings*, 63; Hartman, interviews; Richard Nevins (a member of old Pasadena's society), telephone interviews by Judy Dykman, 1997.
5. "Now the Romantic 'Silver Queen'"; Cable, *Top Drawer American High Society*, 59–60.
6. Hartman, interviews; "One Time Consul of Czarist Russia in Chicago—Was an Officer in Imperial Army," *New York Times*, 28 March 1935.
7. After Nicki's death many in the Russian Nobility Organization were embarrassed to claim they knew him. Some of them attended his funeral, but they all knew the stories of his many shenanigans, especially those involving women. One of those stories was eventually given real credibility. Nicki had at least one illegitimate son, whom he allowed to use his name when his only legitimate child died. The boy grew to manhood, became an engineer, and also married a wealthy woman. For years he avoided meeting dispossessed Russian royalty and did not socialize with the other Engalitcheffs who had emigrated to America after the Russian Revolution. Then, as the Soviet Union fell and enormous problems developed in Russia, he and his wife set out to clear the tarnished Engalitcheff name. More than sixty years after Nicki's death, his illegitimate son donated several million dollars to impoverished children in Russia. Prince Sherbatoff of the Russian Nobility Organization says it was a generous deed that went a long way to restore his father's branch of the family to respectability. Sherbatoff, interview; Nicholas Engalitcheff (member of the Engalitcheff family), telephone interview by Judy Dykman, 1996.
8. "Niece of John S. Bransford," *Salt Lake Tribune*, 28 May 1913; "Mrs. Holmes Backs Film Venture, Miss Adele Blood Will Be Star"; "Actress Testifies Mrs. Bransford Felt 'Blue'"; "Attorney's Illness Halts Will Case"; "Bransford Wins Suit for Estate"; Adele Blood file, Billie Rose Theatre Collection.
9. Francis, 6–7; "Why Adele Blood Deserted the Stage"; Adele Blood file, Billie Rose Theatre Collection.
10. Hartman, interviews.
11. Hartman and Lamb, interviews; Dick Stevens (Hartman family historian), interview by Judy Dykman, 1995; Suzanne B. Engalitcheff to Culver Sherrill, 1938–1942, in possession of Lewis Sherrill (Culver's nephew).

## Chapter 13

1. Marvin J. Bertoch, *Salt Lake City: This Is the Place* (unpublished manuscript, n.d.), Marvin J. Bertoch papers, special collections, Marriott Library, University of Utah, Salt Lake City.

2. "Florida Too Cold, New York Too Hot, and California Too Sad, So Globe Trotting Princess Comes Back Home," *Salt Lake Telegram*, 11 May 1938.
3. Julia Bertoch (daughter of manicurist), interview by Judy Dykman, 1996.
4. Hartman and Lamb, interviews; Blaine Simons (teller with Tracy Collins Bank in the 1930s and 1940s), interviews by Judy Dykman, 1995–1996; S. Engalitcheff to Sherrill, 19 November 1938, in possession of Judy Dykman.
5. Hartman, interviews; Sherrill, 74.
6. Ross. He was probably right. Only a few years later, Patrick Denis's stories of his Auntie Mame made a successful Broadway play and later a motion picture.
7. "Early Mayor of Salt Lake City Dies."
8. Lamb, Hartman, and Simons, interviews.
9. Lamb, interviews.
10. S. Engalitcheff to Sherrill, 1 August 1942; "Death Comes to Utah's Famed 'Silver Queen,'" *Salt Lake Tribune*, 5 August 1942; "'Silver Queen' of Utah Closes Famed Career," *Park Record*, 6 August 1942; Suzanne B. Engalitcheff, death certificate, Department of Vital Statistics, Hartford, Connecticut; Hartman, interviews.

## Epilogue

1. Hartman and Lamb, interviews; Suzanne B. Engalitcheff, probate case 24672, 1942, Third District Court, Salt Lake County, Utah; Suzanne B. Engalitcheff, probate case P-5011, 1942, Pasadena, Los Angeles County, California; "Estate Left by Princess Set at $65,918," *Salt Lake Tribune*, 4 June 1943.
2. Hartman, interviews; S. Engalitcheff, probate case 24672.
3. Hartman, interviews; Ringholz to Dykman; Ringholz, telephone interview by Judy Dykman, 1995. Ray Ringholz interviewed Wallace Bransford prior to his death, and he recalled many family stories dealing with Susie.
4. Lamb, Hartman, and Simons, interviews.
5. "'Silver Queen' Wills 4 Million to Manager," *Los Angeles Evening Herald and Express*, 25 August 1942; "Manager Made Sole Heir of Silver Queen," *Salt Lake Tribune*, 9 August 1942; "Receives Title to Millions," *Salt Lake Tribune*, n.d.; "'Silver Queen' Wills Millions to Manager of Estate," *Salt Lake Tribune*, 26 August 1942; Hartman and Lamb, interviews.
6. Merna Hansen (LDS Real Estate Department), interview by Judy Dykman, 1996; V. Murray, interviews.
7. Boncoraglio to Dykman; Frances Darger (daughter of Susie's Salt Lake City attorney), interview by Judy Dykman, 1995. Darger's father helped Sherrill settle the estate in Utah and later negotiated the sale of the Sherrill Apartments. Sherrill was so pleased with his help that he invited some of the family to visit him in Taorima; Darger remembers a letter from her sister saying it was a lovely place and Sherrill was a gracious host.
8. Boncoraglio to Dykman; Lewis Sherrill (a nephew of Culver), telephone interview by Judy Dykman, 1996.
9. Boncoraglio to Dykman; Margorie Kellogg (friend of the Sherrill family) to Angelo Boncoraglio, in possession of Judy Dykman.
10. Lamb and Hartman, interviews.
11. "Kentucky Colony of City Prominent in Salt Lake's Business and Social Life," newspaper clipping, in Emery-Holmes Scrapbook. Various articles in Margaret Lester's *Brigham Street* discuss the contributions of Salt Lake City's wealthy families to the community.

# Bibliography

## Books

Alexander, Thomas. *Utah the Right Place*. Salt Lake City: Gibbs Smith, 1995.

Alexander, Thomas and James Allen. *Mormons and Gentiles, A History of Salt Lake City*. Boulder, Colo.: Pruett Publishing Company, 1984.

Arrington, Leonard. *Great Basin Kingdom*. Lincoln: University of Nebraska Press, 1966.

*Biographical Record of Salt Lake City and Vicinity*. Chicago: National Historic Records Company, 1902.

Birmingham, Stephen. *America's Secret Aristocracy*. Boston: Little, Brown, and Company, 1987.

Cable, Mary. *Top Drawer American High Society from the Gilded Age to the Roaring Twenties*. New York: Anteneum, 1984.

*Capitol Losses: A Cultural History of Washington's Destroyed Buildings*. Washington, D.C.: Smithsonian Institution, 1979.

Carpenter (first name unknown). *History of Mendocino County and Lake County*. Mendocino Historical Society, 1994 (reprint).

Carr, Stephen L. *Utah's Ghost Rails*. Salt Lake City: Western Epics, 1989.

Ellsworth, S. George. *Utah's Heritage*. Salt Lake City: Peregrine Smith, 1977.

*Encyclopedia Americana*. 1992.

Farriss and Smith (first names unknown). *History of Plumas County, California, 1882*. Burbank, Calif.: Howell-North Press, 1988 (reprint).

Green, Harvey. *The Light of the Home*. New York: Pantheon Books, 1983.

*History of Ray County, Mo*. St. Louis: Missouri Historical Company, 1881.

Kunz, Jeffrey R. M. *The American Medical Association Family Medical Guide*. New York: Random House, 1982.

Lester, Margaret. *Brigham Street*. Salt Lake City: Utah State Historical Society, 1979.

Malmquist, O. N. *The First One Hundred Years: A History of the Salt Lake Tribune*. Salt Lake City: Utah State Historical Society, 1971.

McCormack, John. *Salt Lake City: The Gathering Place*. Woodland Hills, Calif.: Windsor Publications, 1980.

McCutcheon, Marc. *The Writer's Guide to Everyday Life in the 1800s*. Cincinnati: Writer's Digest Books, 1993.

McPherson, James M. *Battle Cry of Freedom*. New York and Oxford: Oxford University Press, 1988.

Meltzer, Milton. *Bread—and Roses*. New York: New American Library, 1967.

*National Park Seminary*. Thompson-Ellis Co., 1936.

*Polk Directory for Salt Lake City*. Kansas City, Mo.: R. L. Polk and Company, 1894.

Poll, Richard D., ed. *Utah's History*. Provo, Utah: Brigham Young University Press, 1978.

Reiter, Joan S. *The Women*. Alexandria, Va.: Time-Life Books, 1979.

*Richmond, Ray County, after the Civil War*. Ray County Historical Society, 1990.

Ringholz, Raye C. *Diggins and Doings in Park City*. Park City, Utah: by author, 1983.

Robinson, Judith. *The Hearsts, An American Dynasty*. New York: Avon Books, 1991.

*Salt Lake City Blue Book, 1894–1917*. Salt Lake City: Salt Lake Lithographing Co.

*San Francisco Blue Book, 1875–78*. Microfilm copy, LDS Family History Library, Salt Lake City, Utah.

Sanborn Map Company. *Salt Lake City, Utah*. New York: The Company, 1890, 1894.

Scheid, Ann. *Pasadena, Crown of the Valley*. Northridge, Calif.: Windsor Publications, 1986.

Sherrill, Culver. *Crimes without Punishment*. Hicksville, New York: Exposition Press, 1977.

Shiver, John A. *Bransford Family History*. Kentucky: McDowell Publishing Company, 1981.

Stevens, Richard L. *Snow Hill Remembered*. Bowie, Maryland: Heritage Books Inc., 1994.

Thompson, George A. and Fraser Buck. *Treasure Mountain Home, Park City Revisited*. Salt Lake City: Dream Garden Press, 1993.

Thorndike, Joseph J. Jr. *The Magnificent Builders and Their Dream Houses*. New York: American Heritage, 1978.

*Utah at the World's Columbian Exposition*. Salt Lake City: Salt Lake Lithographing Co., 1894.

*The World Almanac and Book of Facts, 1991*.

## Articles

"Action to Recover," *Plumas (Calif.) National Bulletin*, 28 November 1901.

"Actress Testifies in Bransford Case," *Salt Lake Tribune*, 19 October 1918.

"Actress Testifies Mrs. Bransford Felt 'Blue,'" *Deseret News*, 19 October 1918.

"Actress to Testify in Bransford Hearing," *Deseret News*, 10 October 1918.

Advertisements, *Argus*, 13 October 1907.

"Albion B. Emery," *Tullidge's Quarterly Magazine*, 1902, 502–3. Salt Lake City: Utah State Historical Society.

"Albion Bernard Emery," *Biographical Record of Salt Lake City and Vicinity*. Chicago: National Historic Record Company, 1902.

"Albion Emery," *Park Record*, 16 June 1894.

"America's 'Silver Queen' Passes through Adelaide," *Salt Lake Tribune*, 25 August 1930.

"Andrew Carnegie," *Biography*. Arts and Entertainment Channel, 1994.

"Arguments in Holmes Case Finished," *Deseret News*, 24 December 1918.

Arsteen, Charlie. "Natural Bridges of White Canyon: A Diary of H. L. A. Culmer, 1905," *Utah Historical Quarterly* vol. 40, no. 1 (winter 1972).

"Asks Russian Divorce Trial," *New York Times*, 2 December 1915.

"The Assouan Dam Won't Be in It," *Detroit Journal*, 14 November 1903.

"Attorney's Illness Halts Will Case," *Salt Lake Tribune*, 16 October 1918.

"A Big Fortune at Stake," *Salt Lake Tribune*, 18 December 1894.

"A Big Fortune Involved," *Salt Lake Tribune*, 22 September 1894.

"Bransford Adds to His Testimony," *Salt Lake Tribune*, 15 October 1918.

"Bransford Attorney Will Case Witness," *Salt Lake Tribune*, 8 November 1918.

"Bransford Takes Stand," *Salt Lake Tribune*, 11 October 1918.

"Bransford Trial Drawing Near to Close," *Deseret News*, 8 November 1918.

"Bransford Wins Suit for Estate," *Salt Lake Tribune*, 26 January 1919.

Brownlow, John B. "Thos. L. Bransford and Col. Colyar's Sketches," unidentified Tennessee newspaper, 19 December 1903.

*California Life*, 21 October 1922, 21 March 1925.

"Chambers Loses the Suit," *Salt Lake Tribune*, 21 January 1895.

"Chambers on the Stand," *Salt Lake Tribune*, 19 December 1894.

"Chambers vs. Emery," *Pacific Reporter*, vol. 45. Salt Lake City: Utah State Law Library.

"Col. Holmes Buys Gardo House for $48,000," *Salt Lake Herald*, 5 May 1901.

"Col. Holmes, Once of Salt Lake, Dies East," *Salt Lake Tribune*, 2 October 1925.

Colyar, A. S. "Reminiscences of Distinguished Men, No. 10," unidentified Nashville, Tennessee, newspaper, n.d.

"Cross Examination of Mrs. Holmes in Trial," *Deseret News*, 7 October 1918.

"Cross Examining of Mrs. Holmes Continues," *Deseret News*, 8 October 1918.

"Death Comes to Utah's Famed 'Silver Queen,'" *Salt Lake Tribune*, 5 August 1942.

"Death of Albion B. Emery," *Salt Lake Herald*, 14 June 1894.

"Death of Hon. A. B. Emery," *Park Record*, 16 June 1894.

"Death of Honorable R. C. Chambers," *The Mining Review*. Salt Lake City, 15 April 1901.

"Death Plucks at the Crown of Britain's King," *Salt Lake Herald*, 25 June 1902.

"Defense Loses in Will Case Decision," *Salt Lake Tribune*, 1 October 1918.

"Defense Opens in Fight for Estate," *Salt Lake Tribune*, 2 November 1918.

"Drawing Hidden Fortune from Earth Finest Method, Avers 'Silver' Queen," *Salt Lake Telegram*, 6 September 1932.

"Early Mayor of Salt Lake City Dies," *Salt Lake Tribune*, 22 May 1941.

"Edwin Francis Holmes," *Pasadena Star News*, 16 March 1916.

*Elite Magazine*, 15 March 1902.

Emery-Holmes, Suzanne. "Beautify Salt Lake City," unidentified newspaper, 27 December 1903.

"Ended Life at Sea on Christmas Eve," *New York Times*, 1 January 1933.

"Epidemic Delays Bransford Hearing," *Salt Lake Tribune*, 13 November 1918.

"Estate Left by Princess Set at $65,918," *Salt Lake Tribune*, 4 June 1943.

"Fight for Estate Nearing the End," *Salt Lake Tribune*, 9 November 1918.

"Fight for Estate Still Drags On," *Salt Lake Tribune*, 5 November 1918.

"Florida Too Cold, New York Too Hot and California Too Sad, So Globe Trotting Princess Comes Back Home," *Salt Lake Telegram*, 11 May 1938.

"Florist Testifies in Will Contest," *Salt Lake Tribune*, 22 October 1918.

"For a Fortune," *Park Record*, 22 September 1894.

"For Love and Affection," *Deseret News*, 20 October 1899.

"Former Husband of 'Silver Queen' Dies on Ocean," *Salt Lake Tribune*, 28 December 1932.

"Former Mayor Succumbs at 84," unidentified newspaper, May 1941.

"Former Utahn Answers the Call," *Park Record*, 2 October 1925.

Francis, Eugene. "Tragedies of the Stage," *American Weekly*, 8 May 1949.

Gates, Susa Young, "The Gardo House," *Improvement Era*, vol. 20 (October 1917).

Godfrey, Margaret. "The Silver Queen," *Salt Lake City*, September/October 1993.

Goodman, Jack. "House in the Cottonwoods Splendidly Isolated," *Salt Lake Tribune*, 27 July 1997.

*Greenville (Calif.) Bulletin*. 13 April 1881, 25 April 1881, 14 September 1881, 13 December 1882, 18 April 1883, 19 March 1884, 4 June 1884, 7 January 1885, 4 February 1885, 1 July 1885, 15 July 1885, 24 November 1886, 8 December 1886.

Heinerman, Joseph. "Brigham Young's Grandest Residence, Amelia's Palace," *Montana, The Magazine of Western History*, Winter 1979.

"Historic Landmark Changes Hands, Amelia's Palace Now Music School," *Salt Lake Herald*, 17 May 1920.

"Hitch in Canal Plan," *Salt Lake Tribune*, 21 January 1903.

"Holmes Hearing Is Renewed in Court," *Salt Lake Tribune*, 29 October 1918.

"Holmes-Bransford Trial Begins Here," *Salt Lake Tribune*, 17 September 1918.

"Holmes-Bransford Trial Halted by Court," *Deseret News*, 3 October 1918.

"Honorable Albion Bernard Emery," *Proceedings of the Grand Lodge Free and Accepted Masons of Utah*. Salt Lake City: Utah Masonic Lodge, 1896.

"Husband Weeps as He Testifies in Trial," *Deseret News*, 15 October 1918.

"Illness of Attorney Delays Holmes Case," *Deseret News*, 16 October 1918.

"Illness of Witness Holds Bransford Case," *Deseret News*, 12 November 1918.

"John Bransford," *Plumas (Calif.) National Bulletin*, 10 January 1895.

"John Bransford," *Salt Lake Tribune*, 24 May 1941.

"John Bransford, American Party Candidate," *Argus*, 10 September 1907.

"John Hayward Sheets," *Journal of the American Medical Association*, 5 May 1928.

"The Leader of Society in Salt Lake," *Goodwin's Weekly*, n.d.

"Leaders Laud Bransford at Final Rites," *Salt Lake Tribune*, 24 May 1941.

"Legal Record," *Argus*, 29 December 1894.

"Lory Snow Dies, U.S. Air Pioneer," *Hartford Times*, 7 May 1954.

"Magnificent New Apartment House," *Salt Lake Tribune*, 27 July 1902.

"Manager Made Sole Heir of Silver Queen," *Salt Lake Tribune*, 9 August 1942.

McCormack, John. "Red Lights in Zion: Salt Lake City's Stockade, 1908–11," *Utah Historical Quarterly*, Spring 1982.

"Men and Events Linked with Great Mines of Park City," *Park Record*, 5 June 1931.

"Milford Bransford," *Park Record*, 26 May 1894.

"Milford Bransford," *Salt Lake Tribune*, 26 May 1894.

"Milford Bransford Deceased," *Plumas (Calif.) Independent*, 26 May 1894.

"Milton Hershey," *Biography*. Arts and Entertainment Channel, 1994.

"Mrs. Bransford Dies in California," *Salt Lake Tribune*, 25 October 1917.

"Mrs. Emery Comes Here to Wed," unidentified New York newspaper, n.d. Courtesy of Stella Inge.

"Mrs. Emery-Holmes Is Bride of Physician at 71," *Salt Lake Telegram*, 19 July 1930.

"Mrs. Emery-Holmes Public Reply to Hughes Supporters," *Salt Lake Tribune*, 9 September 1916.

"Mrs. Emery-Holmes Weds Dr. R. N. Delitch," *New York Times*, 20 July 1930.

"Mrs. Holmes Again on Witness Stand," *Salt Lake Tribune*, 4 October 1918.

"Mrs. Holmes Backs Film Venture, Miss Adele Blood Will Be Star," *Salt Lake Tribune*, 29 January 1918.

"Mrs. Holmes Ends Testimony in Trial," *Salt Lake Tribune*, 5 October 1918.

"Mrs. Holmes Loses Bransford Case," *Salt Lake Telegram*, 26 January 1919.

"Mrs. Holmes Loses Suit against Bransford," *Deseret News*, 25 January 1919.

"Mrs. Holmes May Finish Case Today," *Salt Lake Tribune*, 30 October 1918.

"Mrs. Holmes Sues Bransford for $400,000." *Salt Lake Tribune*, 21 January 1918.

"Mrs. Holmes Takes Stand as Witness," *Salt Lake Tribune*, 3 October 1918.

"Mrs. Holmes Tells Story of Adoption of Foster Daughter," *Deseret News*, 2 October 1918.

"Mrs. Susanna Holmes Loses in $800,000 Bransford Suit," *Salt Lake Herald*, 26 January 1919.

"Nevada Solon Takes Witness Stand in Bransford Case," *Deseret News*, 6 November 1918.

"Niece of John S. Bransford," *Salt Lake Tribune*, 28 May 1913.

"Now the Romantic 'Silver Queen'—Aged 75—May Ditch Her Russian Prince to Marry Boy!" *San Francisco Chronicle*, 10 February 1935.

"One Hundred Fifty Years of *Town and Country* Magazine—The Rich in America," Arts and Entertainment Channel, 1996.

"One Time Consul of Czarist Russia in Chicago—Was Officer in Imperial Army," *New York Times*, 28 March 1935.

"Out of the West," *Buffalo Courier*, 17 February 1903.

Parson, Eugene. "The Striking Career of Thomas F. Walsh," *The Mining American*, 18 November 1916.

"Personality Parade," *Parade*, 15 December 1996.

"Personal Mention," *Greenville (Calif.) Bulletin*, 17 May 1882, 6 September 1882, 17 July 1895.

"Personal Mention," *Park Record*, 15 November 1884.

*Plumas (Calif.) National Bulletin*, 11 January 1868, 21 May 1868, 29 December 1868, 16 March 1887, 6 April 1887.

"Prince & Wife Decide to 'Make Up,'" *New York Times*, 26 August 1915.

"Prince Engalitcheff Wed," *New York Times*, 19 October 1933.

"Prince Vladimir N. Engalitcheff," *New York Times*, 8 March 1923.

"Progress Is Made in Hearing of Will Case," *Deseret News*, 2 November 1918.

"Receives Title to Millions," *Salt Lake Tribune*, 20 (month uncertain) 1930.

"Religious Ceremony Seals Nuptials of 'Silver Queen,'" *New York Herald*, n.d.

"Rites Planned Saturday for 'Silver Queen.'" *Salt Lake Tribune*, 6 August 1942.

"The Rockefellers," *Biography*. Arts and Entertainment Channel, 1994.

Rogers, Jane. "Rogers Family History," *Plumas Memories* vol. 51 (June 1986).

"Romantic History Adds Glamour to Eleventh Showcase Design," *Pasadena Star*, 17 April 1975.

Ross, James M. "From Old Kentucky," *Louisville Courier Journal*, 8 March 1942.

Scott, Patricia Lyn. "Eliza Kirtley Royle," *Worth Their Salt: Notable but Often Unnoted Women of Utah*, ed. Colleen Whitley. Logan: Utah State University Press, 1996.

"Silver King Mine Owner Home with Surgeon Husband," *Pasadena Star News*, 7 October 1930.

"'Silver Queen' of Utah Closes Famed Career," *Park Record*, 6 August 1942.

"'Silver Queen' of Utah Would Conquer Society," *New York Herald*, 2 January 1903.

"'Silver Queen' Seeks Divorce," *Salt Lake Telegram*, 1 November 1932.

"Silver Queen Widow Again," *Pasadena Sun News*, 24 March 1935.

"'Silver Queen' Wills 4 Million to Manager," *Los Angeles Evening Herald and Express*, 25 August 1942.

"'Silver Queen' Wills Millions to Manager of Estate," *Salt Lake Tribune*, 26 August 1942.

"Society Bud of Yesterday Holds Prestige Today," *Salt Lake Tribune*, 11 October 1925.

Society Column, *Deseret News*, 6 September 1904.

Society Column, *Salt Lake Tribune*, 6 September 1904.

"Spectators Barred from Bransford Hearing," *Deseret News*, 11 October 1918.

*State Resources*. Oakland, Calif.: vol. 2, no. 4 (October/November 1890).

"Submitted to Court," *Salt Lake Tribune*, 20 December 1894.

"Testifies Woman Was above Average," *Deseret News*, 1 November 1918.

"Unique Bedset of Pioneers Put on Show," *Salt Lake Tribune*, 24 July 1953.

"Utah Woman Wed in Paris to Physician," *Salt Lake Tribune*, 20 July 1930.

"Utah's Own 'Silver Queen' Arrives for Summer Visit in Salt Lake City," *Salt Lake Tribune*, 12 May 1938.

"Utah's 'Silver Queen' Has Dazzled Washington," *Boston Globe*, 21 April 1902.

"Utah's 'Silver Queen,' 74, Weds 60 Year Old Prince," *Salt Lake Tribune*, 21 October 1933.

"The Vanderbilts," *Biography*. Arts and Entertainment Channel, 1995.

"The Vanderbilts: An American Dynasty." Arts and Entertainment Channel, 1995.

Vann, Korky. "'Gentlemen Hosts' Dance Their Way to Exotic Ports of Call," *Salt Lake Tribune*, 26 October 1997.

"Wallace Bransford Is Still on Stand," *Deseret News*, 14 October 1918.

"Why Adele Blood Deserted the Stage," *Denver Examiner*, magazine section, 3 February 1918.

"Wife's Mental Strength Equal to Husband's, Decides Judge in Bransford Suit," *Salt Lake Herald*, 26 January 1919.

"Witnesses Defend Mrs. Bransford in Trial," *Deseret News*, 4 November 1918.

"Witnesses Testify that Mrs. Bransford Directed Work Intelligently," *Deseret News*, 7 November 1918.

## Unpublished Sources and Government Documents

Armstrong, Lee. Interview by Judy Dykman, 1996.
Author's Club membership records.
Bamberger, Clarence. Interview by Judy Dykman, 1997.
Bertoch, Julia. Interview by Judy Dykman, 1996.
Bertoch, Marvin J. *Salt Lake City: This Is the Place*. Salt Lake City: Papers, special collections, Marriott Library, University of Utah.
Blood, Adele. File in Billie Rose Theatre Collection, New York City Public Library for the Performing Arts, Lincoln Center.
Boncoraglio, Angelo. Letters to Judy Dykman, 1996.
Bransford family scrapbook. Courtesy of Stella Inge.
Bransford File. Plumas County Museum, Quincy, California.
Bransford, John. Autobiography, courtesy of Vadney Murray.
———. Short biographical sketch, courtesy of Vadney Murray.
Bransford, Louise Grace Emery. Probate case 9207, 1918. Salt Lake County: Third Circuit Court, Third Judicial District, in Utah State Archives, Salt Lake City.
Bransford, Milford. Family Bible.
———. Letters to A. C. Ellis, March 1865 and 24 May 1967.
Bransford, Susanne. Scrapbook, Ms B332. Salt Lake City: Utah State Historical Society.
Bransford, Susie E. Autograph book, courtesy of Susanna Hartman.
Brennan, Linda. Interviews by Judy Dykman, 1993–1995.
Brimhall, Sandy. Interviews by Judy Dykman, 1994–1997.
Brown, Teddy. Interview by Judy Dykman. 1997.
Bureau of Census. Coronado, California, 1920.
———. Hollywood, California, 1920.
———. Ray County, Missouri, 1850.
Burgoyne, Robert M. Interview by Judy Dykman, 1996.
Cable, Mary. Telephone interview by Judy Dykman, 1996.
———. Letter to Judy Dykman, 1996.

Chretien, Pat A. M. Interview by Judy Dykman, 1994.
Cone, Mary Ann. Interview by Judy Dykman, 1996.
Cooper, Sarah. Will.
Cram, Zua. Interview by Judy Dykman, 1997.
"Crossing the Plains." Unpublished history of the Bransford family trip to California. n.d.
Crouch, Laura. Interview by Judy Dykman, 1997.
Curtis, Mark. Interviews by Judy Dykman, 1994–1997.
Darger, Frances. Interview by Judy Dykman, 1995.
Dee, David B. Telephone interview by Colleen Whitley, 1997.
Delich, Michael. Letter to Judy Dykman, January 1997.
Delitch, Radovan. Letter to Bill O'Conner, 11 November 1932.
———. Letter to Radisave (no surname given), 1930.
*Directory of Deceased Physicians*. Medical library, University of California at San Francisco.
Elliott, Sally. Interview by Judy Dykman, 1993.
Emery, Albion B. Probate case 102, 1894. Coalville, Utah: Summit County, Utah Territory, in Utah State Archives, Salt Lake City.
Engalitcheff, Nicholas. Telephone interview by Judy Dykman, 1996.
Engalitcheff, Suzanne B. Death certificate, 1942. Hartford, Conn.: Department of Vital Statistics.
———. Letters to Culver Sherrill 1938–1942.
———. Probate case P-5011, 1942. Pasadena, Los Angeles, California, in Los Angeles County Records.
———. Probate case 24672, 1942. Third District Court, Salt Lake County, Utah, in State Archives, Salt Lake City.
Gallivan, Jack. Interview by Judy Dykman, 1997.
Gardner, Mrs. M. C. Interview by Judy Dykman, 1997.
Hansen, Merna. Interview by Judy Dykman, 1996.
Hartman, Susanna. Interviews by Judy Dykman, 1993–1996.
Hogle, Pat. Interview by Judy Dykman. 1997.
Holmes, Edwin F. "Birds and Flowers at El Roble."
Holmes, Edwin F. Probate case 14118–14132, 1926. Kane County, Illinois.
Hotel Utah file, Western Americana Collection, Marriott Library, University of Utah, Salt Lake City.
Jacob, Kathryn A. "High Society in Washington during the Gilded Age: Three Distinct Aristocracies." Ph.D. diss., Johns Hopkins University, 1986.
Jenkins, Mark. Letter to Judy Dykman, 1996.
Kellogg, Margorie. Letter to Angelo Boncoralio.
Ladies' Literary Club membership records.
Lamb, Harold. Interviews by Judy Dykman, 1994–1997.
Lawson, Scott. Interviews by Judy Dykman, 1993–1995.
———. Letter to Judy Dykman, 1997.
Lund, Beverly. Telephone interview by Colleen Whitley, 1997.

Madsen, Carol Cornwall. Interview by Judy Dykman, 1997.

Millsaps, Floralee. Interviews by Judy Dykman, 1993–1995.

———. "Portrait of a Lovely Lady," unpublished manuscript.

Mortensen, A. R. Letter to Mrs. A. W. Naegle, 15 December 1950.

Murray, Jean. Interviews by Judy Dykman, 1994–1997.

Murray, Vadney. Interviews by Judy Dykman, 1993–1997.

National Park Seminary yearbook, 1903.

Nevins, Richard. Telephone interviews by Judy Dykman, 1997.

Newhall, Ann. Interviews by Judy Dykman, 1993–1997.

Park City Museum staff. Interview by Judy Dykman, 1993.

Pasadena Centennial Room and clipping file. Pasadena, California, Public Library.

Plumas County death records, 1867–1900. Plumas County Courthouse, Quincy, California.

Plumas County deed books for 1870s. Courtesy of Scott Lawson.

Plumas County tax records, 1867–1887. Plumas County Museum and Historical Society.

Plumas County voting records 1886–1887.

Ringholz, Raye C. Letter to Judy Dykman, 1993.

———. Telephone interview by Judy Dykman, 1995.

Robinson, Marilyn. Interview by Judy Dykman, 1995.

———. Letter to Judy Dykman, July 1994.

Scott, Patricia Lyn. Telephone interview by Colleen Whitley, 1997.

Sellers, Sue. Interview by Judy Dykman, 1995.

Sherbatoff, Prince. Telephone interview by Judy Dykman, 1997.

Sherrill, Lewis. Telephone interview by Judy Dykman, 1996.

Shipler, Bill and Harry. Collection of glass negatives. Salt Lake City: Utah State Historical Society.

"Showcase of Interior Design, Notes on El Roble Residence." Pasadena Junior Philharmonic Committee information file, 1975, Pasadena, California, Public Library.

Simons, Blaine. Interviews by Judy Dykman, 1995–1996.

Spriggs, Alan. Interview by Judy Dykman, 1993.

Steiner, Frances. Interview by Judy Dykman, 1997.

———. Letter to Judy Dykman, 29 July 1994.

Stevens, Dick. Interview by Judy Dykman, 1995.

Tierney, Lennox. Interview by Judy Dykman, 1996.

Union Pacific Depot Museum, Ogden, Utah. Telephone interview by Judy Dykman, 1994.

Utah Heritage Foundation. Walking tour notes, 1995.

Wells, Laura. Interview by Judy Dykman, 1994.

# Index

## A

*A Woman of No Importance* (Wilde), 67
Air Force, 90, 120
Airis, Edward H., 104
Alexandra, Czarina of Russia, 57
Alta Club, 83, 87, *114*
Amelia Palace, 65, 91. *See also* Gardo House
American Party, 53, 85
American Valley, California, 6
Anchor Mine, 50, 55, 83
Annadale Country Club, 125
Apex Mining, 42
Apperson, Anna, 94
Arizona, 22, 126
Aschheim, M. S., 20-22, 41
Ascot, England, 152

## B

Baalbek, 63
Bamberger family, 65, 104
Barnum, 124
Batavia, Illinois, 120, 122, 126
Beehive House, 61
Belgium, 59
Belle Vista Hotel, 31
Bell, Rex, 149
Berkeley, California, 50, 52, 100
Berlin, Germany, 161
Biltmore, *63*, 81
Bingham, Utah, 22

Blood, Adele, 94, 95, 97, 104, 112, 113, 115–17, *117*, 135, 145, 147, *148*, 149, 151, 159, 164
Blood family, 8, 52, 94
Blood, Frances, 63, 94, 97
Blood, Ira, 94, 173
Blood, Rachel, 20, *43*, 52, *53*, 54, 87, 94, 101, 102, *103*, 112, 113, 117
Blood, Warren H., 20
Blood, William H., 12
Blossom family, 124
Board of Health, 48, 115
Boncoraglio, Angelo, 161, 162
Booth, William H., 88
Boston Conservatory, 49
Boston, Massachusetts, 22, 25, 26, 49, 63, 102, 112
Bowers, Jean, 88
Boyd, Eleanor, 161
Bransford, Albina, *4*, 167
Bransford, Armenith, 4
Bransford and McIntyre, *14*, 15
Bransford and Smith, 8
Bransford and Taylor, 15
Bransford Apartments, 102, *103*, 117, 118, 154
Bransford, Berrell, 4
Bransford, Carter (slave), 5
Bransford, Emily (slave), 5
Bransford, Erma Ellen, 52
Bransford family, 3–6, *4*, 8, 12, 25, 48, 53, 60, 61, 94, 97, 159, *163*
Bransford, Felix, 4, *4*

Bransford, Jackson, 3, 4, 8
Bransford, John, 3, 4, 8, 9, 10–12, 15, 18-21, 24, 26, 31, 32, 37, 40, 41, *43*, 52–55, 57, 62, 65, 81, *82*, *84*, 85, 87, 91, 94, 98, *100*, 101, 104, *108*, 111–13, 115, 117, 119, 120, 140, 151, 152, 154, *155*, 162
Bransford, Laura, *110*
Bransford, Maria, 4
Bransford, Milford, 3–8, *4*, *5*, 10–12, 14, 15, 20, 24, 25, 32, 45, 48, 114
Bransford, Nellie, 9, 12, 20, 25, 31, 32, 40, *48*–50, 53, 54, 61, 66, 101, 104, *108*, 109, *110*, 111, 119, 120, 136, 137, 143, 149, 151, 154–56, 159, 160
Bransford, Parthenia, 4
Bransford, Rachel Blood. *See* Blood, Rachel
Bransford, Rafe (slave), 5
Bransford, Sarah Ellen Cooper. *See* Cooper, Sarah Ellen
Bransford, Stella, *43*, 52, 102, 113, 154, 159
Bransford, Thomas, 3, 4, 7
Bransford Transfer Company, 83
Bransford, Viola Crescent (Ola), 9, 10-12, 20, 24, 25, *25*, 92
Bransford, Wallace, *43*, 52, 54, 98, 100–102, *100*, *103*, 111–20, 151, 154–56, 159, *155*, 162
Bransford, Wallace Jr., *155*

Bransford, Walter Lee, 3, 4, 5, 7
Bransford, Walter Lee Jr., 4, 7
Bransford, Zerrel, 5
Brennan, Matt, 21
Brick, James, 81
Brigham Street, 65
British Columbia, 137
Broadway, 87, 97, 147
Brooks, Lloyd W., 154, 159, 160
Brown family, 104
Brown, Molly, 56
*Buffalo Courier*, 57
Burningham, Stephen, 44
Busch, Adolph, 124

Cable, Mary, 44, 143
California, 4–8, 12, 15, 16, 19, 20, 22, 24, 31, 37, 39, 42, 43, 50, 62, 84, 87, 88, 102, 109, 113–15, 117, 118, 120, 122, 124, 126, 140, 142, 144, 145, 151, 152, 154, 156, 159, 160, 161
California Institute of Technology, 126
*California Life*, 124, *125*
California Limited, 140
Cannon, Martha Hughes, 87
Carleton, Jenny, 55, 126
Carnegie, Andrew, 31
Carnegie Foundation, 126
Carnegie Hall, 147
Carthage, Missouri, 4
Cathedral of the Madeleine, 164
Catholic Church, 164
Chamber of Commerce, 83
Chambers, R. C., 12, 20, 22, 25, 26, 29, *29*, 37, *38*, 39–43, 45, 50, 114, 115
Chateau St. Rodegonde, 98
Chicago, Illinois, 22, 29, 30, 62, 65, 81, 94, 120, 125, 126, 135
Chinatown, 21
Church of Jesus Christ of Latter-day Saints (Mormon), 20, 22, 29, 39, 53, 61, 62. 64, 81–82, 85, 87, 90, 120, 160–62
Churchill, Randolph, 98
Civic Betterment Union, 85, 86
Civil War, 3, 6, 8, 30, 32, 55, 57, 98
Clement, Victor, 64
Coalville, Utah, 39, 40
Cody, "Buffalo Bill", 21

Colbourne, Clara, 50
Colorado, 4, 59, 162
coming out parties, 15, 98
Commercial Club, 21, 83, 84
Confederacy, Confederates, 3, 4
Congregational Church, 33, 61
Connor, Patrick (Colonel), 8
Constitutional Convention, Utah, 37
consumption, 15, 31
Cook family, 5, 8, 109, 122, 161
Cooper, Sarah Ellen, 3, 4, 6–8, 10–12, 15, 20, 24, 25, 32, 40, 45, *45*, 48, *54*, 102, 104, 109, 114, 120, 159
Corbin, Helen Pearson (Corby), 45, 46
Country Club, 83, 88, 125, 147
Crescent Mills, California, 8, 10, 11, 14, 18, 19, 20, 24, 25
Crescent Tailings Placer Claim, 15
*Crimes Without Punishment* (Sherrill), 161
Cross of Danilo, 137
Cullen, Matthew, 40
Culmer, H. L. A., 91
Cummings, Byron, 91
Curtis, Mark, 70

Dadiani, Prince of Georgia, 136
Daly, John J., 24, 26, 37, 41
Daly Mines, 24
Daniels, Gertrude, 126
Davis, Edward Cader (Reverend), 97, 115
Dayton, Ohio, 90
Deas, Harry Beverly, 60
de Bertrand, Danise, 136, 137
Deer Valley, Utah, 21, 162
Delitch, Radovan (Rada), 137, *138, 139*, 140, 142–44, *158*, 160
Delmonicos, 54
DeMille, Cecil B., 149
Denver, Colorado, 62, 63, 144
Depression, 30, 120, 140, 142, 143, 152, 154
Deseret Mandolin Orchestra, 66
*Deseret News*, 65, 101, 151
Detroit, Michigan, 82
Dickson, W. H. (Judge), 40–42, 115

Dodge, W. H., 40
Donner Lake, California, 6
Donner Party, 6
Durand family, 124

earthquake, 94, 97
East Millcreek, 104
Eastern Star, 26
Einstein, Albert, 126
El Roble, 102, 109, 122, 125, 126, *128–33*, 135, 137, 142, 149, 151, 159
*Elite Magazine*, 58, 59, 65, 81, 126, 151, 152
Emery, Albion B., 18, 22, *22*, *23*, 24–26, 29, 31–33, 37, 39–45, 48, 50, 59, 83, 100, 102, 112, 114, 137, *158*
Emery, George W., *30*
Emery-Holmes Apartments, 102
Emery, Louise Grace, 16, 26, *27*, 43–45, 47–50, 52–55, *53–54*, 57, 65, 92, 94, 97, 98, 99, 100–102, 104, *110*, *111–13*, 110–19, 145, 147, 151, 162
Engalitcheff, Nicholas, 135–37, 143–46, *144–46*, 158
Engalitcheff, Vladimir, 135
England, 3, 60, 126, 143, 144, 152, 161
Europe, 1, 55, 62, 97, 98, 115, 126, 140, 142, 144, 149, 151, 152, 154, 159
Evans and Early Mortuary, 1, 156
Evans, Levis, *113*
Evans, Rachel, *113*
Evans, Stella, *113*
*Every Woman*, 97
Exeter, 50

Feldman, J. B., 100, 120, 159
Feldman, Letitia, 159
Ferry, Mont, 164
Ferry, William F., 37
Fielding, Temple, 161
Fifth Avenue Hospital, 137
Finn Hall, 21
Fitzgerald, John A., 18
Flood, James, 94
Florida, 151

Flourney, Margaret (Maggie), 10, 18, 19
Folsom, Amelia, 61, 62, 68
Folsom, William H., 62
Fort Douglas, 104
Fort Hall Indian Reservation, 22
Frémont, John Charles, 4
Frick, Joseph E., 118

G. A. R., 125
Gallivan, Jack, 44
Gardo House, 61, 62, 65, 66, 68–80, 88, 101, 114, *114*, 117, 120, 151
Genesee, California, 18
George Fisher and Sons, 142
Germany, 59, 114
Gilded Age, 1, 30, 31, 54, 55, 63, 81, 92, 120, 142, 150, 162, 164
Glendenning, James, 41
Gold Rush, 94
*Golden Giant*, 21
Gould, George Jay, 98
Graham, Fred, 66
Grand Tour, 15
Grant Brigham F., 172
Grant, Heber J., 54, 172
Great Basin, 5, 167
Great Lakes, 55, 83
Great Salt Lake, 82, 84, 85, 104
Green Hotel, 124, 142, 144, 152
Green Mountain Mine and Mining Company, 11, 14, 24
Greenville Band, 25
*Greenville Bulletin*, 15, 24, 25
Greenville, California, 8, 15, *16*, 20, 24, 25
Guyer family, 124

Haggin, James Ali Ben, 39, 42
Hale, George Ellery, 126
Hamilton, G. B., 169
Hammerstein, Oscar, 136
Harkness family, 124
Harris, Jay Tarvin, *54*, 61, 98, 109, 143, 149, 156, 159
Harris, Gage, 149
Harris, Susanna, 3, 7, 109, *109*, 110, 140, 142, 143, 149, *149*, 151, 152, 156, 159, 160, *160*, 162

Hartman, Chris, 151
Hartman, Harris, 151
Hartman, Susanna. *See* Harris, Susanna
Hathaway, Jane, 135
Hawaii, 31, 32, 41, 45
Heald's Business College, 10
Hearst, George, 26, *39*, 42, 94
Hearst, Phoebe Apperson, 31, 52, *52*, 94, 98
Hearst, William Randolph, 94, 96, 98
Hershey, Milton, 31
Hitler, Adolph, 1, 154
Hogle family, 104
Hogle Investments, 160
Hollywood, California, 91, 122, 143, 147, 149
Holmes, Carleton, 50, 55, 90, 91, *110*, 126
Holmes, Edwin F. (Colonel), 50, *51*, 54, 55, 57, 59, 61–62, 64–66, *67*, 81, 84–85, 88, 90–92, 98, 101, 102, 104, 109, 112–14, 117, 120, 122, *123*, 125, 126, 135, 137, *158*, 159
Holmes, Harriett, *110*, 122
Holmes, Hellen, 91
Holmes, Olive, *110*, 91, 120
Holy Cross Hospital, 81
Holz, Joseph, 16
Hope, Dawn, 117, 135, 147, *147*, 151, 159, 164
Hope, Wandell, 117
Hopkins, Mark, 94
Hot Springs, Virginia, 113
Hotel Barclay, 145
Hotel Utah, 49, 140, 151, 154
House of Windsor, 115
Houston, Grizzelle, x, 92, 120, 154, 156
Huddart Floral, 66, 104
Hughes, Charles Evans, 87, 88
Hunt, William, 63
Hyte, William, 104

I. Magnin, 125
Idaho, 22, 61, 62, 83
Idaho Falls, Idaho, 61
Illinois, 61, 85, 170, 182
Imperial Quartz Mining Company, 12

income tax, 30, 120
Independence, Missouri, 4
Indian Valley, California, 6–8, 10, 12, 15, 16, 18, 22, 25, 52, 94
influenza, 115–17
Ivanhoe Holding Company, 42
Ivers, James, 40, 64, 140

Jackling, David, 49
Jeffers, Robinson, 126
Jennings, William, 61, 64
Jerome, Jennie, 98
Jews, 20, 59
Jonas, Alberto, 66
Judge family, 65, 104, 115, 164
Judge, John, 26, 37, 40–44
Judge, Ivers, and Keith Livery, 40
Judge, Jennie, 44, *45*, 65
Judge, Katherine, 65
Judge Memorial High School, 164

Kahn, Emanuel, 40
Kamas, Utah, 21
Kearns family, 164
Kearns, Jennie Judge. *See* Judge, Jennie
Kearns, Thomas, 26, *26*, 29, 33, 37, 39, 44, *45*, 50 64, 65, 84, 115
Keeley Institute, 82
Keith, David, 26, 29, 32, 33, 37, 39–42, *41*, 49, 50, 55, 64–65, 85, 164
Kennedy family, 162
Kentucky, 3
Kind, Martha Royle, 66
*King of Kings*, 173
Knutsford Hotel, *43*, 49, 61, 65

Lamb, Harold Jr. (Hal), 92, *93*, 102, 154, 159, 162
Lamb, Harold V., 24–26, 28, 43, 45, 50, 90–92, *92*, 102, 104, *110*, 115, 118, 120, 151, 154
Lamb, Joe, 92, *93*, 154, 159
Lamb, Susan, 92, *93*, 154, 159
Lamb, Willis G., ix, 18, 20, 24, 25, 28–29, 32, 33, 39, 40, 45, 50
LDS Business College, 65

Legion of Honor, 137
Lent, 41, 42, 65, 136
Leonard, Edna, x, 154, 162
Liberal Party, 22, 24, 29, 53, 82
Lion House, 61, 114
London, Belle, 85, 86, 86
London, England, 15, 57
Los Angeles, California, 84, 113
Louis XIV, 63
Louise Grace Emery Apartments, 103
*Louisville Courier*, 4
Louisville, Kentucky, 4, 154
Loyal Legion, 125
Lyon, Nathaniel, 166

### M

Madrid, Spain, 152
Maidu, 6
Maine, 22, 151
Malmquist, O. N., 154
Manhattan Island, New York, 151
Marlborough, Duke of, 98
Marshall Fields, 62
Marshall, John A. (Judge), 40, 62, 115
Maryland Hotel, 142
Masons, 7–8, 15, 21–22, 24-26, 25, 29, 32–33, 83, 88
Massachusetts, 22, 25
Mayflower Mine and Mining Company, 26, 29, 41, 42
McCornick, W. S., 37, 40, 55
McCune, Alfred, 62, 65
McGinnis, 8
McKinney, 14
McNally family, 124
Mediterranean, 65, 145
Mendocino County, California, 7
Merritt, S. A. (Judge), 40, 42
Mexican War, 3
Michigan, 55, 85, 92, 120
Milan Cathedral, 63
Missouri, 3–7, 15, 49
Missouri River, 49
Mitchell, Craig, 44
Moffatt, A. T., 41
Monte Carlo, 152
Morehouse family, 124
Mormon. *See* Church of Jesus Christ of Latter–day Saints
Moscow, Russia, 55
Moulton, Arthur W. (Reverend), 1

Mt. Olivet Cemetery, 1, 32, 92, 104, 114, *163*
Mt. Wilson Observatory, 126
Murphy, "Black Jack," 21
Murray, David, 64
Mussolini, Benito, 1
*Mystery of the Desert* (Culmer), 76, 91

### N

Naples, Italy, 145
National Geographic Society, 91
National Park Seminary, 57, 97
Natural Bridges, 91
Neff, John, 104
Nevada, 4–7, 21, 112
New Deal, 154
New Mexico, 126
New Orleans, Louisiana, 152
New York, 2, 14, 30, 44, 48, 49, 54, 57, 59, 63, 65, 81, 94, 97, 98, 126, 135–37, 143–45, 147, 151
New York City Municipal, 143
*New York Herald*, 59
*New York Times*, 136, 137
Newhouse family, 65
Newhouse, Ida Stingley, 64
Newport, Rhode Island, 63, 98, 151, 154
Nicholas II, Czar of Russia, 57
Niles Mandolin Orchestra, 66
Nims, 37
Nob Hill, 94
Noel, Herbert James, 147
North Carolina, 63
North Hollywood, California, 147
Northland Mining Company, 26, 29, 41, 42
Norwalk, Connecticut, 2, 156
nouveaux riches, 30, 31, 59, 97–98, 115, 120, 162

### O

Oakland, California, 12, 167
Oakwood, 104, *105*–8, 109, 112, 120, 149, 151
Ogden, Utah, 24, 85, 91
Ontario Mine, 25, 37, 41
Oquirrh Mountains, 22
Orient, 84, 117
Orleans, New York, 54

Orphans Nursery and Day Home, 88
Ouray, Colorado, 59

### P

Palermo, California, 37
Pape and Bowmans, 21
Paris, France, 15, 98, 137, 140, 143, 151
Park City, Utah, ix, 20–22, 24–26, 29, 33, 37, 39–43, 45, 55, 83, 85, 88, 101, 122, 151, 152, 164
*Park Record*, 21, 22, 24, 40
Partridge, Evelyn, 135
Pasadena, California, 91, 94, 102, 112, 122, 124–26, 135, 137, 140, 142, 144, 152, 161
Pasadena Playhouse, 126
*Pasadena Star*, 125
Paul, James, 98
Petaluma, California, 7, 8
Peterhof, 57
Philadelphia, Pennsylvania, 98
*Picture of Dorian Gray*, 97
Pinchot, Gifford, 81
Plaza Hotel, 2, 49, 117, *134*, 135, 147, 156
Plumas County, California, 6, *7*, 8, 10–12, 14–16, 18–22, 25, 53
polygamy, 62, 82
Pope Leo, 1
Post Office, 21, 24
Postle Company, 126
Potter, Palmer, 94
Prevaricators Club, 15, 52
Progressive Movement, 3, 81, 82, 85, 88
prostitution stockade, 86, 86
Prou, Baroness, 98

### Q

Quessenbury family, 3, 60
Quessenbury Hardware, 3
Quessenbury, Susan, 3, *4*, 5, 7
Quincy, California, 5, 6, 12, 18, 52
Quincy-Indian Valley Road, 12

### R

Radical Republican, 8
Rawlins, Athol R. and Joseph L., 115, 116

Rawlins, Ray, and Rawlins, 115
Ray County, Missouri, 4
Red Cross, 88, 114, 115, 120
Remeny, Edouard, 21
Reno, Nevada, 6, 8, 12, 20, 21
Republican Party, 37
Richmond Apartments, 159, 160
Richmond, Missouri, 3, 4, 6, 159, 160
Ridges, Joseph, 12, 62
Riley and Toweys, 21
Rockefeller family, 162
Rogers-Evans Insurance, 85
Rome, Italy, 15
Roosevelt, Franklin Delano, 154
Roosevelt, Theodore, 81, 88
Ross, James M., 154
Rowland Hall, 43, 50, 116
Russia, 55, 57, 84
Russian Consulate, 135
Russian Nobility Organization, 145
Russian Orthodox Church, 136, 137, 143
Russian Revolution of 1917, 135

Sacramento, California, 20
Salisbury, O. J., 65
Salt Lake City and County Building, 115
Salt Lake City, Utah, 1, 5, 20, 22, 26, 29, 32, 39–41, 43, 44, 48, 49, 61, 63–66, 81–85, 83, 87, 88, 90, 91, 98, 100, 102, 104, 112, 113, 115, 120, 140, 151, 152, 154-156
Salt Lake County, 84, 115
Salt Lake County Court House, 115, 116
*Salt Lake Herald*, 62, 65
*Salt Lake Telegram*, 65
Salt Lake Theatre, 66
*Salt Lake Tribune*, 44, 65, 101, 151, 154
Saltair, 81, 82, 85
Salvation Army, 88
San Francisco Blue Book, 12
San Francisco, California, 10, 12, 18–20, 24, 31, 37, 50, 52, 62, 94, 97, 144
*San Francisco Chronicle*, 94, 144, 146
San Pedro Railroad, 84

Santa Barbara, California, 162
Santa Fe Railroad, 126, 140
Scandinavian, 57
Scheid, Karl, 66
Serbia, 137
Sheets, John, 18
Shelbourne Farm, 120
Sherrill Apartments, 160
Sherrill, Culver, 140, 144, 151, 152, *152*, 154–56, 159, 160–62, *161*
Shipler, William and Harry, 104
Silver King Mine and Coalition, 29, *34*, 40, 41, 43, 59, 85, 100, 140
Snow, Cornelia (Corney), 122, 172
Snow, Lory, 88, 89, 90, 91, *110*, 120, 152, 164
Sonoma County, California, 7, 8
South Berwick, Maine, 22
Southern Eureka Mining Company, 15
Southhampton, New York, 44
Spafford, William H., 104
Spiro, Solon, 41
Springfield, Missouri, 4
St. Petersburg, Russia, 57
Stanford, Leland, 94
Steinway, 77
Stephens, Harold M., 115, 118, 119
stock exchange, 53, 85
Strawberry, Utah, 21
Sullivan, John L., 21
Summit County, 29, 37
Swede Hall, 21
Swedish royal family, 98

Taormina, Italy, 161, *161*, 162
Taylor Plumas Mine, 14
Taylorsville, California, ix, 8, 10–12, 15, 16
Taylorsville Lyceum, 16
Taylorsville Rescue Lodge 215, 15
Taylorsville School, *11*
Temple Square, 62
Test Oath Law, 4
Texas, 4, 92, 126
Tooele, Utah, 22
Tournament of Roses, 102
Tracy Collins Bank, 154, 160

Trans-Siberian Railroad, 55
Treasure Mountain, 21
Treganza and Lamb, 92
Tribune Building, 154
Tribune Printing Company, 61
Twelfth National Irrigation Congress, 85

Uintah Masonic Lodge, 21
Ukiah, California, 7
*Under the Gaslight*, 21
Union. *See* United States
Union League of Chicago, 125
Union Pacific Railroad, 39
United States, 3, 4, 8, 14, 22, 31, 39, 55, 57, 81, 85–86, 94, 98, 114, 124–26, 137, 164
United States Supreme Court, 62
University of Chicago, 120
University of Utah, 91
Utah, 1, 8, 12, 15, 20–22, 24–26, 29, 30, 33, 37, 39–44, 48–50, 53–55, 59, 62–66, 81–85, 88, 91, 98, 100, 102, 104, 112, 115, 117, 119, 120, 125, 140, 143, 145, 151, 159, 160, 164
Utah Central Railroad, 39
Utah Eastern Railroad, 39
Utah House of Representatives, 29
Utah Lake, 84
Utah Mexican Rubber Company, 85
Utah State Bank, 85
Utah Supreme Court, 26, 42, 118
Utah Symphony, 88
Utah Territory, 37, 62
Utah Valley, 84

Vanderbilt, Alva, 63, 87
Vanderbilt, Consuelo, 98
Vanderbilt, Cornelius, 31
Vanderbilt family, 31, 44, 59, 63, 81, 87, 88, 98, 115
Vanderbilt, George Washington, 63, 81
Vanderbilt, Gloria, 44
Vanderbilt, William Kissam, 63
Victoria, Queen of England, 57
Vienna, Austria, 152

## W

Waldorf Astoria, 54
Walker family, 66, 104
walkers (male escorts), 135–36, 136
Wall, Enos, 21, 62, 65, 109
Walsh, Thomas, 59, 59
Wandemere, 81
Wasatch Mountains, 21
Washington Square, 5
Waterman Smelting Company, 22
Weber, John L., 40
Weir, Thomas, 65, 164
Wells, Heber M., 64
Westchester Country Club, 147
Western Union, 14
Westminster College, 164
Whitehouse, Alice, 98
Wilde, Oscar, 67
Wilson, Millicent, 98
Wilson, Woodrow, 88
Windsor, Marie, 149
Woodruff, Wilford, 62
World wars, 30, 90, 114, 137
Wright Brothers, 90
Wrigley famly, 124

## Y

YMCA, 164
Young, Brigham, 61, 62, 65, 68
Younger, H. B., 21